WESTMINSTER

John Garrett MP is the author of *The Management of Government* and *Managing the Civil Service*. He has been described as 'the doyen of public sector consultants', 'knowing more about public expenditure planning than anybody else of his generation' (*The Times*) and as 'wittily waspish' (*Independent*). Actively involved in Civil Service and Parliamentary reform for twenty-five years, he has been a Labour front-bench spokesperson on Energy, Industry and the Treasury. He has served on a number of committees, including the Treasury and Procedure Select Committees and the Public Accounts Committee. Labour MP for Norwich South since 1974 (excluding 1983–1987), he lives in London and Norwich.

WESTMINSTER
Does Parliament Work?

JOHN GARRETT

VICTOR GOLLANCZ

LONDON

First published in Great Britain 1992
by Victor Gollancz Ltd

First Gollancz Paperback edition published 1993
by Victor Gollancz
A Cassell imprint
Villiers House, 41/47 Strand, London WC2N 5JE

A catalogue record for this book is
available from the British Library.

ISBN 0 575 05624 X

Photoset in Great Britain by
Rowland Phototypesetting Ltd, Bury St Edmunds, Suffolk
and printed in Great Britain by
Guernsey Press Co. Ltd, Guernsey, Channel Isles

For
Georgia
Rose
Sophie
Wendy

We have met the enemy, and he is us!

WALT KELLY: *Pogo*

Contents

Preface

There are a number of informative books about how Parliament works, usually dwelling on our quirks, ornaments and foibles, but few that attempt to fathom why it does not work effectively. As a Member of Parliament I have become increasingly concerned about how ineffectual Parliament has been in dealing with the overwhelming and continually growing power and the authoritarian style of British government. Twenty years ago, Professor John Griffith, in my view the most acute analyst of our constitutional systems, wrote that 'the House of Commons in its attempts at reform which touch the governmental, rather than the parliamentary, process is not infrequently treated with an indifference unthinkable in many other countries.'[1] He understated the case: in my time most attempts by the House of Commons to reform even the parliamentary process have also been treated by the executive with arrogant indifference. My growing concern about, and resentment of, this situation have prompted me to write this report on Parliament.

I have spent most of the last twenty-five years examining and attempting to improve the management of public authorities, either as a management consultant or as a Member of Parliament. The principles behind the general analysis which I have attempted to apply throughout this book derive from this experience. It considers the apparent purposes and functions of Parliament and whether its authority, structure and systems enable it to fulfil them. Chapter 1 considers the purposes; the succeeding chapters examine the structure, systems and functions of Parliament.

A golden rule of management consultancy, dinned into me on my first assignment thirty years ago, is to avoid becoming caught up in the client organisation's problems. Objectivity is all. This injunction is not easy to comply with when the organisation is as wayward, illogical and indifferent to improvement as Parliament and when the contingent issues of citizens' rights and democratic accountability matter so much for the health of our society. Exasperation, despair and hope continually intrude on cool analytical prescription. However, I have tried to separate personal prejudice from professional enquiry by putting the more opinionated and tendentious elements of the book in Chapter 1 and the relatively objective analysis in the following 'functional' chapters. In each of those chapters, I follow a conventional format in first considering the development of a parliamentary function (e.g. the scrutiny of legislation, audit) and the present arrangement of authority, practice and procedure, and then proposing some reforms which I consider practicable. By practicable, I mean improvements which could be implemented by an extraordinarily progressive and determined Leader of the House, acting with the support of the Prime Minister, in one Parliament (or somewhat longer) – a proposition which itself strains at the limits of practicability.

I am conscious that the book ranges from the protection of fundamental freedoms to some minor features of the daily life of an MP, but I've always found that in endeavouring to comprehend an institution, it's the details that lead you to define the culture.

The reader may well divine my personal biases, as a Europhil Tribunite with a deep distrust of civil service mandarins and the judiciary, and a belief that most of the inadequacies of Britain's social and economic performance are due to the class-ridden amateurism which invests the management of most British institutions, including Parliament.

Some of my colleagues have accused me of wanting to see Parliament run more efficiently. Uniquely, I think, 'efficiency' is a pejorative term in Britain, implying inhumanity, miserliness and, perhaps worst of all, indifference to tradition. In fact, Parliament seems to me to be highly efficient in that each year it processes thousands of pages of legislation, produces hundreds of reports and airs countless grievances at remarkably little cost. This book primarily considers whether or not Parliament is *effective*, whether it achieves its purposes, a different and more complicated matter. My view is that with some entirely feasible reforms, some more resources and very much more assertiveness, Parliament could become considerably more effective.

Some of my colleagues will also produce criticisms of this aspiration (indeed, they already have). First, they say a more effective House would require MPs who are technocratic paragons – button-cute, rapier-keen, owl-wise (to paraphrase Sid Perelman) executives, instead of the plain folk we have at the moment. Secondly, they deem it sacrilege to apply a managerial term like effectiveness to this great 'cockpit of the nation' where political parties battle for the nation's soul, where a single speech by a modern Pericles can turn the tide, win the day and bring proud ministers to heel, and consider that any suggestion of introducing system and order into this chaotic glory is uncomprehending and potentially undemocratic.

Both arguments are mistaken. First, whatever the background, training and interests of a Member of Parliament, it seems to me that he or she could probably do a better job if they were better resourced and empowered. Secondly, an analysis from a managerial perspective does not imply a managerialist prescription: it is just a useful way of looking at any institution. Comparing what an institution does with what most people (including the people in it) think it does and then speculating on what it could practicably do; examining its powers, structures and systems and how they might feasibly be improved, is not to advocate corporatism nor the stifling of conflict. Parliament essentially provides a forum for debate and struggle between political parties. It seems to me that the debate could be better informed and the struggle made more comprehensible to the people who sent us here if our arrangements were reformed.

Parliamentary reform usually receives little attention in Parliament and there is currently no very active campaign for it in either House. I would guess that the only improvements likely to be endorsed by my fellow members at the time of writing are a small change in the hours of sitting and a modest improvement in the standard of accommodation – and even to these proposals there would be vocal opposition from some hair-shirt radicals and some enthusiastic guardians of the public purse. The more technical issues which exercise me – such as the lamentable lack of informed scrutiny of public spending and the inconsistent and erratic examination of legislation – would generally not be recognised as significant problems. Parliamentary reform rarely has much weight behind it. Occasionally, a Leader of the House (Crossman, St John Stevas) attempts to push it along, but for most of the time it is seen as a backwater issue and to advocate it with any enthusiasm is to risk being typecast at least as unworldly and probably as a crank.

However, we cannot much longer ignore the constant growth of external pressures for change in our parliamentary arrangements. The remorseless process of European integration and the growing claims of the European Parliament; the increasing demand for the formulation and entrenchment of citizens' rights; the continual growth in the power of government and the appearance of new forms of government organisation which further distance the administration from parliamentary scrutiny, all make a re-examination of what Parliament is for and what it does, and could do, important topics today.

I am aware that my tone is generally critical. I am acutely aware that most people in the world consider our Parliament a model of democratic freedom and that many are willing to sacrifice their lives to achieve something like it. I start from the assumption that Parliament is so fundamental to our national life that its present servility to government should not be allowed to continue. In my experience, most British institutions slowly petrify into monuments. This book is intended to help keep the blood flowing.

This book originated with a suggestion from Peter Hennessy; in the end I am very grateful for it. My thanks go to Liz Knights, my editor at Gollancz, and Caroline Taggart, copy editor; Roz Cullinan for producing the text and for her diligent research; Joanna Elson for helping with editing and typing and the staff of the House of Commons library for dealing with my countless enquiries. I am grateful to Joyce Quin, Professor J. A. G. Griffith, Professor Andrew Likierman and Bob Sheldon for their comments on particular chapters. I would also like to thank the many members of the staff of the Commons and Lords and the Members of Parliament of all parties who submitted to being interviewed. Andrew Bennett and Graham Allen, members of that very rare breed nowadays, MPs who are concerned about parliamentary reform, were particularly helpful.

Heinemann Ltd have kindly allowed me to quote passages on financial control and state audit from my book *The Management of Government*. I am also grateful to Little Brown (UK) Ltd for permission to quote from Ted Short's *Whip to Wilson* and to Fontana, an imprint of HarperCollins, for permission to quote from *Politics of the Judiciary* by Professor John Griffith.

Finally, I am indebted to the Norwich Labour Party and the voters of Norwich South for giving me the opportunity to represent the City of Norwich and to study Parliament from the inside.

JOHN GARRETT
Westminster, 1992

I

A Running Commentary on Decline

Under the auspices of the Know-How Fund, set up by Mrs Thatcher in 1989 to advise the countries of Eastern Europe on how to emulate British freedom and enterprise, Mr Roger Sands, Clerk of the House of Commons Overseas Office, visited the Parliaments of Poland, Hungary and Czechoslovakia. He found that many of the distinguished characteristics of the British parliamentary system were not immediately attractive to the new democracies. Our system, he pointed out, gives 'almost unchallengeable power' to a government which enjoys a secure majority in the House of Commons and the new democracies naturally wanted to have effective checks on the power of government. 'The new politicians of central Europe are not disposed to be impressed when told (for example) that the agenda of the House of Commons is determined by the government after informal consultations conducted by a government official; that a valid vote requires the participation of only 40 out of 650 members; or that we regard it as the responsibility of government rather than Parliament to ensure that the laws which we pass are technically correct.'[1]

Mr Sands' report usefully illustrates the central theme of this book: that in matters large and small the power of government over Parliament is far too great for government to be properly accountable to Parliament and to the electorate.

The present achievement of the evolution of our constitution has been to replace a despotic monarch with an autocratic government. In the seventeenth century James I said, 'I will not be content that my power be disputed upon, but I shall ever be willing to make the reason appear of all my doings and rule my actions according to my laws.' 'That view,' said Professor John Griffith in a lecture given in 1981,[2] 'is not far removed from that of the executive of today, acquiesced in by the

Commons.' In the same lecture he observed that the executive today has more control over the Commons than had James's successor, Charles I. (Appropriately, among its most objectionable practices are the ruthless use of the Royal Prerogative and Crown Immunity.)

In every function of Parliament, government throws its weight, not only against any opposition to its will, but against enquiry, scrutiny and discussion. Inexorably, government advances, leaving Parliament, in the words of Austin Mitchell, 'heckling the steamroller'. Many of the limitations government imposes on Parliament have no statutory authority: the rules governing the appearance of civil servants before Parliamentary committees and the determination of what legislation Parliament may examine, for example. Parliament may still live up to John Stuart Mill's description of it as the Nation's Committee of Grievances and Congress of Opinions, but that is not much to weigh against the power of modern government. If, according to the dictum of the late Lord Armstrong of Sanderstead, the task of the British civil service is 'the orderly management of decline',[3] then an objective observer might well say that the main achievement of Parliament these last forty years or so has been to provide a running commentary on decline.

One of the causes of this weakness has been the traditional dominance of the debating chamber and the more lowly status of investigatory and legislative committees in our legislature. The chamber may occasionally provide the stage for some heroic performances, but in the main it encourages histrionics and meretriciousness. There is still a lot to be done to shift the style of the House of Commons from theatre to serious and penetrating scrutiny of government. The thought has occurred to me from time to time that the superficiality of the Commons, the subservience of content to presentation, may derive from the fact that it houses many more lawyers than managers. This imparts a style which concentrates much more on events and exploits than on systems. Systems thinking focuses on the flow of consequences from a policy decision to its impact on a community and on drawing conclusions from that sequence. Parliament rarely thinks in that way.

Parliament exists to scrutinise legislation, but badly drafted bills are pushed by ministers through the legislative process without adequate consideration before, during or after it. Parliament has no access to specialist lawyers who could advise it on the quality of drafting. The present government refuses to allow the use of a procedure which would enable Parliament to take evidence from ministers and experts on the meaning and purposes of a bill. The consequences and effects of legislation are virtually never formally followed up by Parliament, so that it has no way of learning by experience how to improve legislation or the way in which it is considered or managed.

Because delay is the main weapon in the hands of the opponents of legislation, it is often described as an effective one, but there is little evidence that it has any appreciable effect. Most of the time, governments get all the legislation they want, when they want it, often at the expense of rational discussion. The number of bills (all of them important and contentious) on which discussion has been cut short by the government has risen from six in the years 1950–1960 to forty-three between 1979 and 1990. Recently one major bill (on reforming the poll tax) was pushed through all its stages in a single day. Any institution which can be forced in short order to enact the Community Charge Bill, the Football Spectators Bill, the Dangerous Dogs Bill, the Security Service Bill (and, in the last decade, forty-eight local government bills), when all rational observers could see that to do so would be ridiculous, must have something seriously wrong with it. In addition, while about 2,500 pages of primary legislation are put to the Commons every year for extensive debate, there are some 10,000 pages of delegated legislation, often just as important, which are hardly discussed and cannot be amended.

Parliament exists to examine, and to authorise, government spending. In fact, it rarely considers spending in any detail and billions of pounds worth are usually authorised on the nod. Attempts to provide more time in the Commons for the examination of spending have usually failed in the face of government opposition. Select Committees rarely examine spending programmes and can do nothing to alter them. Those committees employ no accountants and very few other expert staff who could advise them in these matters. As a result of the recent establishment of government agencies – over fifty of them at the time of writing, dealing, for example, with social security benefits, training, defence research – the committees find themselves swamped by more and more information which they cannot absorb or comprehend. Parliament's cursory examination of spending (it devotes many hours to considering minor taxation) is, as Winston Churchill observed in 1905, 'a series of farces'.[4]

To be fair, there is one exception to these strictures. The only achievement of Parliament in wresting power from government in living memory was the recovery of control of our state audit system by the Commons' Public Accounts Committee in the National Audit Act of 1983. This came after a seventeen-year campaign conceived and promoted *outside* Parliament – and for years actually resisted by Parliament – until it was gradually worked on to the parliamentary agenda. We shall see that government finds it very hard to admit this defeat and in the long run hopes to reverse it.

Parliament exists to call ministers to account for their decisions, their policies and the way in which their departments are managed. Debates and questions in the Commons are not particularly daunting for a competent and well-briefed minister, especially if he or she can produce a flippant reply. The threat is even less now that executive functions of government are being shifted from departments of state, whose ministers have to answer personally and directly to Parliament, to agencies whose chief executives do not. While Select Committee hearings may occasionally give ministers a hard time, the committees do not have the means to carry out serious policy evaluation, nor the assessment of public needs, and they have never shown much interest in examining the quality of management of government departments.

There seems to be very little awareness of what Select Committees *could* do (or what they were capable of doing a hundred years ago). Committee chairmen reportedly spend their meetings together considering the budget for travel abroad and the distribution of the few days available for debates on committee reports, not discussing the need for a research budget nor the scope for co-ordinated scrutiny of government policies. They show no signs of being aware of current ideas of 'networking': creating relationships between groups to bring a variety of skills, experience and viewpoints to bear on a problem. They have not grasped the idea of moving like a flotilla instead of as individual raiders. They would mount a more effective challenge to government if, for example, they joined together to carry out studies of issues which cross departmental boundaries (poverty, discrimination, energy saving).

The superficiality and lack of ambition of most of the Select Committees means that a determined government can usually get away with concealing any important failure for a long time. Meticulous scrutiny of the government by Parliament is essential in a country where the administration is run by a higher civil service noted for its articulacy and refinement of thought rather than its technical qualifications.

When we come to Parliament's role in seeking the redress of the grievances of individual citizens or groups of complainants, the story is more cheerful. There are a number of ways in which a member can confront a minister with a constituent's complaint and by which attention can be drawn publicly to an injustice. Every year, many thousands of people benefit from the ability of a Member of Parliament to intervene on their behalf. However, this service tends to be patchy and haphazard in that many, probably most, people do not know how an MP can help them, or are too diffident to approach their local member and MPs vary in their interest and competence in welfare casework. Members of Parliament and their staff are given no formal training in counselling, consumer law, welfare rights or immigration procedures. This element of a member's work increases constantly and is clearly inadequately resourced.

Even in its purely domestic affairs, the government has refused to provide Parliament with the resources it needs. Its requests for modern information technology equipment have been rebuffed. Members, their staff and the staff of the House have worked in squalor for decades: on a number of occasions work on new office buildings has been stopped by the government on economy grounds. It has taken thirty years to provide one small, refurbished office building and it will be well into the twenty-first century before every MP has an office. Parliamentary pay and pensions are a subject few MPs want to talk about, but the fact is that governments have subjected members and their families, and still subject their survivors, to hardship and charity handouts. With MPs' pay, you always get the feeling from the authorities that it is a gratuity for time lost from a regular job (which, for too many, it is). None of this is by chance: it is a conscious act by the government to keep Parliament in its place and to see to it that it is ill-equipped to challenge, to check and to scrutinise.

Some features of the weakness of Parliament and its subservience to government are underlined if we apply to it some of the criteria of a management audit. How does the organisation relate to the external world – pick up signals from its environment, inform its public – in a systematic way? It is remarkable that so important an institution in our democracy has virtually no means of outreach, to use a fashionable term. It does very little to inform the nation about its purpose, or its procedures, or its history. It also does little to inform itself about developing issues in Britain, Europe or the world. Parliament's Public Information Office and Education Unit have modest budgets; Parliament itself is very hostile to visitors (while this book was being written it daily proclaimed itself as being closed to the public when it was actually open); it tends always to show its worst face to the media and does not explain what it is doing. It has no capacity to carry out, or commission, field investigations of voters' views on current issues nor professional studies of the operational effectiveness of government. It has scant means of modelling or simulating the effects of government decisions. It has no independent source of advice on prospective developments in the EC, on which it is constantly misinformed, nor any presence or listening post in the EC Commission or the European Parliament. It has no independent source of research or information on new technologies, nor on social or economic developments. Virtually all its information comes from government, a lot of it doctored. As Parliament has no research capability of its own, it is always likely to be misled by evidence from government and other public bodies – look at the way it was deceived for years by official analyses of the economics of nuclear power and of renewable energy sources, and how little it has known of nuclear weapons programmes and the improprieties of the secret services.

While Parliament is silent in its own cause, fifteen main government departments now spend £150 million a year (much more than the total cost of running Parliament) on pumping out favourable publicity about themselves. The Department of Employment, a notorious producer of bogus good news and massaged facts, alone spends £20 million a year on publicising its achievements. The media barrage laid down by a government's news managers can drown out any objective appraisal or dissent – witness the effort behind publicising the 'victories' of Prime Ministers at European summit meetings in which Britain actually had to admit it was too impoverished to join the European mainstream.

Since no Parliament can bind a future Parliament, and since without a written constitution it is very difficult to entrench citizens' rights, theoretically our parliamentary system could quite easily lead to totalitarianism and to the acquiescence of Parliament in its own destruction. The safeguards we have are a liberal tradition and a willingness to play fairly by the rules. Our liberties depend on a gentlemanly pact. Unfortunately, when gentlemen are not in charge you get the behaviour of the police during the miners' strike; the withdrawal of trade union rights; arbitrary deportations; the *Spycatcher* prosecution; and a shameful record at the European Court of Human Rights. Many people now think that we need the protection of a written constitution and a bill of rights. The growth of feeling on this point shows how ineffectual our parliamentary system has been in assuring our fellow citizens that their liberties are properly defended.

Opinion surveys show that Parliament is not highly regarded (in a recent survey only 15 per cent of respondents would count on Parliament to safeguard their rights) and MPs are usually low in the league of popular esteem. Given the way that Parliament and MPs are treated in the tabloid newspapers and the limited education in citizenship offered in our schools, that may be understandable. However, a low level of regard for parliamentary democracy is not confined to the ordinary voter. In the course of my professional career, I have often been disturbed by the extent to which many of the senior civil servants I have met despised Parliament and its members and were indifferent to its right to be informed or assisted. I will also never forget meeting chairmen of nationalised industries in 1983 to discuss the proposal that the House of Commons Public Accounts Committee – our senior Select Committee – should be empowered to investigate the use these industries made of the money supplied to them by Parliament. The chairmen found the idea simply outrageous. They declared that they would strenuously resist any such interference and some of them threatened to resign if the proposal passed into law. Their reaction to this modest demand – that Parliament should seek to find out what happened to money that Parliament had provided – made it clear that these public servants had not only a deep hostility to a democratically elected legislature, but also an exceptionally limited concept of public accountability. Some leaders of trades unions in the nationalised industries were easily persuaded to support them. Needless to say, the government took the same view and the nationalised industries escaped parliamentary audit.

Public awareness of the form and scope and purpose of parliamentary democracy, of government and of other institutions is disappointingly low in Britain. In my experience, most people have only a hazy idea of what Parliament does and primarily associate it with antic behaviour and wrangling. Most customers at my advice surgeries have little grasp of the relationship of Parliament to government or of the respective relationships of central government, county and district authorities.

A survey carried out in 1985, and the most recent we have, showed that the public thought the most important part of an MP's job was to express voters' concerns about national issues (69 per cent); deal with constituents' personal problems (53 per cent) and attend meetings in the constituency (24 per cent).[5] In general, the public had little interest in Parliament and did not think it did its job very well. At about the same time, back-bench MPs considered that their most important role was to make a contribution to the national debate (47 per cent); to act as a check on the executive (45 per cent); and to act as a spokesperson for local interests (42 per cent). Half of them thought that the role of the backbencher was 'fairly satisfactory' and 13 per cent that it was 'very satisfactory'. They thought that constituency work was 'the best part of the job', followed by 'participation' in law-making and 'just being there' at the centre of things.[6]

This seems a fairly low level of aspiration for people who have put themselves out sufficiently to get into Parliament. 'Constituency work' in this context was probably not so much dealing with welfare cases as being a person of standing and influence in the constituency, with access to most aspects of its community life and ostensibly having the power of intercession with public authorities. A genuinely valuable feature of this role is that an MP has very rapid feedback on the effect of government policies or decisions: social security claimants or the managers of local industries are quick to let an MP know if they are disadvantaged by the actions of government. When Parliament has so little effective power, representing a constituency can be an absorbing occupation: it is infinitely expandable, it gives an MP a subject on which to be authoritative and admired, to feel influential and to achieve some tangible results. Government ministers and civil servants tend to flatter, and thereby encourage, the MP as local spokesperson and advocate (and on the whole would prefer that he or she was nothing else), because they know that an overload of constituency work drives out political thought and persistent scrutiny.

Although job descriptions have been produced for MPs (by the Top Salaries Review Body), the variety of ways in which the job is done means that it is impossible to generalise about its content. Some MPs are parliamentarians for more than any reasonable definition of full time; some have outside occupations which might justifiably be thought full time. As one journalist put it, 'There is a world of difference between an influential MP in a safe seat with a wallet full of lucrative consultancies and one going flat out in a marginal.'[7] Many concentrate on constituency or regional matters, others on particular policy areas. If an MP with a reasonable majority can retain the confidence of the few members of his or her constituency party or association, he or she can define the job however they wish. The organisation and culture of the parties in Parliament also vary dramatically: the Parliamentary Conservative Party is tightly disciplined and organised and acts as a collective. The Parliamentary Labour Party acts in a spirit of free and individual enterprise with less regard for organisation or command.

Public perceptions of the House of Commons are not improved by seeing its behavioural style in the chamber, particularly now that its most exciting occasions are televised. A leader in *The Times* summed it up: 'The modern Commons behaves like the playground of a boys' school. Opposition spokesmen lean back on the front bench with their feet up, guffawing and nudging each other. When the House is full, members trying to speak are shouted down. Britain's Parliament is designed for confrontation. Ministers are cheered by their own side and jeered by the other. A sensible, soft-spoken woman – or man – does not show up well at the dispatch box.'[8]

Over the last twenty years, long-serving members agree that there has been a noticeable deterioration in behaviour in the Commons chamber. The barracking, or drowning out, of speakers – apparently organised, or at least condoned, by government business managers – is an ominous development. The Commons has a short attention span and much prefers aphorisms to facts. The 'good' Commons speech is characterised by an aggressive delivery and political point-scoring. Speakers who are either quiet or on the pedantic side of intellectual get short shrift. One conventional explanation for this behaviour is that we have debates, not the stiff and formal speechifying of other legislatures, and debating implies liveliness and frequent interruptions. Another is that since the debating chamber is based on the size and shape of the small Royal chapel in which it started, the opposing sides are in close proximity face to face and a combative style is inevitable. However, both these conditions apply in the House of Lords and in standing committees, where behaviour is much more civilised. It seems more likely that raucously macho behaviour has become acceptable and that a crowded Commons works itself up into a collective fugue not untypical of packed assemblies of the British male. Anyway, the Speaker, part of whose function is to see that the rules of debate and standing orders are observed, could put a stop to it simply enough by being less indulgent, by naming constant interrupters and by refusing to call the worst offenders to speak or to ask questions.

Occasionally, and particularly when both main parties are divided on an issue, of which the best current example is European integration, debates can reach a very high standard, though a prized oratorical tradition is on the wane as a new generation of politicians are trained in the brisk reactions required by television rather than the unfurling argument of the public platform. The influence of the media on political style has been a feature of the last decade or so. This applies not only to the style of delivery – the importance of the 'sound bite', the right clothing, the ability to twinkle on the television – but also to the mind-set of leading contemporary politicians, many of whom appear to focus much more on tomorrow's press release than on the issues of the coming decade. This febrile short-termism drives out any thought of strategy in government: the main concern of ministers has been to get a feel-good news item in the top media slot every day. It has also led in the 1980s to the emergence of the hooligan minister. The government of 1979 to 1992 must be unique in that it has enabled some politicians to rise to Cabinet status solely on the basis of aggressive behaviour.

It is probably just as well that the Commons chamber is declining in importance. Attendance there is now usually very low for speeches other than by ministers, shadow ministers and a few others who could galvanise (Michael Foot, Tony Benn, Norman Tebbit). For most of the time a back-bench speaker can expect an audience of twenty or fewer, virtually all of whom will be waiting to speak. This is a much lower attendance than would have been usual twenty or thirty years ago, largely for the humdrum reason that MPs now have offices to go to instead of having to pass the time in the chamber. In addition, constituency correspondence, committee work and the demands of the media have increased enormously in recent years. The desperate search for material by new local radio stations and freesheets, in addition to the demands of the long established media, has substantially increased calls on the time of an active MP.

The workload of a conscientious back-bench MP who undertakes his or her share of committee work, is frequently available to constituents, plays a part in developing his or her party's policy and sees to it that he or she is up to date on the issues in which they specialise, can be a heavy one. Very few managers in industry or government or members of the professions work such long hours of what Bagehot called 'distracted routine'.[9] For those whose families live in a distant constituency the life is often lonely and the burden on spouses, particularly wives, is heavy: it has been said that most MPs' partners operate as single parents. The workload of a minister or a shadow minister and the burden on their families are even heavier. In the Home Office and the Northern Ireland Office they must be intolerable.

Parliament is extremely unrepresentative in composition: women form only 9 per cent of its membership (and less than 1 per cent of MPs are from ethnic minorities). Clearly, this situation is due largely to the attitudes of local political parties when they select parliamentary candidates. The Liberal Democrats and the Labour Party are trying to persuade or require local parties to select more women. These attempts will not be very successful if they are not accompanied by moves to change those features of the routine and atmosphere of the House of Commons which are inimical to the participation of women. The hours, and particularly the voting late at night, make life very difficult for women MPs with young families, even if they live in London, and there are no crèche facilities. Many women also find the aggressive, confrontational debating style of the Commons unsympathetic and daunting. Women members tend to be treated patronisingly or ridiculed by the Commons (though not by the Lords) and the media. The catcalls during Clare Short's speech in 1988 on banning 'glamour' photographs in newspapers ('Show us yours') were shameful, and the recent reporting in a serious newspaper of an excellent speech by Diane Abbott was limited to a description of what she was wearing.

In the chapters that follow, I will set out proposals for change and improvements to our parliamentary system. A number of these ideas have been around for years. Some reformers – the new constitutionalists – will find them too modest, but, as I suggested in the preface, the purpose of this book is to make *practicable* suggestions for improving the effectiveness of Parliament in the foreseeable future, and to build very carefully on existing practices.

If we *were* starting from scratch and designing an effective legislature on a blank piece of paper, I doubt if the Westminster model would be a starter. The founding fathers of the United States knew what they were doing when they drew up a constitution based on the separation of powers of the executive, the legislature and the judiciary, and on a system of checks and balances. Our combination of powers – having the executive drawn from members of the legislature – weakens both. The legislature loses effectiveness because well over a hundred members, among the brightest and best of the largest party, are in the government, and scores more want to be, and as many in the main opposition party hope to be in government. This is not a formula for a Parliament strenuously seeking to assert its powers against government. The limitation of ministers to members of the Commons or Lords can also be a handicap for government. Sir John Hoskyns, a former government adviser, put it brutally: 'For the purposes of government, a country of fifty-five million people is forced to depend on a talent pool which could not sustain a single multi-national company.'[10] There is more than a little truth in this observation. British government departments are in general not very well directed by a combination of mandarins and politicians, both invariably innocent of any experience of, or qualification in, management or technology. It seems odd that none of the proposed new constitutions on offer, including the most radical (by Tony Benn), proposes the separation of powers, with a Chief Minister free to choose an administration from able sympathisers wherever they may be, and a legislature whose members have a strong incentive to challenge the government rather than to prepare themselves for a place in it.

A less revolutionary fresh start might concentrate on reorganising the Commons. Investigatory committees are so much more effective a means of scrutiny than plenary debates that anybody redesigning our system would surely adopt the practices of newer legislatures and organise it into large standing commissions, combining the functions of the present Select and Standing Committees and meeting more or less continuously. These commissions would be specialised by subject and department (e.g. agriculture, defence, Welsh affairs) and would both scrutinise legislation and carry out investigations of spending, policy and the management of government departments. Plenary sessions in the chamber would occupy no more than a week or so in each month and would review the recommendations of the commissions.* Parliament could start to move in this direction now, by giving formal powers to examine legislation (and more resources) to Select Committees.

Leaving aside these radical ideas, some modest shifts in the balance of power are now urgently needed, notably from the government to the Speaker and from the government to the House of Commons Commission (the all-party committee of MPs which runs the place). The first shift would be intended to give Parliament more control over legislation and a greater power to defend citizens' rights. Most of the advocates of the strengthening of civil rights in Britain propose the establishment of commissions or committees with powers to circumscribe government's ability to limit, or prevent the advance of, those rights. Given that the European Convention on Human Rights (see Chapter 2), will doubtless eventually become law in this country, it would be much less complicated and, most important, evolutionary if the Speaker, advised by the Clerk of the Commons, were given the power to invoke special procedures for lengthy deliberation when these rights were threatened by legislation. It will appeal to those anxious to guard our parliamentary tradition if the

---

* Before the First World War the Independent Labour Party adopted a policy of the 'municipalisation' of Parliament, or government by all-party committees, as in local authorities. These committees would be chaired by ministers and would supervise departments and scrutinise legislation. The idea was to allow more participation and independence to backbenchers. It was rejected by the Labour Party Conference in 1930.

Speaker (established 1377) and the Clerk (established 1315) could be the foundation of these reforms. The Clerk is the senior officer in the service of the House of Commons and is adviser to the Speaker, committees and members on practice and procedure. In addition to chairing debates, the Speaker protects the rights of members and minority parties, acts as a spokesperson for the House and chairs the House of Commons Commission. The speaker renounces party affiliation on taking on this role, and its political independence is a great and under-exploited strength of our system. He or she already has the power to refer some exceptional bills for more extensive consideration, and his or her role in the scheduling of legislation, in supervising the quality of legislation (see Chapter 3) and in organising the timetable of the House could be developed. On the other hand, the Speaker and the Clerk should not be expected to direct, manage and substantially develop parliamentary services and a Chief Executive of the House of Commons – a professional manager – should be appointed to do so.

The House of Commons Commission should be given far more resources than it now has for staffing the Commons, particularly for employing qualified staff in a new Research Department and in a Department of the Opposition, and for providing staff and equipment for MPs and their offices. In response to these improvements, MPs should be obliged to declare, in the short run, and relinquish, in the longer term, their outside earnings and any staff provided by outside organisations. If all these changes increased the cost of Parliament by 20 per cent, and they might, it would still be minuscule in relation to the cost and importance of the issues with which it deals. This is where we need a Leader of the House – the Cabinet minister who has a responsibility to defend the rights of the Commons – with nerve, who will request the money and put up with the criticism. Parliamentarians have been trained by our media to feel an excruciating sensitivity about parliamentary costs: catering, pay, pensions, travel, research, accommodation, even repairing the building – any costs, all costs – and tend, with hypocritical timidity, to back away from supporting any investment in making Parliament more effective.

One important reason why Parliament requires more staff for research and analysis is that it needs to become much better informed about developments in the European Community. The information on this subject provided by government is hopelessly partial and inadequate. For example, if our Parliament knew more about the aspirations of the European Parliament and more about the legislative style and attitudes of other EC national Parliaments, a lot of the misunderstandings and hostilities of recent years could have been avoided. Our Parliament needs its own sources of information and a capacity to process it. The Procedure Committee, which examines and reports on our rules and practices, recently considered whether the two committees which examine European legislation, some of it very complex, should have expert advisers. It reported that such assistance would not be appropriate because the committees were concerned with legislation, and legislative committees have never before had advisers; because experts would produce a burdensome amount of paper; and because they would cost a small amount of money in fees. Reading these fatuities, from a committee which was once a force for reform, makes me wonder if I am in a serious legislature.

It is obvious that the British government has already permanently ceded to the EC important powers in the fields of trade and industry and civil rights, and that it will inevitably cede further powers in monetary and economic management, environmental protection and employment rights. Our European partners understand that a member nation has to relinquish sovereignty in these areas in the course of forming a single market. Since most of our partners have far more successful economies than we have and since in general they are more progressive in social and employment rights than we are, it is difficult to see why outdated notions of sovereignty should impede the process. However, the present constitutional arrangements of the EC are wholly inadequate for this transfer of sovereignty. So far, we and our partner democracies have been ceding powers to the secretive Council of Ministers for implementation by the unelected Commission. The Commission will have to be made fully accountable to the European Parliament. It is not as if the European Parliament would be snatching powers from our Parliament: they have already been taken by the Commission. The European Parliament should take back from the central institutions of the EC powers which used to be exercised by the national legislatures. Whatever our self-deceptive reliance on opt-out clauses, we are clearly on the road to democratic federalism, in the sense that important and increasing powers will be exercised on behalf of member states by EC bodies and their use will have to be scrutinised by a democratically elected European Parliament.

Mrs Thatcher, in the debate on the Maastricht Treaty in early 1992, contrasted European arrangements unfavourably with the 'supremacy' of the British Parliament, echoing the xenophobic self-satisfaction so prevalent in discussions of European affairs. One thing that is clear from every chapter of this book is that far from being supreme, our Parliament has too often been supine, particularly when her boot was on its neck. The reforms of my time, principally the creation of more effective Select Committees, have been hailed as giving Parliament a new voice, but compare their reports today with those of Select Committees of the last century – particularly on social conditions – and you can see how generally pallid, deferential and under-researched they are (see Chapter 4).

It is time that Parliament developed, or, seen from a historical perspective, redeveloped, a mind and will of its own. It must exist for more than the legitimisation of whatever government wants to do. If it is to examine legislation, then it should demand to know the justification and purposes of new laws (and the effects of old ones). If it is to approve government spending, then it should do so in a professional and competent way and demand to know what outputs and results are expected, and achieved, from expenditure. If it is to scrutinise the decisions of ministers, then it should put an end to secrecy.* It should also develop a comprehensive system of investigatory committees which, for example, could extend parliamentary scrutiny to policies on women, on security and on the judicial system. If it is to redress grievance and provide easily accessible advice to citizens, then it should be properly funded and equipped to do so. If it is to establish and fortify citizens' rights, then it must urgently take a hand in reforming the selection and training of the judiciary. Particularly, it should learn to fulfil the informing, expressive and educative functions that Bagehot thought it had as 'the great engine of popular instruction'.[12] Parliament should sell itself. It should have the facilities for displaying, communicating, teaching to visitors, tourists, children, teachers and scholars what a living Parliament does.

In practice, the purpose of our Parliament is to provide the members of a government and to scrutinise its proposals and its actions – to the extent that government will allow. However, it seems to me that, contrary to constitutional theory, there are some important functions in which *Parliament* should have an independent locus and a standing neither conferred by the monarch nor in the gift of government. One is to audit the spending it authorises; another is to educate our citizens in

---

* In the debate on yet another Freedom of Information Bill in January 1992 the responsible minister actually said, 'Open government is about the *voluntary* creation by the government of the conditions for an informed democracy [my italics].'[11]

Parliamentary democracy; a third is to improve the quality and intelligi-
bility of legislation; a fourth is to protect and advance civil rights; a
fifth is to enact and supervise freedom of information and a sixth is to
oversee the responsible transfer of authority to the European Parliament. At present, our Parliament has no machinery to carry out any
of these functions other than the first. There is a territory here
waiting to be claimed for parliamentary democracy. The flag should
be planted by the Leader of the House and I have to say that very few
of them in my lifetime have ever shown any inclination to do so. The
job of Leader of the House, which the *Civil Service Yearbook* describes
as being 'to uphold the rights and privileges of the House as a whole',
appears to have been transformed into acting as the Cabinet's major-
domo.

For these, and for its dependent functions, Parliament will still need
an Upper House to share the workload. Some simple reforms of the
present House of Lords – the removal of the hereditary element and
bishops – are necessary until such time as we have carefully designed
the structures of a new constitutional settlement which includes the
definition of powers of a democratically elected Upper House.

A final point. I cannot see that significant progress towards the
reforms I propose will be made unless there is a stable government of
the left and centre. Modern Conservatism has little truck with ideas of
strengthening the powers of Parliament or with defining or extending
civil liberties. Departing from the self-imposed restriction that this book
should not venture far from the immediately practicable, I must confess
that writing it has led me to the conclusion that electoral reform will be
a necessary precursor to any lasting constitutional reform. The exclusion
from power of the progressive majority in Britain has led to the primitive
state of our rights as citizens, the marginalisation of Britain in Europe
and the subjugation of our Parliament. I come to this conclusion with
some regret. As a socialist, compromise was not the secular grail which
drew me into politics and has led me on through an extremely precarious
career, but I never anticipated the impact of the ideological Right in
power, or the destructive polarisation and the damage to democracy
which followed it.

Parliament will be subjected to growing pressures in the coming
decade: from demands for a new constitutional settlement and better
protected civil rights, from the European Community, from its own
inability to cope with ever-increasing legislation and a rising flood of
information, and from scientific and technical advance. It needs to take

a few crucial powers into its own hands so that overweening government
are made more accountable to it. Our Parliament can adapt to these
new demands if it has the vision and the determination.

2

Rights

In recent years there has been growing concern about the encroachment by the government on civil liberties in Britain and the inadequate protection of the rights of citizens offered by our constitutional arrangements. This has led to campaigns for a variety of written constitutions, for a Bill of Rights and for the incorporation of the European Convention on Human Rights into UK law. These campaigns appear to have had a significant effect on public opinion. A MORI 'state of the nation' poll in April 1991 showed large majorities in favour of a Bill of Rights. A second MORI poll in October 1991 showed that only 15 per cent thought that the House of Commons should be responsible for protecting citizens' rights, while 40 per cent thought that they should be protected by a court with a more representative judiciary (only 8 per cent trusted 'the kind of judges we have now') and 34 per cent thought that it should be protected by the European Court of Human Rights.

Britain is one of the very few democracies which has no written constitution: a single document establishing the structure and authority of national and subordinate levels of government and their limits, and defining the electoral process, citizens' rights and a judicial system for redressing constitutional grievances. Most countries set out these powers, relationships and rights in a constitution which is 'entrenched', i.e. amendable only by a process which involves a difficult and complex series of legislative actions, or by referenda. Instead, in Britain, we have a body of statutes and court judgements which do not define fundamental rights but establish what is unlawful, and conventions and usages which allow basic freedoms.

The main constraints on government in Britain, elucidated by A. V. Dicey in the last century, are 'the rule of law' and the 'sovereignty of Parliament'. Neither principle is unambiguous. The rule of law implies that there can be no encroachment on the liberty of the individual without due legal process, and the sovereignty of Parliament asserts that

Parliament is pre-eminent in the making of law. However, in recent years, a number of judgements on human rights in British courts have attracted strong criticism and the limitation of government power by Parliament has been negligible. Since under our arrangements no Parliament can prevent a future Parliament from undoing anything it has done, no rights can be permanently safeguarded. The result is that 'British governments enjoy the greatest degree of political power of any advanced democracy in the world.'[1]

The growth in the untrammelled power of government led Lord Hailsham to assert in 1976 that government control of Parliament, the party machine and the civil service had led to an 'elective dictatorship'. Our constitutional arrangements were wearing out, he said, and the solution was nothing less than a written constitution which limited the powers of Parliament.[2] Governments since then have substantially extended their powers (in the fields of trade union law and local government, for example) and the charge now has considerably more force, though Lord Hailsham does not seem to have returned to it in recent years. The lack of any permanent constitutional rules, coupled with the fiercely adversarial politics of the last twenty years or so, have meant that in many areas concerning citizens' rights there has been more or less constant conflict. Basic principles which have long been settled in other democracies – the right to strike, the powers of the Upper House, the rights of public servants and the formation and role of the judiciary – are still matters of controversy in Britain.

There is a disturbing amount of evidence that citizens' rights in Britain are inadequately protected, by the best international standards, and have been further weakened in recent years. Amnesty International's 1991 Report *United Kingdom Human Rights Concerns* described Britain's record in this field as one which seriously undermined confidence in its legal safeguards. It referred to the difficulty of redressing miscarriages of justice, notably in the Guildford Four and Birmingham Six cases; actions by the security forces in Northern Ireland; inadequate procedures for complaints against the police; the arrest, imprisonment and deportation of Arab residents at the time of the Gulf War without the right of appeal to the courts, and severe restrictions on people seeking asylum in Britain. The employment legislation of the last decade has also led to workers' rights which are more limited than in other countries of the EC. Also in 1991, the international human rights group Helsinki Watch reported that Britain fell far short of protecting the freedom of expression guaranteed by conventions and international agreements to which it was a party, quoting the growth of police powers and the erosion of the independence of broadcasters. It is worth noting, however, that Britain is the only EC member state with race relations legislation and that neither the Treaty of Rome, nor the EC Social Charter offer specific legal protection for ethnic minorities.

Concern that 'our political, human and social rights are being curtailed while the powers of the executive have increased, are increasing and ought to be curtailed' led in 1988 to Charter 88's campaign for a written constitution. 'No country can be considered safe whose freedoms are not encoded in a basic constitution,' the authors of the Charter said. It proposed that a British constitution should include a Bill of Rights and should establish freedom of information, proportional representation, a democratically elected second chamber, an independent and reformed judiciary, legal remedies for the abuse of power by government and an equitable distribution of power between local, regional and national government.

Far-reaching new constitutions have also recently been proposed by the Institute of Public Policy Research, by the civil rights group Liberty, by the Liberal Democrat Party and by Tony Benn. The IPPR constitution would have the effect of significantly circumscribing the power of government and of the Commons by creating an Upper House with equal powers on constitutional matters and a number of standing commissions with powers in the fields of human rights, electoral law and judicial appointments. Tony Benn's Commonwealth of Britain Bill ventures more widely: into the abolition of the monarchy and the disestablishment of the Church of England; the creation of a presidency and of an Upper House of the People; and the appointment by the Commons of a Human Rights Commissioner. The effect of the Benn bill would be to establish the supremacy of the House of Commons in constitutional matters.

Conservative governments have had no sympathy with constitutional reform and the Labour Party has preferred to concentrate on such separate issues as freedom of information, trades union rights and policing and penal policy. The Liberal Democrat Party has a number of constitutional proposals, including a more powerful Upper House, a supreme court and autonomous regional governments. However, there is an increasingly potent influence at work in this domain. Our membership of the EC has meant that many issues of civil rights and the rights of employees fall within the competence of European institutions –

the Court, the Commission and the Parliament – and individuals and organisations increasingly look to Europe for remedies.

A Bill of Rights

The Universal Declaration of Human Rights was proclaimed by the General Assembly of the United Nations in 1948. This was the first step in the establishment of an International Bill of Human Rights and Fundamental Freedoms, which was launched in 1976 with the promulgation of the International Covenant on Economic, Social and Cultural Rights; the International Covenant on Civil and Political Rights; and the Optional Protocol on Civil and Political Rights.

The covenants require nations which ratify them to recognise and protect human rights and the protocol enables the Human Rights Committee of the UN to consider applications from individuals claiming to be victims of violations of the Covenant on Civil Rights, having exhausted all available domestic remedies. The Covenant on Political and Civil Rights requires a ratifying nation to protect its people by law against cruel, inhuman or degrading treatment and to guarantee their right to a fair trial and protection from arbitrary arrest and detention. It proclaims freedom of thought and expression, of peaceful assembly and of association. The Covenant on Economic, Social and Cultural Rights recognises the right to work, to fair wages, to social security, to adequate standards of living, to health and education, to form and join trade unions, and to freedom from hunger.

Many of the provisions in these covenants have been incorporated in national constitutions and bills of rights. In 1976 Britain ratified both covenants, but British governments have refused to ratify the protocol. Only recently (in December 1991), after much pressure at home and abroad, has Britain ratified the UN Convention on the Rights of the Child of 1989, entering reservations (claiming the right not to comply) on areas such as juvenile custody, immigration, nationality and child labour where British legislation differs from it. Even as Britain signed this convention it was in breach of it, because in Scotland we sentence children to life imprisonment without limit of time.

The Council of Europe, formed in 1949 (see Chapter 11), made the protection of human rights a condition of membership and drafted a 'Convention for the Protection of Human Rights and the Fundamental Freedoms', known as the European Convention on Human Rights. This is an international treaty which has been ratified by all twenty-one member states of the Council of Europe. It has sixty-six articles and eight protocols and specifies much the same rights as the UN Covenant on Civil and Political Rights. It was largely drafted in the Home Office and Britain was the first country to ratify it in 1951, against the advice of the then Lord Chancellor, Lord Jowett, who foresaw that eventually it would have to be legislated into British law. Most signatories have since incorporated it into their domestic law and have constitutional courts which review the compatibility of their domestic legislation and government decisions with the principles of the convention and define and limit the powers of their legislatures in the field of human rights. In Britain, the convention has not been enacted in law, but in 1965 the government accepted, on a temporary basis, the right of an individual citizen to petition European judicial institutions on an alleged violation of the convention. This right has since been renewed at five-year intervals, but never made permanent.

Once a citizen of a signatory nation alleging a violation has exhausted the remedies available in his or her own country, the case can be considered in the first instance by the European Commission. The Commission accepts only about 3 per cent of petitions as admissible, and these are subject to an attempt at conciliation with the parties concerned. The proceedings of the Commission are in secret. The Commission sends its opinion on an unsettled qualifying case to a Committee of (Foreign Affairs) Ministers of the Council of Europe, which may rule on the case or send it to the European Court of Human Rights. The Court consists of judges nominated by member countries. If the Court finds for the complainant it may issue a judgement which binds the defaulting state to remedy its action, usually by amending its legislation. This process is supervised by the Committee of Ministers.

Of all member countries, Britain has the worst record for violations of human rights as defined in the convention. More complaints have been registered with the Commission by British citizens than by those of any other country, which is not surprising since they cannot take alleged violations to British courts. The British government has been found guilty of one or more violations of the convention in twenty-seven cases up to the end of 1990, virtually double the number of any other country and nearly one-fifth of all such judgements. We have been found guilty of inhuman and degrading treatment of terrorist suspects in Northern Ireland; degrading punishment in birching juveniles in the Isle of Man; discrimination in immigration control; interference with the rights of prisoners; telephone tapping; interference with the freedom of speech of newspapers; inadequate protection of the rights of parents whose children have been taken into care; wrongful treatment of life-sentenced prisoners; inadequate safeguards for detained mental patients; and the dismissal of workers on account of the operation of the closed shop. More than a hundred British laws and regulations have had to be amended or repealed to comply with the judgements of the court. Proposals to extend the authority of the convention, to cover violations of rights by government decisions and practices, have been opposed by the British government.

One problem for complainants to the European Court is that its procedures are too lengthy and costly. It is not unusual for a case to take five or six years, often because of requests for extensions of time by the British government. There are proposals to speed up the process, including omitting the participation of the Committee of Ministers whose role, as a political body involved in a judicial process, is anomalous. Legal aid for such cases is limited and is not available until a case has been admitted by the Commission.

The convention has been criticised from a humanitarian point of view in detail and in general. For example, it allows a life to be taken in preventing the escape of a person lawfully detained, it allows the death penalty (in time of war) and the detention of alcoholics, drug addicts and vagrants. There are conflicting views on whether or not it could restrict British abortion law. A wider objection is to the exemption clause which follows the statement of principle in each article. Thus, the article granting the right to peaceful assembly, freedom of association and the right to join a trade union is followed by this clause:

> No restrictions shall be placed on the exercise of these rights other than such as are prescribed by law and are necessary in a democratic society in the interests of national security or public safety, for the prevention of disorder or crime, for the protection of health or morals or for the protection of the rights and freedoms of others. This Article shall not prevent the imposition of lawful restrictions on the exercise of these rights by members of the armed forces, of the police or of the administration of the State.

To the British eye, unaccustomed to such formulations, these restrictions appear to offer a pliant judiciary all the scope it would need to negate the right expressed in the article.

However, Britain's miserable record before the Court of Human

Rights has led to a growing demand for 'repatriation' of the convention – incorporating it into British law – so that alleged violations can be heard in a British court and so save the time and money of complainants. More fundamental arguments have been put by Liberty (the National Council for Civil Liberties): 'It would provide the UK's constitutional and legal system with explicit and positive recognition of basic human rights ... would compel legislators, administrators, police officers and members of the judiciary to be concerned systematically and consciously with human rights ... Judges would have to grasp human rights concepts which, at present, are not found in our law ... the incorporated Convention would also help to generate a tradition of human rights which is presently lacking in the UK.'[3]

As long ago as 1976 the government published a discussion paper which set out the case for and against incorporation. The advantages were:

a. its provisions, being drafted in general terms, would be open to reinterpretation by future generations in accordance with their needs;
b. its special status could mean that it provided an effective and quasi-permanent check on oppressive action by future governments and indeed Parliaments;
c. it could be held to ensure conformity with current international obligations (which themselves are framed in general and quasi-permanent terms);
d. it would help to provide a more systematic concern with fundamental values, and more informed public discussion about them; and would bring about corresponding changes in current methods of making, applying and interpreting the law as a whole.[4]

The paper came to no conclusion as to the weight of these advantages. The Standing Advisory Commission on Human Rights in Northern Ireland in 1977 and the House of Lords Select Committee on a Bill of Rights in 1978 both recommended incorporation.

The several proposals for a British Bill of Rights which have appeared in recent years take different approaches to the problem of entrenchment: i.e. how to stop, or at least delay, a government repealing the legislation at any time. The IPPR's suggestion is to create a Human Rights Commission to assist individual complainants, to investigate breaches of a Bill of Rights and to challenge legislation which is inconsistent with it. The IPPR and the Liberal Democrats propose that a Bill of Rights could be amendable only by a two-thirds majority in the House of Commons. Liberty proposes not only a two-thirds rule, but a Human Rights Scrutiny Commission, with powers to attach warnings to a bill indicating that it is in breach of human rights legislation. Legislation so identified would have to be re-enacted after five years. The courts could overturn legislation in breach of the bill unless these special parliamentary procedures were invoked.

The Labour Party has taken a different approach in producing a proposed Charter of Rights. At first opposing the incorporation of the European Charter or the devising of a domestic bill of rights, the party proposed a number of 'individual and specific' Acts of Parliament which set out citizens' rights. These, involving some forty items of legislation, would cover freedom of information; privacy; the security services; equal opportunities; immigration, citizenship and asylum; children; legal rights; rights in employment and to assembly. The preamble to Labour's charter said that the traditional European approach to rights by means of general statements of principle was not appropriate to Britain, though it conceded that European countries had taken individual rights more seriously than Britain. The party considered that rights would be made a reality only through specific legislation backed by a programme of action and said it would urge other EC countries to follow its lead. Its approach to entrenchment was via a new, elected Second Chamber: '. . . It will have the power to delay, for the lifetime of that Parliament, changes to designated legislation dealing with individual or constitutional rights. In this way, we will effectively entrench our Charter of Rights . . .'[5] Any government that sought to erode people's rights would have to present the issue to the people at a general election.

In June 1991, Roy Hattersley, then Labour's Shadow Home Secretary, announced his conversion to what he would 'loosely call' a Bill of Rights on the 'intellectually trivial but politically important' argument that supporters of civil liberties would not believe the Labour Party's intentions without one; on its usefulness for setting the proper ideological mood and because it might protect those freedoms which individual items of legislation did not cover. It was intended that this 'statement of principles' would have the full force of law and would guide and govern the courts where the specific law was silent.

The Judiciary

Hitherto, the major political parties have resisted incorporation of the European Convention into British law either because they maintain that British citizens have adequate protection under existing law (a position that scarcely bears examination) or because of the power it would give to the judges who would have to interpret the convention and rule on alleged breaches of it. Unelected, unrepresentative and immovable judges, it is said, would take essentially political decisions. The general view on the left, where fear and loathing of British judges are deeply ingrained, is that by background, training and social class they would invariably take an authoritarian and unprogressive view of citizens' rights. This view was best summed up by Professor John Griffith in his influential book *Politics of the Judiciary* in 1985:

> My thesis is that judges in the United Kingdom cannot be politically neutral because they are placed in positions where they are required to make political choices which are sometimes presented to them, and often presented by them, as determinations of where the public interest lies; that their interpretation of what is in the public interest and therefore politically desirable is determined by the kind of people they are and the position they hold in our society; that this position is a part of established authority and so is necessarily conservative and illiberal. From all this flows that view of the public interest which is shown in judicial attitudes such as tenderness towards private property and dislike of trade unions, strong adherence to the maintenance of order, distaste for minority opinions, demonstrations and protests, indifference to the promotion of better race relations, support of governmental secrecy, concern for the preservation of the moral and social behaviour to which it is accustomed, and the rest.[6]

Alex Lyon, a former Labour Home Office Minister, has pointed out that the majority of the judges serving in the European Court are trained to understand issues of social policy, whereas British judges are not: 'Thus British barristers are promoted to the bench without any understanding of the complex nature of social policy. When they have to apply their minds to such cases, the result is often born of their own political prejudice ... I support a law on human rights, but it has to be created under a different judicial system.'[7]

Our arrangements for appointing judges have led to a remarkably unrepresentative selection: two women and no members of ethnic minorities among the eighty-odd High Court judges, and of some 430 circuit judges fewer than twenty women and only one member of an ethnic minority. Overwhelmingly public school and Oxbridge-educated, narrow in social origin, establishment in attitude, quaint in dress, they are widely distrusted as champions of citizens' rights. Recent opponents of a Bill of Rights have written: '. . . Many of the restrictions on political freedom which have taken place in the 1980s have not been as a result of legislation but have been judge-made initiatives authorising the extension of executive power. Some of the most significant restrictions on the freedom of assembly, freedom of movement and the freedom of the press were imposed by the courts, not by Parliament. The harsh reality is that we need to be protected by Parliament from the courts, as much as we need to be protected from the abuse of political power.'[8]

The suspicion of our senior judges is reinforced by the fact that they are appointed by the Prime Minister and their appointments are not subject to parliamentary scrutiny. To give extensive new powers to an élite of unaccountable political appointees hardly seems a sensible way of advancing human rights in Britain.

It is clear that changes in the arrangements for judicial appointments are seen by most reformers as a necessary adjunct (or precursor) to a codification of rights. One remedy which is gaining support is that we should adopt the German practice of having a career judiciary whose members are trained and examined in a lengthy apprenticeship from their mid-20s. The Law Society, in a discussion paper of March 1991 on judicial appointments, suggested that the field of recruitment should be widened, that criteria for appointment should be clarified and published and that a Judicial Appointments Commission, including judges, lawyers and 'a strong lay element' should be established to advise the Lord Chancellor on appointments. This commission should also examine the possibility of a career judiciary. The Institute of Policy Research recommended, as part of its proposals for a written constitution, a similar Judicial Services Commission with responsibility for judicial appointments which would be 'obliged to ensure the independence of the judiciary, that it fairly reflects all sections of society and regions of the UK and that it enjoys the confidence of the public'.

These proposals would open up the method of selecting judges, particularly if the qualifications and experience of candidates were published – as they are for candidates for the European Court of Human Rights. Reform of the judiciary is well beyond the scope of this book, but it is worth noting that in the absence of a Commons' Select Committee to oversee the Lord Chancellor's department there is no parliamentary forum even to consider the issue. If such a committee is established (see Chapter 4) it could at least undertake comparative studies of the selection and training of judges and promote a public debate on a subject about which far too little is known; it should also have the right to examine proposed appointees to the highest judicial positions. Two modest proposals that could make a contribution to the reform of our judiciary are that judges should retire at sixty-five and that they should, with other public servants, make a declaration of their membership of masonic societies.

Judicial Review

One area of civil rights in which judges have been more active in the last decade is judicial review of administrative action. Judicial review is the power of the superior courts to examine the legality and validity of the use of administrative powers by public bodies and, where necessary, to invalidate those actions. In 1974 there were 160 applications for leave to seek judicial review and in 1989 there were 1,580. The focus of these cases is narrow, with 40 per cent concerning immigration and the next largest category concerning prison discipline. The growth in applications (of which about 15 per cent have been allowed) has been due to the simplification in 1977 of the rules governing the procedure, the success of some well-publicised cases and an increased willingness on the part of judges to intervene in government administration. The grounds of challenge to a decision include illegality (the authority misconstrued the law); procedural impropriety (the person affected was not given a fair hearing); irrationality or unreasonableness, and the abuse of power. These grounds are not set out in any statute or code.

Governments have been stung by the increasing, but often exaggerated, willingness of the aggrieved to resort to judicial review into inserting 'ouster clauses' in legislation, which establish that a decision made under that particular act may not be called into question by any court (Security Service Act, Interception of Communications Act). Apparently alarmed by the increase in judicial review, in 1987 the Treasury Solicitors' Department and the Cabinet Office produced *The Judge Over Your Shoulder*, a guide for civil servants on how to deal with the threat of judicial review. Somewhat tetchy in tone, it said that 'scarcely a day went by' without the *Times* Law Reports containing one or more cases where someone was challenging the decisions of public bodies. In fact, judicial review has not been the revolution it has been claimed to be. Applications are difficult to organise: the permission of a court has to be obtained to bring a case, there are time limits and there are no reliable guidelines on what is admissible. One extensive study concluded, 'It appears to have played a minimal role in the redress of grievance and has provided the community with a very partial and limited check against government illegality.'[9]

Freedom of Information

An issue which has regularly been the subject of campaigns associated with citizens' rights and constitutional reform over the last twenty-five years has been the need to repeal our exceptionally repressive official secrets legislation and enact a statute conferring a general right to information about the activities of government. The Official Secrets Act originated in 1889. Section 1 dealt with spying and Section 2 with breaches of trust by officials. In 1911 a scare about the supposed activities of German spies led to an act (passed in one day, with virtually no debate) which tightened up Section 1 and widened the scope of Section 2. Section 2 became a 'catch-all' clause which made it an offence to communicate or receive any kind of official information without authority.

In 1968 the Fulton Committee on the Civil Service proposed the reform of official secrets, but no action was taken until the failure of a prosecution against the *Sunday Telegraph* in 1971 led to the setting up of the Franks Committee, a departmental committee of the Home Office. The Franks Committee recommended that Section 1 of the Official Secrets Act be replaced by an Espionage Act and Section 2 by an Official Information Act which would define categories of information the disclosure of which would injure the security of the nation and the safety of the people. In 1976 the Labour government undertook to legislate on the lines proposed by the Franks Committee, but took no action. In 1979 the Conservative government announced it would legislate on official secrets, apparently promising to limit the penalties under Section 2; it then introduced a Protection of Information Bill which was so heavily criticised that it was withdrawn.

Meanwhile, a campaign had started for the enactment of a Freedom of Information Act, along the lines of Swedish and American 'right to know' laws. The author and Robert Sheldon proposed such legislation in a Fabian tract of 1973; a policy committee of the ruling Labour Party drew up a Freedom of Information Bill in 1978 and in the same year the Liberal MP Clement Freud introduced a similar private member's bill which was not supported by the Labour government; in 1981 a bill brought in by Labour's Frank Hooley was defeated by the Conservative government. In 1988 a Conservative backbencher, Richard Shepherd, introduced a Protection of Official Information Bill, based on the 1979 proposals, which was also defeated by the Conservative government.

Most proposed Freedom of Information Bills are based on the United States Freedom of Information Act of 1966, which requires the US government and its agencies to make available to citizens, on request, all documents and records except for those defined in nine categories of exemptions. These exempted areas include secret national security or foreign policy information; personnel or medical files; trade secrets; law enforcement investigations; reports on financial institutions and geological information. As the release of information under the act was still resisted by government agencies, Congress passed amendments in 1974, over a Presidential veto, which reduced delays in the production of information, ended excessive charging for information, reduced the costs of litigation to enforce disclosure and enabled the courts to decide whether information had been improperly classified by a government agency. In 1978 President Carter reduced exemptions from the act and required highly secret classifications to be justified to an Information Security Oversight Office.

At the time of the defeat of the Shepherd Bill the government undertook to introduce legislation to repeal Section 2 of our Official Secrets Act and in 1988 it enacted an Official Secrets Bill. This did nothing to increase information available to the public, gave the government total power over what should be classified as secret and allowed no defence on the basis that what had been revealed was in the public interest. The result is that we still have official secrecy laws that are repressive and undemocratic. In January 1992, the Liberal Democrat Archie Kirkwood introduced another private member's Freedom of Information Bill which failed to make progress. In an illuminating speech, the minister speaking in the second reading debate said that open government should be voluntarily created by the government; that freedom of information legislation had the potential for distracting officials and ministers; that it would lead to a considerable diminution in the powers of the House, would significantly erode Westminster traditions and would expose ninety-two miles of shelved files in the Public Record Office to access.[10]

Clearly, the enactment of a Freedom of Information Bill should be a priority for a reforming government. It should establish the principle of access to official information held by public bodies, with carefully drawn exemptions relating to national security and foreign relations, law enforcement, commercial confidentiality and personal privacy. The burden of proof for withholding information should rest with the public bodies concerned and the act should specify arrangements to refer any refusal to provide information to a court or tribunal.

A Way Forward

The case for a written constitution is not yet compelling given the absence of any general agreement on what it might contain and the existence of an unreformed judiciary into whose hands its interpretation would fall. Given the hostility of the Conservative Party, it is difficult to envisage such agreement in the absence of electoral reform which would give stability and continuity to progressive governments in Britain and enable it to survive. The idea of 'having rights' is so weak in Britain at present that the existence of a declaratory statement of rights, via the incorporation of the European Convention, would at least provide a set of principles against which to test the actions of public bodies and would help to create a consciousness of human rights throughout society, from school onwards.

This does not obviate the need for specific legislation as well. It certainly requires a massive change in the recruitment of judges and the supervision of their selection and progression by a Judicial Commission. Parliament also needs to be significantly strengthened in this area, by establishing a Legal Affairs Select Committee and a Joint Committee of Commons and Lords on Human Rights, to scrutinise legislation and government decisions which affect the rights of citizens. In the long run, one of the most useful functions of a reformed Upper House would be to endow it with powers of delay against the repeal of human rights legislation. In the mean time, the problem of 'entrenching' such legislation could be at least partially dealt with by evolutionary changes to the roles of the Speaker and the Clerk of the House. They now have powers to rule on the admissibility of bills and on appropriate procedures for handling them. The Speaker, advised by the Clerk, could be given the power to identify legislation which apparently infringed the Convention or a Bill of Rights and to require a more protracted process for its enactment: full Select Committee hearings prior to presentation, and/or a two-thirds majority and/or a period of delay before implementation.

3
Legislation

This chapter briefly describes the process of producing new law, from the introduction of a bill to its passage as an act of Parliament. Parliament spends more time on this function than any other, and the scrutiny of bills is often protracted, with lengthy periods of technical discussion by a few interested members punctuated by outbreaks of hectic conflict. The process is on the whole unsystematic in that there is usually little prior examination by Parliament of the purposes of a bill, insufficient expert analysis of its content and likely consequences during its progress through the system, and no formal arrangements for considering what its implementation achieved when put into practice. The chapter concludes with a consideration of how the process and its results might be improved.

Government Bills

A government bill is drafted by parliamentary lawyers on the instructions of the officials of a government department. At first reading its title is announced and it is then printed and made publicly available. Usually after an elapse of two weekends, there is a second reading debate on the principles and purposes of the bill. Non-controversial bills are occasionally referred to a Second Reading Committee. After the second reading, which virtually all bills pass, usually on a vote, the bill goes to its committee stage where it is usually considered by a Standing Committee formed specially for the purpose. A Standing Committee consists of not fewer than sixteen, nor more than fifty members, but, at the time of writing, before the April 1992 election, it usually consists of some eighteen Members of Parliament appointed by a Committee of Selection in proportion to their party's representation in the Commons (eleven Conservative, six Labour, one Liberal Democrat). They examine and debate the bill clause by clause. Amendments to the bill are proposed by the opposition members and are usually resisted by the ministers serving on the committee, who are advised by a team of civil servants, and votes take place. Amendments and additions may also be proposed by ministers to reflect their department's second thoughts or to improve the drafting of the bill.

At peak times of the year, there might be ten Standing Committees in action. They begin by meeting in the mornings on Tuesdays and Thursdays and usually move on to afternoon and sometimes evening sessions.

When a bill has completed its committee stage it is reported, as amended, to the House. It then goes to its report or consideration stage on the floor of the House, when further amendments can be moved. The final Commons stage is the third reading, a brief debate on the bill as amended. The bill is next sent to the Lords where, after a second reading debate, it is considered by a committee of the whole House. There it may be amended and the amendments are sent back to the Commons, where they may be accepted, or further amended, or returned to the Lords for more consideration. In the event of a failure to agree the will of the Commons prevails, after a year's delay. The Lords has no power to amend a money bill. The bill then receives the Royal Assent and becomes law.

Some bills are initiated in the Lords and then go to the Commons and finally back to the Lords in the same stages.

In 1989–90, thirty-four government bills, out of thirty-six introduced, went all the way through to Royal Assent and occupied 372 hours on the floor of the House of Commons. Government bills are by far the largest category of business handled in the Commons, usually accounting for 25–30 per cent of the time available.

For most bills an informal timetable for the stages of a bill is agreed by government and opposition. Strongly contested bills often make very little progress in Standing Committee – on the 1980 Social Security No. 2 Bill, Clause 1 was still under discussion after forty-four hours in committee; on the 1983 Transport Bill, Clause 2 (of twelve) was under discussion after eighty hours; on the 1983 Telecommunications Bill, Clause 3 (of eighty-four clauses and six schedules) after 110 hours (the same clauses had been discussed for over a hundred hours in the preceding Parliament); on the 1989 Water Bill, Clause 8 (out of 180) after seventy-five hours. Remarkably, the first *two days* of the committee stage of the European Communities Bill on the floor of the House were taken up with points of order. When a bill is or may be bogged down in this way the government brings in an allocation of time, or guillotine, motion to cut short debate and to fix a date, or a number of sittings, for the completion of the bill.

Once guillotined, the detailed timetable for the remainder of the bill is recommended to the Standing Committee by a business sub-committee. The guillotine motion is invariably hotly debated, with the opposition alleging that democratic discussion has been stifled and the government maintaining that the bill was being filibustered and that the opposition never hesitated to use the procedure when it was last in government.

On the face of it, all these procedural stages and the lengthy discussion in each would seem to prove that Parliament is exceptionally thorough in its examination of legislation and textbooks usually assert that it does the job rather well.

The most exhaustive examination of parliamentary scrutiny of government legislation was published by Professor John Griffith in 1974.[1] He found that the success rate for opposition amendments in committee in the sessions 1967–68 to 1970–71 was about 2 per cent. His conclusion was that 'on only sixteen occasions in three sessions was the government of the day forced in committee, either by defeat in a division or by pressure there exerted, to modify a part of a principle. And if we consider such modification to be one of the main purposes of committee scrutiny of government proposals, this surely represents a very small achievement.'[2]

The second reading debate on a bill is a typical floor-of-the-House set-piece occasion. A minister opens the debate, which usually starts at about 4 p.m., followed by an opposition shadow minister from the front bench. There is then a general debate and a front-bench spokesperson and a minister wind up for each side and there is a vote at 10 p.m. For all but the most controversial bills attendance is thin after the opening speeches and consists of the members who know that they are likely to be called by the Speaker, having notified the Speaker's office of their wish to speak. These debates are often of a relatively high quality because many of those who speak from the back benches are knowledge-able about the subject or have a constituency interest in it.

John Stuart Mill, writing in 1861, considered that 'a numerous assembly is as little fitted for the direct business of legislation as for that of administration' and thought that laws would be better made by committee.[3] It is true that he thought that such a committee should be composed of experts, because he considered the Commons to be a 'tribunal of ignorance', but the point he made still has force. The principles of most bills would usually have as effective an examination if they were referred to a Second Reading Committee rather than to the House as a whole. This procedure is very rarely used, and only for minor bills, apparently because ministers (and shadow ministers) like the media coverage they get from appearing at the dispatch box. The possibility of television coverage of the proceedings of a Second Reading Committee might change this view. However, the reference of bills to these committees could usefully be increased.

When a bill gets into Standing Committee it is supposed to be scrutinised clause by clause and amended and improved in the light of discussion. This intention is rarely achieved, for a number of reasons, mostly bad. First, the aim of the government side in a Standing Committee is to get the bill through that stage as quickly as possible and unaltered by the opposition. So government backbenchers are enjoined to keep silent and the minister is concerned to give away nothing which would bring credit to the opposition. Opposition members are usually encouraged to propose as many amendments as possible, to vote often and to talk at length. The more controversial the bill, the less the progress made, until the government loses patience and guillotines the discussion. After that, when the bill has to make progress according to a timetable, the atmosphere changes and a more sensible discussion ensues, with both sides usually participating in a more intelligent way.

Secondly, bills are often drafted in a hurry and badly. It may be that the ministers and civil servants in the originating department are not sure precisely what they want and parliamentary lawyers are not properly briefed. Sometimes the department is still consulting with interested parties on the purpose and content of the bill when an opportunity arises to introduce it, which, if foregone, would postpone it indefinitely. Departments like to grab every opportunity for a place in the legislative timetable.

Thirdly, all but a few specialists serving on a Standing Committee on a technical bill (on, say, the regulation of financial institutions) have some difficulty in understanding its details and it is not necessarily the case that any available specialists would be put on it. The Whips might feel that they could cause trouble for their own side if they knew too much about the subject. It is not uncommon to find a minister presenting a bill, and replying to opposition speeches and questions, with very little grasp of its details and relying on material hurriedly handed to him by his panel of civil servants.

John Stuart Mill expressed this problem rather fiercely: 'It is an evil inherent in the present mode of managing these things, that the explaining and defending of a bill, and of its various provisions, is scarcely ever performed by the person from whose mind they emanated, who probably has not a seat in the House. Their defence rests upon some minister or Member of Parliament who did not frame them, who is dependent on cramming for all his arguments but those which are perfectly obvious, who does not know the full strength of the case, nor the best reasons by which to support it, and is wholly incapable of meeting unforeseen objections.'[4] Once again, Mill favoured the use of experts 'in the confidence of government' to present bills, a solution which is never likely to be acceptable, though the use of the Special Bill Procedure (see below) would make a contribution to it.

If ministers have a hard time mastering the details of a bill, those speaking for the opposition have it much worse. At least the minister has a team of civil servants briefing, rehearsing and prompting him or her. The support staff for the main opposition spokesperson on a bill is likely to be one researcher paid for by 'Short money' (see Chapter 10) and then only if he or she is a Shadow Cabinet member. If a bill concerns the interests of a trading association, consumer or pressure group or trade union, suggested amendments and briefing material will be sent to members of the committee and occasionally such an organisation will help the opposition. Nowadays the minister provides committee members with 'notes on clauses' which help to elucidate the dense legalese of a bill, but they are brief, often partial and of limited value.

The result is that the legislative dice are heavily loaded in favour of the government and usually the only people who have mastery of the contents of the bill are the civil servants who produced it. The many hours spent on a committee stage are usually frustrating and unproductive for most of the participants.

Many of these problems can be illustrated by what happened with the Companies Bill of 1989, on which the author led in committee for the opposition. The bill, consisting of 166 clauses, 17 schedules and 240 pages of impenetrable jargon, was the first major bill regulating company law for nearly a decade and amended seven other acts. It implemented an EC directive on company accounts and another on auditing and the accounting profession; amended and extended provisions for the investigation of companies; changed the arrangements for the registration of company charges and for the disclosure of interests in shares; regulated mergers and takeovers; altered the insolvency laws; brought in major changes in the regulation of the financial services industry (which were needed because of weaknesses which had been discovered in legislation passed three years earlier) and made other amendments to company law. It was really three bills: one to comply with EC regulations, one to try to patch up and consolidate complex existing legislation and a portmanteau bill into which the Department of Trade and Industry (DTI) tossed its backlog of ideas for improving the law relating to companies and financial institutions.

It became apparent from the introduction of the bill in the Lords in January 1989 that not only had it been hurriedly drafted, but that the government were making it up as they went along. What had happened was that the DTI had found itself having to meet an EC deadline for the implementation of a directive and had decided to attach all other company legislation it had on hand to that opportunity. On important areas of the bill – company charges, the regulation of auditors, insolvency – it was still consulting with organisations which would be affected by its provisions. One of its most objectionable features was that it contained many clauses which allowed the DTI to fill in the details later by statutory instruments which the House would not be able to amend.

After a second reading debate of five hours in the Lords, the bill moved into committee there for six days, spread over two months, during which the government incorporated 400 of its own amendments. Most of the debates were brief and inconclusive. When the bill came to the Commons, its second reading was put on from 11 p.m. to 1.40 a.m. the night before local council elections, so that attendance was thin. Important parts of the bill – on accounting standards and regulation of the City, for example – were still missing, four months after its introduction to Parliament.

In the Commons Standing Committee, the bill was considered for fifteen two-and-a-half-hour sessions in May and June 1989. Consideration consisted of a series of very short debates on amendments proposed to the bill by the government and the opposition, requiring very close concentration on the part of the half dozen or so members taking an active part. At the conclusion of this stage the government's own amendments had reached the thousand mark and included no fewer than fifteen new clauses which were introduced on the last day of the committee's sittings. These new clauses, in effect a new Financial Services Act, introducing extensive measures to regulate the City and provide investor protection, were discussed for only four hours. They had been available in print for one week, a time quite insufficient to enable consumer groups and other interested parties to consider them. The relevant explanatory notes provided by the government for members of the committee were available only two days before the new clauses were discussed.

On 25 October the bill came to the floor of the House for a third reading debate. At midnight, after seven hours of debate, with over seventy groups of clauses and schedules still to be discussed the Leader of the House announced that the bill would be guillotined the following day. Discussion of the bill therefore had to be completed in a further four and half hours (ending at 1 a.m.), with barely any time being devoted to the examination of important new government powers.

The Companies Bill was a good example of Parliament (and government) at its worst. The legislative process on a highly technical bill was simply ineffective. The issues were far too big and complex to be taken in one bill. It was rushed and exceedingly badly drafted and for much of the time the government was not clear about what it wanted. The Leader of the House admitted in the guillotine debate that the discussion in committee had been constructive and that there was no evidence of obstructive tactics.[5] However, he thought that 'the elected government are entitled, on reasonable terms, to look to the House for the passage of their business.' Experience in operating the act since it became law shows that it is still full of ambiguities and that another Companies Bill will be needed before long to clear up the mess. In addition, the act as passed contains forty-six delegated powers which the government can exercise at any time by statutory instrument and which could be used to change its effect without any further parliamentary scrutiny.

Spatchcocked legislation of this kind is depressingly common. The abolition of the Inner London Education Authority was added to an Education Bill towards the end of its committee stage, key clauses in the Children Bill governing child care were introduced a few weeks before the bill left its committee and the Broadcasting Bill (on TV franchises) changed its aims in committee.

Some of the problems with the Companies Bill could have been avoided if the government had allowed it to go through an investigatory stage before it was debated in an adversarial-style committee. Such a procedure exists (see below), but is not used nowadays. Committee sessions in which MPs could have taken evidence on the purpose and likely consequences of the bill would have shown how ineffective and ill-prepared much of it was and would have obliged the government to have thought it through more carefully before bringing it forward.

This bill illustrates another feature of the inadequacy of much legislative oversight by Parliament. The ministers presenting it in committee, where the detailed scrutiny was supposed to take place, were advised by a team of specialist civil servants – in fact, several teams, who changed according to the subject under discussion. The opposition had no such support. They were served by one temporary research assistant, a very able young man straight out of university, who managed (often at very short notice) to mobilise a few sympathetic outside advisers, mainly accountants and consumer protection specialists, to produce briefs and amendments on the most obviously controversial parts of the bill. There was no time or available expertise to permit detailed opposition questioning on the content or merits of important sections of the bill. The debate was hopelessly one-sided and the investing public and others affected by the measure were not adequately served by the parliamentary scrutiny it received.

Private Bills

A private bill confers particular powers or benefits on an individual or an organisation. Any citizen has the right to promote a private bill before Parliament. There are at least seven types of private bill, conferring permission to carry out certain construction works (e.g. roads, railways, harbours); for local authorities to undertake new activities or to produce regulations; for companies and public institutions to merge; for modifying existing laws where primary legislation is not needed; and for particular cases of divorce, inheritance or naturalisation. Most private bills are promoted by local authorities or statutory undertakings such as water companies and British Rail. The greatest use of the Private Bill Procedure since the middle of the last century has been for the construction or extension of railways and one or two railway bills are still presented in each Parliament.

Twenty to thirty private bills are considered in the Commons each year and 80 per cent of them are unopposed. Those that are opposed and have to be debated involve about ten evenings and around twenty-five hours of time on the floor of the Commons each year.

The promoters of private bills employ firms of parliamentary agents to carry out the complex procedures of drafting and publicising a bill and negotiating with possible objectors before and during its passage through Parliament. The process begins with a petition to the Chairman of Ways and Means (a deputy Speaker) who decides whether the bill shall start in the Commons or the Lords. In the Commons, the title of the bill is read out. If any member wishes to oppose it, he or she simply shouts, 'Object', to block its progress and may then put down a blocking motion. If opponents persist, time has to be found for the bill to be debated. After a second reading debate, if the bill is approved by the House it goes to a private bill committee. If there are petitions against it, and the petitioners are accepted as having a genuine personal or community interest by the Court of Referees (a committee of senior backbenchers) the bill will go to an opposed bill committee. If there are no objections to it or they have been withdrawn, it will go to an unopposed committee. In the Commons these committees consist of four or five MPs who consider whether the purposes of the bill are proper and desirable and, in the case of an unopposed bill, question the promoter. In the case of an opposed bill, the committee has to listen to evidence brought by the promoters and petitioners against the bill and the promoters have to prove the value of the proposed legislation. Both sides usually employ barristers and call witnesses who are examined on oath. After the committee stage, the bill has a third reading, which may be debated, and then goes to the Lords, where it may also be referred to an opposed committee for a similar examination. Some private bills start in the Lords and then move to the Commons in the same stages.

Private bills must complete their stages in both Houses before the end of a parliamentary session or they fall and have to start again. On application from the promoters, they may (on a motion) be carried over to the next session or may be the subject of a revival motion in the next session. Either motion is debatable. If the discussion on a private bill on the floor of the House is protracted, a closure motion is required to end debate with a majority of a hundred members in favour.

This is an extraordinarily complicated, time-consuming and expensive way of obtaining planning permission for public works. Many members find it irksome and inappropriate and in recent years some have decided to block all private bills in order to protest at the use of the procedure.

The matters raised in most private bill proceedings are little different from those in local planning enquiries held all over the country every day. Indeed, the Harbours Act of 1964 offers the choice between the Private Bill Procedure and an application under the act to alter a harbour. Since the inspector's report on a planning enquiry is made to a

minister, Parliament can always require the findings of such an enquiry
to be debated, as in the Sizewell nuclear power station case in 1987. It
has long been suspected that the promoters of a development may use
the Private Bill Procedure in order to avoid the delays of planning
enquiries or may deliberately include in their schemes minor elements
which do need parliamentary approval, so as to take advantage of the
Private Bill Procedure. Fees have to be paid to Parliament for promoting
or petitioning against a private bill, but until recently they had not been
increased for a hundred years or so and in a recent year amounted to
around £8,000, while the costs to Parliament were estimated at
£300,000: Parliament has been providing a service to promoters for
virtually nothing. The fees paid by promoters to agents and counsel for
opposed private bills usually amount to more than £60,000.

Dissatisfaction with the concept of private bills was brought to a head
in the 1980s by procedural controversies over several of them. In 1981
a bill for a bypass round Okehampton was thrown out by its committee
and then confirmed by the government. This was the first time that a
report by a Private Bill Committee had been overruled, so wasting the
time of members and the money of petitioners. In 1985 a bill was
introduced to alter the line of a railway in the course of constructing a
relief road in Edinburgh and a Commission's enquiry into the matter,
under the Scottish Private Bill Procedure, lasted for fifty-two days before
it was referred to a Parliamentary Committee which confirmed the Commission's approval. The Felixstowe Dock and Harbour Bill, to extend
Felixstowe dock, was presented in November 1984 and was finally
passed in May 1988 after forty-one hours in the chamber and eighty-six
hours spread over five months in committee. It was widely felt that a
public enquiry would have been more effective.

At about this time it became apparent that a number of cities were
interested in building rapid transit rail systems to ease traffic congestion
and that most of them would be promoted by private bills (a dozen or
so since have been). The House therefore faced the prospect of many
hours of debate on matters of purely local interest.

A farcical twist was given to this subject in January 1991 when the
Southampton Rapid Transit Bill (which the author introduced) came
before the House of Commons. The bill was to permit the City of Southampton to build a light railway system round the city centre. It was supported by the Labour-controlled City Council by a two-to-one majority
and surveys showed that locally it had popular support. It started in the
House of Lords in November 1988 and received a second reading in April

1989. The Lords considered it in committee for seven days in November 1989, taking evidence from promoters and petitioners, and visiting the site. In May 1990 the Lords approved the bill in a third reading debate and in the same month it came to the Commons, where it was blocked until the end of the parliamentary session by some Conservative members representing the area. In January 1991 it was the subject of a revival motion to enable it to continue its progress through the Commons. A transport minister said in the revival debate that the government took a neutral position on the merits of the project (though it had supported a number of similar proposals). After three hours of debate 138 Conservative MPs and ministers voted against the motion, and the bill and the project were consequently lost. It was alleged that the Gulf War Cabinet had been adjourned to allow some ministers to vote on this motion! So, after two years and four months in Parliament, after an expenditure of some £750,000 by Southampton City Council and countless hours of the time of council officials and councillors, the whole exercise came to nothing.

In 1988 a Joint (i.e. Lords and Commons) Committee on Private Bill Procedure issued their report.[6] It found that the main opponents of the procedure were petitioners, because they thought the procedure gave the initiative to promoters and because planning enquiries were less intimidating, more local, less adversarial, less arbitrary and gave more facilities for objectors. They thought that planning inspectors were more expert than MPs and found it valuable that they had to give reasons for their decisions which were reviewable by the courts on points of law. The main defenders of private bills were promoters, who found the procedure quicker, considered that 'Westminster was more willing to experiment than Whitehall'[7] and thought that MPs were more disinterested and made up for their technical ignorance with political wisdom.

The committee concluded that local planning enquiries had many advantages over the Private Bill Procedure. It made a number of recommendations to reduce the use of the procedure, including requiring promoters to prove that private legislation was necessary and, as far as possible, to use other means, particularly local planning enquiries, to obtain authorisation for their projects. It also proposed simplifying the procedure, making blocking more difficult, and recommended raising the fees payable to Parliament to £10,000 per bill (still a derisory sum).

The government replied to the report in June 1990.[8] It generally agreed that proposals for railway and rapid transit projects and more harbour measures could be considered and approved outside Parliament. These changes might reduce the numbers of private bills that reached Parliament each year by about half. It welcomed most of the suggestions for speeding up and raising the charges for using the procedure. It has not yet taken any further action on the matter.

These changes seem likely to remove some of a long-standing burden on the House, but it is far from clear why the procedure should continue to exist at all. If the current proposals are carried through, the matters which will continue to be the subject of private bills will be the construction of river barrages (which could be dealt with by planning enquiries); the regulation of markets (most of which could be handled by local government legislation); the deconsecration of cemeteries and companies wishing to change their constitutions (which could be achieved by application to a court or tribunal). Private legislation could and should be dispensed with entirely.

Private Members' Bills

Members of Parliament may introduce bills in one of three ways: by ballot, under the ten-minute rule or by what is known as Ordinary Presentation under Standing Order 58. Virtually all of those which are successful are introduced by ballot.

Under the ten-minute rule a member may propose a bill on a Tuesday or Wednesday in a brief speech which may be followed by a brief speech from an opponent. Proposers queue at the Public Bill Office, sometimes all night, to get the opportunity to introduce their bills. They are rarely serious attempts at legislation but offer means to obtain some publicity on the need to change the law. No ten-minute-rule bill has been enacted since 1983–4 and only about twenty-five since 1945.

Under the Ordinary Presentation procedure a member may present a bill which stands little chance of being debated but enables the member to have 150 copies printed and to set out his or her proposals on a subject. Four or five a year are passed into law. In the 1990–91 session such bills concerning the protection of badgers and the breeding of dogs were passed, but Tony Benn's comprehensive Commonwealth of Britain Bill was not.

Balloted private members' bills are usually serious attempts to introduce legislation. About 400 members usually enter an annual ballot in which twenty are drawn by the Speaker in order. Thirteen Fridays are allocated for discussion of these bills, of which seven are allowed for second readings. Most members have a bill, or a subject, in mind when they enter the ballot, but those who are successful soon receive many suggestions for bills. Once a member has been drawn in the top dozen or so he or she is contacted by pressure groups which usually have a draft bill on the shelf. Government departments also have 'handout' bills available which they offer to members who have been successful in the ballot on the understanding that the department will offer support during the stages of the bill. These are bills for which the government cannot find time or which it wishes to keep at arm's length. They stand a good chance of getting through and appear to be increasing in number: in 1989–90 seven of the top twenty appeared to be in this category.

There are some complicated ways of blocking the progress of private members' bills if they are in any way controversial or disliked by the government. After going through Committee and other stages, between five and ten are passed in each parliamentary year, most of them fairly uncontentious. Recent ones have concerned the wearing of seat belts by children, malicious communications, the registration of buildings for marriage and rights of way.

A few have succeeded in spite of opposition from the government, a notable example being the National Audit Act 1984, which strengthened parliamentary scrutiny of government spending (see Chapter 6). The most fiercely contested in recent years have been those concerned with attempts to weaken the provisions of the Abortion Act 1967 (itself a private member's measure) which have led to MPs being deluged with letters, illustrated postcards, petitions and, on one occasion, models of foetuses. The 1992 private member's bill to protect wild mammals (i.e. end hunting with hounds) provoked a comparable level of controversy.

There have been a variety of procedural attempts to increase the time available for the consideration of private members' bills, particularly controversial ones, but on the whole the present arrangements seem to be reasonable. One development which should be watched is the growing tendency for private members to introduce bills provided by the government – a trend which could, in time, change the nature of a valuable procedure.

Delegated Legislation

'There is now general agreement about the necessity for delegated legislation; the real problem is how this legislation can be reconciled with the processes of democratic consultation, scrutiny and control.' (Aneurin

Bevan MP, in evidence to the Donoughmore Committee on Delegated Legislation, 1932.)

An Act of Parliament very often confers powers on ministers to make consequential rules or regulations which have the force of the parent act. These are known as secondary, subordinate or delegated legislation, and the most common form is the statutory instrument. Other forms include administrative orders, regulations, rules and codes of practice (which are increasingly used in such areas as health and safety at work, social security and criminal evidence). The scope of delegated legislation has never been defined by Parliament or the courts and it is very difficult to chart its boundaries. Wherever they are, we can be sure that government is trying to extend them. There is a large fuzzy area round the edge, in government 'directions' to public bodies which may or may not be construed as legislative in effect. The whole field has been called executive law, theoretically breaching the constitutional principle that only Parliament can make law.

There are many examples of 'enabling' or 'blank cheque' legislation which delegates very extensive powers to ministers. Particularly notable are the European Communities Act 1972 and the Social Security Act 1986. The latter attracted much criticism in both Houses because of the exceptionally wide powers it conferred on ministers to introduce or change social security schemes and 'the dearth of information offered about what the powers were and how they would be used'.[9] The Local Government Bill of 1991 gave extraordinary powers to the Secretary of State for the Environment to reorganise, and change the powers of, individual local authorities by statutory instrument after receiving advice from a commission appointed by him. Particularly objectionable are so-called 'Henry VIII clauses' which allow ministers to amend or repeal primary legislation by statutory instrument, analogous, it is said, to that monarch's Statute of Proclamations (1539). The same Local Government Bill included such a clause, allowing the Secretary of State for the Environment to extend compulsory competitive tendering for local authority services. It was deleted in the Lords as unconstitutional, but restored by the government when the bill returned to the Commons.

There are usually about 2000 statutory instruments made each year, nowadays amounting to some 10,000 pages of legislation (about four times as much as primary legislation). About a third of them, apparently uncontentious, are not subject to any parliamentary procedure, but just become law on a given date. Some become law unless Parliament passes a motion (called a prayer) calling for their annulment, usually within forty days; this is known as the Negative Procedure. Others (affirmative instruments) require a resolution in order to be implemented. The procedure to be applied to an instrument is decided by the minister concerned and is set out in the parent or enabling act. Virtually no instruments can be amended or altered.

Two committees on statutory instruments, a joint Lords/Commons committee and a Commons committee for taxation and money-raising matters, scrutinise these instruments to see if they are in accordance with the enabling act and to warn the House when the procedure has been abused. They may not consider the merits of an instrument, but can report if the authority of the parent act has been exceeded or if it involves an unusual use of the powers of the parent act or if its meaning is in doubt. They may not demand a debate on an instrument. Virtually every week the Joint Committee reports on instruments that have been drafted in a slipshod way or are unclear or otherwise out of order. In the 1988–89 session the committee reported over 120 as defective. A good example of a defective instrument was the Community Charges (Registration) (Scotland) Regulations 1988. In a debate on this instrument in March 1988,[10] the Chairman of the Joint Committee on Statutory Instruments, Bob Cryer, said that there was a strong case that the regulations were beyond the powers the House had given to the Secretary of State for Scotland in the parent act. The poll tax registration officer was being delegated powers to ask for documents and to ask questions of poll tax payers: 'There is clear sub-delegation to a civil servant to make the law,' he said. The instrument was passed by a government majority regardless. Not infrequently, the government puts a motion to approve an instrument to the House of Commons while the Joint Committee is still deliberating on it.

Debates on statutory instruments are usually held if there is evidence of significant opposition to them and may take place on the floor of the House or in a standing committee if a motion to do so is made by a minister (there are six of these committees).

For many years there have been vigorous complaints about the increasing use of statutory instruments by governments as a means of producing legislation which cannot be discussed at any length, and cannot be altered by Parliament. 'Some have depicted this state of affairs as an abdication by Parliament from its principal constitutional role in favour of the executive. Acts of Parliament, sponsored by government departments and passed into law with the acquiescence of a docile parliamentary majority, give the executive sweeping legislative powers; and safeguards against the abuse of these powers are inadequate,' wrote one recent commentator.[11]

A particularly violent attack on the use of delegated powers was made by the Lord Chief Justice, Lord Hewart, as long ago as 1929 in a book called *The New Despotism*. This led to the appointment of a committee on ministers' powers which found nothing much to worry about. Concern has since surfaced from time to time, but the use of delegated legislation has steadily grown.

The arguments for delegated legislation are that it can be used for highly technical details which would otherwise overload a bill; it can be used to update fees, fines and financial limits; it can bring parts of an act into force when practicable; it can be used to modify or amplify an act in the light of experience; and it can enable emergency action to be taken under the general provisions of the act. Governments like it because it gives them flexibility and time for second thoughts and is efficient from their point of view in that it stops Parliament from delaying the process of legislation.

While most statutory instruments are uncontroversial, many nowadays put important and unsupervised powers into the hands of government and they are difficult to challenge in the courts. Andrew Bennett, who has served on the Joint Committee for fifteen years ('one of the most boring committees I have ever sat on'), has described their growing and dangerous use: 'I would suggest that a major change in the nature of instruments has occurred. Provisions that in the past would have been contained in primary legislation are dealt with in delegated legislation.'[12] He refers to the wide powers conferred by the Education Act 1986, the way in which Child Benefit regulations have been used in a manner that was never envisaged in the Child Benefit Act 1975 and the regulations under the Electricity Act 1990 which allowed the government radically to alter the arrangements for electricity privatisation. He also points out that social security payments, affecting a million or more people, can be changed by instrument when far less significant tax changes may be the subject of hours of debate in the House and in committee.

Lord Donaldson, commenting in the Court of Appeal on changes by the Department of Social Security to the severe disability premium, said that the regulations allowed the Secretary of State 'to prescribe that black is white and nothing is something ... This just will not do.'[13]

Changes in the premium deprived up to 400,000 people of a benefit worth over £28 a week.

This is not the only example of massive changes in social security rules introduced by statutory instrument. In April 1992, two instruments came into force which reduced the definition of full-time work for income support and family credit purposes from twenty-four to sixteen hours. This had the effect of reducing by £60 the weekly income of a couple with two children where one partner had a twenty-hour-a-week job paying £40. Worse still, on 21 August 1991 Statutory Instrument 1878 was introduced and came into force when the House was not sitting. It banned people from claiming backdated benefits due to official error – in Strathclyde alone there were at that time 30,000 claims totalling £6 million. Statutory Instrument 1531 of 1991, concerned with the suspected keeping of explosives, gave the police powers of forcible entry into dwellings without warning, power to evict occupants of a dwelling and power to charge with an offence if a suspect remained silent.

Lord Rippon of Hexham, in a recent conference on delegated legislation ('I believe what is happening today is – in the words of Lord Simon – a constitutional outrage'), pointed out that a clause in the Children Bill – piloted by the Lord Chancellor himself – gave extraordinary powers to the Secretary of State to modify or repeal a large part of the bill by regulation and to add to the powers and duties of local authorities in any way he saw fit.[14]

The Joint Committee on Statutory Instruments observed in a memorandum to the Procedure Committee: 'Secondary legislation has increased not only in volume but in scope. Instead of simply implementing the nuts and bolts of government policy, statutory instruments have increasingly been used to change policy, sometimes in ways which were not envisaged when the enabling primary legislation was passed.'[15]

The Statutory Instruments Committee has also complained about the way its findings are treated by the government. Referring to the numerous occasions when it reports faulty instruments to the House, it commented, 'At present, there is no formal mechanism for ensuring that necessary corrective measures are taken and in the absence of a power to amend instruments, this has resulted in instruments of uncertain legality taking effect. In former times, it is the committee's impression, departments paid great attention to reports from the committee . . . This seems to be less the case now and some departments respond to points taken by the committee in a truculent manner and refuse to repair the faults in instruments. The committee finds that it is not acceptable that so little account is taken of its work . . .'[16]

It has also pointed out that it receives no prior explanation of how statutory instruments are intended to be used when the enabling powers are debated; that affirmative instruments can be debated before it has reported on them; that it cannot take evidence from witnesses other than government officials nor report on codes of practice which are increasing in number and are rarely examined by the House of Commons.

Andrew Bennett also asks, 'Who scrutinises the regulations ministers do not make? The answer is no one. I could give a very long list indeed of regulatory powers that were conferred on ministers and not used when and how Parliament intended.'[17] He quotes examples of ministers taking powers to make regulations, perhaps as a result of campaigning by pressure groups, and then 'destroying any balance there was in the legislation' by making some regulations and not others so that the pressure groups then have to lobby for the regulations to be made. For example, ministers succumbed to pressure to make provision for marine conservation areas in the Wildlife and Countryside Act 1981, but have since designated only one.

A valuable study of delegated legislation by Keith Puttick draws attention to the way it can be used to accumulate legislative power:

> Another phenomenon is also apparent. This is the 'storing up' of legislative and administrative powers. In this respect, powers to make delegated legislation are particularly advantageous for the purposes of carrying out the administration's longer term and less well formulated policies . . . In some instances it is obvious that rule-making powers are assumed well in advance of any serious consideration as to how they will eventually be used.[18]

The use of delegated legislation on the scale we see today is clearly an abuse of Parliament; primary legislation should as far as possible specify the powers which are intended to be taken under it. Delegated legislation should also be more easily amendable by the House. The Statutory Instruments Committee should be given more information and more powers: i.e. ministers should explain to it how they propose to use an instrument; it should be able to take evidence from outside experts; it should have the right to examine codes of practice and similar instructions and directions and it should be able to prevent a doubtful instrument from coming into effect without being debated. Andrew Bennett makes the sensible recommendation that ministers should report to Parliament annually on those regulatory powers which they possess and have not used, together with a brief explanation of why they have not been used. It would be equally useful if each department also reported annually on the delegated powers it had acquired and used. This would not necessarily diminish the practice, but it would enable us to map the terrain. None of these proposals would be difficult to implement and they would oblige ministers to think twice before pouring out legislation which avoids proper parliamentary scrutiny. It is nearly twenty years since the use of delegated legislation was last examined by Parliament. In that time the growing use of executive law, or government by decree, has seriously weakened parliamentary scrutiny.

The Royal Prerogative

The Royal Prerogative is the expression used to denote what remains of the power of the Crown to legislate without the authority of Parliament. Since the monarch acts with the advice of the government, the procedure enables a government to produce primary legislation without parliamentary consent. Furthermore, this legislation may not be challenged in the courts. It is not clear what the limits of the Prerogative are. In the last ten years, some 1400 orders have been made under it. When ministers are questioned about them, the usual answer is that they deal with such matters as the grant and amendment of Royal Charters, the government of dependent territories and reports of the Judicial Committee of the Privy Council (the Superior Court for present, and for a number of former, colonies). This makes the procedure sound innocuous and quaint. However, it is also applied to the making of international treaties, the declaration of war or blockade, the disposition of the armed forces, the regulation of the civil service and the making of hundreds of appointments (ministers, peers, chief executives). The government used it to enable the United States to bomb Libya from bases in England in April 1986 and to commit British military forces in the Gulf War. The debate on this decision in the House of Commons was on a motion which could not be amended, instead of a statement of policy to which the opposition could have moved a reasoned amendment.

Tony Benn observed at the time, 'This is the first time in the history of this country that British troops have been sent into battle under foreign command, using the Royal Prerogative of war-making to do so, without the House having had an opportunity to express its view on any motion other than that we adjourn.'[19] He contrasted the handling of the matter in the Commons to that in the American Congress where both Houses debated and voted on a resolution on military action.

Under the Royal Prerogative the government can forbid a subject to leave the country; jury vetting guidelines, Home Office rules about granting passports and the establishment of a criminal injuries compensation scheme were also promulgated under it. When it was used to ban membership of trade unions by staff of the government intelligence establishment, GCHQ, in January 1984, the government argued successfully in a subsequent court case that not only were such powers not open to judicial review but instructions given in exercising them enjoyed the same immunity.

It is clearly very unsatisfactory that a citizen can challenge in court the operation of a statute but not an order issued under the Royal Prerogative which has the same effect as legislation. It is time that this feudal anachronism was ended. A number of prerogative powers could be enacted in legislation: the regulation of conditions of employment of civil servants should be governed by a Civil Service Act and powers in the field of civil liberties could be replaced by Home Office legislation.

The principle of Crown Immunity derives from the Royal Prerogative. The sovereign enjoys a number of immunities derived from the antique 'prerogative of perfection' (i.e. 'the king can do no wrong'), including immunity from writ and from liability to income tax and having the status of preferred creditor in commercial transactions. The most controversial issue raised by Crown Immunity is that under it government departments and many public bodies are not bound by a wide range of protective legislation, such as health and safety and food hygiene laws, planning regulations and the Rent Acts. For example, the NHS could not be prosecuted for filthy hospital kitchens until the National Health Service and Community Care Act of 1990 removed much of the Crown Immunity enjoyed by the NHS.

A series of questions to government ministers put down by Jack Ashley has established that thousands of establishments operated by the government are immune from prosecution under food hygiene, health and safety and environmental protection legislation.[20] The fifteen ministers replying to his questions said that their policy on Crown Immunity was to consider every case on its merits and if there was evidence of inadequate standards they would consider how best to deal with the circumstances.

Crown Immunity is another feudal relic which should not be allowed to enable public bodies to ignore legislation which applies to other organisations.

Timetabling Bills

We have seen that a guillotine motion imposes a compulsory allocation of time on the consideration of a bill and is usually put down by the government when a bill has made very little progress, usually after eighty to a hundred hours in Standing Committee. Many guillotine motions are justified, though some are palpably unfair and lead to inadequate discussion on important later clauses in a bill or on amendments to it. The guillotine arrangements for the Council Tax Bill in December 1991 involved the Standing Committee meeting for three ten-hour days a week, two of them running from 10.30 a.m. to 2 a.m. the next day.

Guillotine debates last for three hours on the floor of the House and are exceptionally unrewarding. In recent years the use of the procedure has grown substantially: between 1945 and 1970 it was used twenty-two times while in Mrs Thatcher's eleven years forty-three bills were guillotined.

For years, there has been widespread support for the idea that all bills should be timetabled after their second reading and should be allocated time in committee which would allow reasonably full, but not protracted, examination and debate. This arrangement would allow a balanced discussion of the bill, would encourage participation by government backbenchers and would avoid the need for guillotine debates.

In 1985 the Procedure Committee considered the case for automatic timetabling. What it called the 'classic objections'[21] to the idea were that it was not possible to anticipate the points of debate that might arise during the progress of a bill; that government might find less need to respond to argument because the passage of the bill would be assured after a certain time; that the absence of a timetable allows the opposition to use its power of delay to secure concessions from the government and that government supporters would take a larger part in debates in committee and would thereby reduce the opportunities for the opposition to participate.

A memorandum to the committee from the Study of Parliament Group (an association of officials of the Lords and Commons, academics and former MPs) dealt summarily with these objections: it said that timetabling could be sufficiently flexible to modify the overall allocation of time; that there was no obvious instance in recent history when the opposition had managed to obtain a substantial concession from the government by delay alone and that there was little to be said for a system which discouraged government backbenchers from participating in proceedings on government legislation.[22]

The Procedure Committee devoted attention to what it called the 'time-hallowed argument' that delay is the major weapon available to opponents of legislation and could find very few examples where delay had had any effect at all.

Its conclusion was that there was a pressing need for timetabling for a small number of highly controversial bills, a proposal supported by nearly 73 per cent of the 323 MPs who had answered a survey question on the matter. It proposed the establishment of a Legislative Business Committee which would examine the likely progress of every bill and, if it considered that a bill would require more than twenty-five hours in Standing Committee, would recommend a maximum number of hours for the committee stage. The detailed allocation of time would be decided by a business sub-committee formed from the membership of the Standing Committee.

After nearly a year the government tabled a number of motions on the Procedure Committee's recommendations, but not the one on automatic timetabling, so the Chair of the Procedure Committee tabled an amendment which would give effect to the proposal for a one-year experiment. On what was ostensibly an unwhipped vote, the proposal was defeated by 'an unprecedented turn-out of ministers and parliamentary private secretaries',[23] in alliance with the opposition front bench. Apparently, both front benches objected to an independent Legislative Business Committee having any hand in deciding the use of time in the House.

The Procedure Committee persevered with the topic and in 1986 put forward another possible solution.[24] It recommended that one-third of the members of a Standing Committee should be nominated as a business sub-committee to recommend a timetable for the bill after it had been in Standing Committee for six sittings (fifteen hours).

It is clear that the absence of timetabling leads, on about half a dozen highly controversial bills each year, to delaying tactics in committee which are pointless and extremely boring and to an equally pointless debate on a guillotine motion. The committee then resumes its work and can usually examine the rest of the bill adequately before time runs out. The best solution was the Procedure Committee's original proposal, that Parliament, rather than the government, should establish a timetable for such bills. In February 1992, the Leader of the House indicated that the government was now willing to consider the timetabling of bills.

Special Standing Committees

The Procedure Committee of 1977–78 (see Chapter 4) considered that there should be some way of allowing the committee which is to consider a bill to examine and establish the factual and technical background to the proposed legislation before proceeding to debate its clauses: 'In order to achieve this the committee should be free directly to question those who have drafted the proposed legislation and those who implement it as to the purpose of the legislation, the evidence on which clauses are based, the degree and content of any prior consultation with outside interests, the effects which the legislation is expected to produce and the problems which will be involved in its implementation. They should also be free to consult those who will be principally affected by the legislation.'[25]

The committee thought that such a procedure would lead to more informed and better aimed criticism of the text; might do away with many 'probing' (i.e. exploratory) amendments; might encourage more consideration of the problems of implementation and thereby lead to better drafting in the first place; and should also satisfy the interests principally concerned that proper attention had been paid by Parliament to their opinions about the proposed legislation.

It recommended arrangements, now known as the Special Bill Procedure, to enable committees on bills to have a limited number of sittings in Select Committee form, i.e. calling witnesses and receiving written evidence, before moving to a conventional examination of the bill. It thought that the investigatory sessions of such a committee should be limited to three two-and-a-half-hour sessions in public. It hoped that a variety of bills, including bills of some substance, would be the subject of this new procedure in order to give it a fair trial and that it would, before long, 'become accepted as the "normal" committee to which the great majority of bills stand committed'.[26]

The recommended procedure was accepted by the government, thanks to the efforts of the Leader of the House, the then Mr Norman St John Stevas, on a sessional basis from 1980–81 to 1983–84 and was incorporated in the standing orders of the House in 1984. It was used for three bills in 1980–81, one in 1982–83 and one in 1983–84, all of them uncontroversial. Since then it has not been used.

A Procedure Committee in 1985 commented that all the evidence it had received on the operation of Special Standing Committees was enthusiastic.[27] Its report quoted persuasive evidence as to the value of the procedure from the Solicitor-General. He said that he had served on three Special Standing Committees and on one of them, concerned with the Criminal Attempts Bill, he had had the salutary experience of cross-examining two leading authorities on criminal law as to the likely effect of a bill about which he was already experiencing a 'sinking feeling':

> 'At the end of the final sitting of the Special Standing Committee the draftsman informed me that not only did the bill not do what it was supposed to do, but that it could not be made to do it.
>
> 'It is unnecessary to relate here the unorthodox and urgent steps that were then taken to recast that part of the bill in time for the resulting vast array of amendments to be on the paper when the ordinary Standing Committee first met the following week. The point is that it was better that those defects became apparent before the ordinary Standing Committee began its examination of the bill rather than, say, half way through the process. I gratefully recognised this at the time and have never forgotten it.'

The Solicitor-General's conclusion about the procedure was:

> 'It is very remarkable how the operation of the special procedure stimulates the interest of the members of the committee, and brings them together even though their respective opinions may remain sharply divided. In my experience it engenders the feeling, both among members and among witnesses, that here at least the House of Commons is permitting itself to do important work in a mature manner, and is doing it well.'[28]

Other witnesses referred to the way in which the few Special Standing Committees which had been established had enabled members to be better informed as a result of hearing evidence and had led to important changes in legislation which might not otherwise have been made.

It is disturbing that a procedure which offers so greatly to improve the scrutiny of legislation is not used. It would have been an ideal way of handling the Companies Bill referred to earlier. The government would have had to put the bill in far better order before bringing it to the House, because ministers and civil servants could never have faced public examination of its provisions without more consultation and thought. It would certainly have led to better drafting and hence fewer government and opposition amendments. An attempt to get the Companies Bill put to a Special Standing Committee was voted down by the government, which clearly fears this way of examining legislation. Ministers appear to think that it might prolong a committee stage, but in fact it is much more likely to shorten it. The most likely explanation is that ministers know that much of the legislation they bring forward is so inadequately prepared that they could not explain, let alone defend, it under cross-examination and that outside experts would make their proposals untenable. The thought of public demolition of a government bill, perhaps televised, is more than they can stand.

All this indicates that an investigatory stage in a committee's consideration of a bill is potentially a very valuable procedure. Any suggestion that it might be used to delay the progress of legislation could be countered by timetabling all bills. What is needed is a standing order which makes the procedure mandatory for all but the most minor bills.

Uncontroversial bills could also be much more frequently considered by Second Reading Committees and removed from the floor of the House altogether. A few are handled this way now by agreement between the parties: for example in 1990 the Overseas Superannuation Bill, the Raoul Wallenberg Memorial Bill and the Caldey Island Bill. Given the number of occasions when there are so few members in the chamber for a second reading debate that the Whips have to go round drumming up speakers, there seems to be far wider scope for the use of the procedure.

Pre-legislative Committees

The practice of establishing an ad hoc committee to look into a matter of public concern is the oldest parliamentary use of committees and in the past their reports often led to legislation. However, the use of pre-legislative committees to consider the form and content of proposed legislation has died out in recent years. Some Select Committees have conducted enquiries, generally thought to be useful, on forthcoming legislation – e.g. the Home Affairs Committee on the 'sus' law and the Transport Committee on the licensing of heavy goods vehicles – but the practice is uncommon. The 1967 Procedure Committee believed that the House 'should be brought in at an earlier point in the legislative process so as to allow discussion by Parliament of subjects and details

of potential legislation before the government finally prepare a bill.'[29]
The opposition Chief Whip of the time observed that a minister preparing a bill consulted all sorts of outside organisations but 'the one lot of
people he never consults in any way before he prepares it are members
of the House of Commons.'[30]

The committee felt that there was considerable scope for the use of
ad hoc pre-legislative committees so that members, as well as ministers,
could hear the views of interested parties on prospective legislation. The
Leader of the House and the Prime Minister (Harold Wilson) supported
the idea as likely to lead to the better drafting of bills. This Procedure
Committee also proposed that the annual Queen's Speech on the
government's programme for the session should be accompanied by
explanatory white papers giving more information about proposed legislation.[31]

Since neither that Labour government nor its Conservative successor
gave the House the opportunity to express a view on this proposal,
the Procedure Committee returned to the matter four years later.[32] It
recorded that since 1900 nearly half of pre-legislative Committees had
given rise to identifiable legislation and recommended that such committees should be used, at least for non-controversial legislation. Oddly,
the next time the procedure was used was to consider the highly controversial issue of a wealth tax. Predictably, the Wealth Tax Committee of
1974–75 was a disaster, producing a number of contradictory minority
reports and ending in allegations of leaks. The procedure was tried once
more in 1975–76, for legislation on direct elections to the European
Assembly, and then fell into abeyance.

The use of Royal Commissions and similar committees of enquiry
also died after 1979 because Mrs Thatcher disapproved of them. There
is a case for objective enquiries by commission into persistent national
concerns which Select Committees cannot find time to tackle. Sir Douglas Wass, in the 1983 Reith Lectures, suggested the supervision of the
police, the social security system and the financing of higher education
as such issues.

Understanding the Law

A major problem with British legislation is that much of it cannot be
understood, even by experts. Much unproductive time and cost is
devoted in the courts to establishing its meaning. One source of this

problem is that instructions given to parliamentary draftsmen by officials in government departments are increasingly detailed and elaborate and another is that nearly all legislation involves numerous amendments of previous legislation.

British, unlike European, law is drafted in the greatest achievable detail so as to indicate its application in every possible circumstance. In contrast, the tradition in Europe is to draft laws in general terms and to leave detailed interpretation to the courts. In 1975 a committee under Sir David (now Lord) Renton was established to consider the preparation of legislation[33] with a view to improving the clarity of statute law. The committee's report commented that British statutes often 'contain a mass of detail without clearly expressing the purposes or the principles which have prompted it'.[34]

It also recorded widespread criticism of legislation by the legal profession and other users. Among the complaints it received were that our laws used obscure and complex language of elusive meaning and uncertain effect; that the desire for certainty led to over-elaboration; that the internal structure of legislation was illogical and unhelpful to the reader and that the lack of clear connection between various acts made it difficult to ascertain the state of the law on any given matter. It quoted the views of the Law Society on the language of statutes:

> Legalistic, often obscure and circumlocutious, requiring a certain type of expertise in order to gauge its meaning. Sentences are long and involved, the grammar is obscure, and archaisms, legally meaningless words and phrases, tortuous language, the preference for the double negative over the single positive, abound.[35]

The Renton Committee made eighty recommendations for the improvement of drafting, about half of which were implemented by the government, though to this day very little has been done about clarity, the use of simple language and improving scrutiny before legislation. Lord Renton has recently returned to the issue, suggesting that the Law Commission, a body established to make proposals to the government for the examination of the law and its revision, should report on a proposal to legislate and should itself publish a draft bill. He has also suggested that each bill should be prefaced with a statement of purpose to make its intentions clear.[36]

Looking at Results

The process of legislation, involving hours of detailed consideration in committee in the Commons and in the Lords, appears to be painstaking and thorough. Yet most of those participating would agree that much of the time is unproductively spent. Virtually all the changes made to a bill before it becomes law are the result of the government having second thoughts after receiving outside representations or correcting its own mistakes in drafting. As the Renton Committee pointed out, a bill and an act represent conflicting needs. A bill is a document considered by a lay audience who want to establish the purpose and effect of each clause. An act is a document for use by professionals to establish the consequence of each clause for a particular case or individual.

There is little purpose in recommending that governments should bring forward less legislation or that they should spend more time in preparing it or that they should allow more time for consideration. On the other hand, there ought to be the basis for a deal which would allow more informed and thorough scrutiny of bills, which is desperately needed, and still allow a government to get them through in much the same time as it does now.

Timetabling of all controversial legislation by an all-party committee chaired by the Speaker would give the government the certainty it needs and would still make room for improved examination. It will be argued that if government members had the majority on such a committee they would be under pressure to give less time than the opposition would want. However, a committee of senior backbenchers who no longer have to ingratiate themselves with their parties' leadership is likely to take an objective view. The idea that delay is an essential weapon of opposition and that filibustering a bill is in some way damaging to a government is hardly believed by anybody today.

The detailed examination of bills should be preceded by white papers or descriptive documentation which are far more explanatory than the memoranda and notes which accompany bills under the present arrangements. Most bills should go through the apparently abandoned special procedure of an investigatory stage in committee. Relatively non-controversial legislation could be preceded by pre-legislative committees, a useful procedure now also largely abandoned.

Once a bill is enacted, it is virtually unknown for there to be any review of how it has actually worked. If an act is seen to be a failure, it is simply followed in due course, or when there is time, by amending legislation, and the whole routine is gone through again. There is a good case for post-legislation committees, which could be set up on a motion by the opposition, preferably consisting of members who saw the bill through Standing Committee. This idea was briefly considered by the 1971 Procedure Committee,[37] which proposed that ad hoc post-legislation committees should look at acts which clearly needed amendment as a result of court judgements, difficulties in interpretation, impracticability in everyday use or the nature of delegated legislation made under their authority. It suggested that such a committee, appointed from both Houses, would take evidence from officials and outside witnesses and could consider the draft of an amending bill produced by the government. At the time the proposal was supported by the Leaders of both Houses and the opposition Chief Whip in the Commons, but nothing came of it.

There is also the problem of the gross imbalance between the resources of the government and the opposition in dealing with legislation. 'Short Money' (see Chapter 10) goes some way to enabling the opposition to employ expert staff, but not nearly far enough. A Department of the Opposition is needed, staffed by civil servants on secondment, lawyers, parliamentary draftsmen and experts who could give the kind of support to opposition spokespersons that ministers get from civil servants. Such a development would go a long way towards reducing the dominance of the government. We would get better legislation as a result and civil servants would have useful experience in serving a shadow administration.

Finally, there is the issue of Parliament's rights in scheduling, and in supervising the quality of, legislation. It is one of the quirks in our system that the so-called 'usual channels' between government and opposition, through which deals are done on the parliamentary programme, is the Private Secretary to the government Chief Whip. This civil servant serves each government and occupies a position of great delicacy and trust: the post has been filled by only three men since 1919. The arrangement works to the satisfaction of the government and the government in waiting. However, in the last resort, the government has control of the use of the time of the legislature. There is a good case for having the Speaker chair a meeting of representatives of the parties, to discuss forthcoming business and to settle procedural issues before agreeing the legislative programme. It is also unsatisfactory that the government employs parliamentary counsel to draft legislation, while Parliament has no access to this expertise. The Clerk's Department or a new Research Department (see Chapter 4) should have the responsibility for providing it.

4

Investigation

Select Committees, of members selected to examine and report on a matter, have been appointed for the past 400 years. Until the middle of the nineteenth century they were mainly concerned with the affairs of the House and its membership. Then they began to carry out important investigations of social issues (unemployment, poverty, Highland distress) and of government actions (the conduct of the war in the Crimea) and their work often led to legislation or changes in administration. Occasionally, Select Committees were set up to examine government financial estimates (e.g. in 1848 on the expenditures of the army, the navy and on the management of woods and forests). In the 1880s their use declined and they were largely replaced by Royal Commissions and departmental committees.

The modern structure of investigatory Select Committees began with the demand for a small committee, rather than the entire House of Commons sitting as a Committee of Supply, to examine proposed items of expenditure. As early as 1888, for example, the Hartington Committee recommended that a Select Committee of seventy members should examine certain estimates, but this proposal was not accepted by the government. In 1902 a Select Committee of the House of Commons was appointed 'to inquire whether any plan can be advantageously adopted for enabling the House, by Select Committee or otherwise, more effectively to make an examination, not involving criticisms of Policy, into the details of National Expenditure'. This Committee on National Expenditure reported in 1903. It considered that 'the examination of estimates by the House of Commons leaves much to be desired'. Estimates were used in practice 'mainly to provide a series of convenient and useful opportunities for the debating of policy and administration, rather than for the criticism and review of financial method and the details of expenditure'. The committee recommended the establishment of an Estimates Committee, with the power to send for witnesses and papers 'not of a secret character'. The Estimates Committee should examine a class of the estimates for the current year not exceeding one-fourth of the whole, this class having been selected for them by the Public Accounts Committee. The selected estimates should be debated by the House when the Estimates Committee had reported on them. Increased information should also be afforded to members, showing the comparative growth of estimates and a fuller explanation of the reasons for new expenditure.[1]

Winston Churchill, in the 1905 speech referred to in an earlier chapter,[2] complained about the lack of consideration of the report of 1903. Policy on expenditure was a matter for the Cabinet and the House of Commons, he said; the audit of expenditure was adequately dealt with by the Public Accounts Committee and the Treasury, but between these two there was a lacuna or middle ground which he called the 'merit' of expenditure and upon that no control adequately or effectively operated at that time.

In April 1912 Lloyd George, as Chancellor of the Exchequer, proposed that a Select Committee on Estimates should be set up.[3] He referred to the gigantic growth in expenditure, from £71 million in 1872 to £186 million in 1912. This had been due to the enormous increase in the cost of battleships, the increased cost of the Post Office, the new cost of pensions and the need to help local authorities with their obligations for education and sanitation. A committee was needed to examine the question of getting value for the money expended. The House of Commons had not within living memory exercised any control over expenditure, he said: the clerks of the Treasury were the only check. In every Supply Debate, members had called for more expenditure: the House had never put itself in the position which every representative of the Treasury had to put himself (i.e. to seek to *limit* spending). The House should establish an Estimates Committee as an experiment on the lines proposed by the committee of 1903.

The proposition was attacked by Austen Chamberlain in the following debate as either useless or 'in the highest degree mischievous': he thought that a committee of the kind suggested would lessen the responsibility of ministers for public expenditure and it would be difficult to get any members of standing to devote themselves to that class of work. Earl Winterton thought that very few members were competent to discuss the estimates and the proposal would put an unnecessary burden upon officials. Despite these objections, Lloyd George's motion was carried and the Estimates Committee was set up in May 1912 with fifteen members.

The working of the Estimates Committee was reviewed by the Select Committee on Procedure in 1932.[4] It felt bound to say that various attempts to make the Estimates Committee an effective instrument for the control of public expenditure had failed. The committee had done good work from time to time, but the difficulties in their way had arisen because they were powerless to deal with policy, they did not receive the estimates in time, they had no staff to survey the whole field of public expenditure and no definite days were allotted for a discussion of their reports in the House. This Procedure Committee recommended that the Estimates Committee be enlarged, that it should consider matters of policy, that it should regularly survey the relation of total public expenditure to the national income and that it should be provided with an independent technical staff adequate for its functions. At least three days should be set aside by the House for a definite consideration of its report. In May 1933 Neville Chamberlain, Chancellor of the Exchequer, in a brief oral answer, gave the government's reply to the Procedure Committee's recommendations.[5] The Estimates Committee could not deal with matters of policy without encroaching on the powers of executive government, he said. Where questions arose in which policy and administration overlapped, if administration was the predominant factor the government had no objection to the committee making recommendations, so long as it interpreted its terms of reference with discretion. The committee could not employ a body of technical officers, but the government was willing to place at its disposal several officers from the Treasury who would act as assistants to the Treasury official already attached to the committee. The government was in sympathy with the request for opportunities to discuss the reports of the committee, but the matter would have to be considered further.

The Procedure Committee next returned to the question in 1946.[6] It discussed the purposes of the Public Accounts Committee and the Estimates Committee: the first was to ensure financial regularity in expenditure and the second to criticise expenditure on the basis of economy and 'sound business principle'. Though the functions of the two committees were distinct, their subject matter was the same. The Public Accounts Committee worked on the appropriation accounts and the Estimates Committee worked on the estimates, but estimates in one year became appropriation accounts in the following year and, for long-term schemes and projects involving expenditures over several years, the work of the committees overlapped. The Procedure Committee proposed a merger of the functions of both committees into a single Public Expenditure Committee, with sub-committees. The government rejected this proposal.

An important step in the development of Select Committees was taken in the 1956–57 session with the establishment of a Select Committee on Nationalised Industries which was soon generally accepted as a success. Harold Wilson, in a speech at Stowmarket in July 1964, said, 'We have seen how effective certain select committees – Estimates, Public Accounts and Nationalised Industries – have been in getting to the heart of some national problems by summoning witnesses, taking evidence and reaching agreed conclusions, cutting right across party controversies. I believe this could be taken further . . .' Encouraged by this atmosphere of reform, the Procedure Committee of 1964–65 suggested that 'the House should possess a more efficient system of scrutiny of administration'[7] and proposed a new structure of specialist sub-committees developed from the Estimates Committee, with powers to enquire into how departments carried out their responsibilities and to examine estimates and expenditure. The Leader of the House at the time, Herbert Bowden, said that the government opposed these ideas because they were very anxious that such a committee 'should not get into the position where discussion of financial control and keen scrutiny of the expenditure of departments is lost and replaced by policy decisions'.[8] In the 1965–66 and 1966–67 sessions the Estimates Committee tried to go ahead anyway and appointed seven sub-committees, on such areas as Economic Affairs and Building and Natural Resources. This development was stopped by the Estimates Committee being run down in membership by the government so that it could no longer cover all its new subjects.

At the end of 1966 a new Leader of the House, Richard Crossman, declared his enthusiasm for Select Committees and proposed two new ones on an experimental basis: a 'departmental' committee on Agriculture, to scrutinise the work of the Ministry of Agriculture, Fisheries and Food, and a 'subject' committee on Science and Technology, to examine the development of science and technology throughout the government. A year later, Mr Crossman revealed that 'our original intention was that a departmental committee should spend one session on each department and then move on'[9] and then announced that the Agriculture Committee would be wound up. He thought that the subject committee on Science and Technology was different and satisfied a very important need and should survive. The Agriculture Committee fought hard to remain in existence and was finally abolished in early 1969.

Concurrently, two other departmental committees – on Education and Science, and Overseas Aid – were established and so were other subject committees – on Race Relations and Immigration (1968) and Scottish Affairs (1969).

In July 1969 the Procedure Committee produced a report on the 'Scrutiny of Public Expenditure and Administration'[10] in which it returned to the ideas it had set out in its report in the 1964–65 session. It recommended that the Estimates Committee should become a Select Committee on Expenditure with eight 'functional' sub-committees, each assisted by expert staff, but went much further than its earlier report by proposing that the sub-committees should examine the management methods of departments in implementing policies and of the strategies behind public expenditure programmes. It also suggested that they should be able to assess the efficiency with which departments set and realised their objectives.

The government's reply to the 1969 report said that it was going to review the whole committee system, but this review was not completed before it lost office. The new Conservative government brought out a green paper, *Select Committees of the House of Commons* in October 1970.[11] It recommended an Expenditure Committee with seven sub-committees (General; Defence and External Affairs; Environment; Trade and Industry; Education; Arts and Home Office; Social Services and Employment) and with the right to question ministers on their policies, to scrutinise public expenditure programmes and projections and to enquire into departmental administration. It proposed that the departmental Education and Science and Overseas Aid Committees should be wound up and that the subject Select Committees on Science and Technology, Race Relations, Nationalised Industries and Scottish Affairs should continue 'for the remainder of this Parliament'. This scheme would mean that the House of Commons would have the opportunity of watching the Expenditure and specialist committees in operation side by side and at a later stage would be able to decide in the light of practical experience whether to deploy more of its Select Committee resources in one direction or the other.

The government's proposals were accepted and the Expenditure Committee began work in early 1971, with terms of reference which included the examination of the policy objectives of ministers and the effectiveness of civil service management. Later, the government gave way to pressure and in February 1973 reappointed the Overseas Aid Committee. Meanwhile, the Procedure Committee had proposed to enlarge the Expenditure Committee so that a sub-committee on Taxation and Finance could be formed, which might develop 'into an independent Select Committee on Taxation and Economic Affairs'.[12] The Treasury opposed this proposal, which was repeated in the Procedure Committee's report in the following session, though the government did set up ad hoc select committees to examine corporation tax, a proposed tax credit scheme and a proposed wealth tax.

The Expenditure Committee reviewed its work in a report in the 1971–72 session.[13] It proposed that its sub-committees should report direct to the House, instead of through the full Expenditure Committee; that adequate time should be allowed for debating its reports and that departmental observations on its reports should be issued within two months. The government's views on this report were largely dismissive: it did not approve direct reporting, there was no promise of further debating time and there was no promise to issue departmental replies in a fixed time, though departments should always do their best 'to reply expeditiously'.[14]

After the elections of February and October 1974, the demands for greater parliamentary scrutiny over government policy and spending increased in strength and frequency. The Leader of the House in the earlier part of the period (Edward Short, now Lord Glenamara) was sympathetic and in June 1976 the government approved the setting up of a special Select Committee on Procedure 'to consider the practice and procedure of the House in relation to public business and to make recommendations for the more effective performance of its functions'.

The Procedure Committee 1978

The Procedure Committee of 1977–78 produced the most radical and far-sighted report of any committee of its kind: 'epoch-making' in the words of the Leader of the House, Norman St John Stevas, who did most to try to implement its proposals. 'The essence of the problem,' it reported, 'is that the balance of advantage between Parliament and government in the day-to-day working of the constitution is now weighted in favour of the government to a degree which arouses widespread anxiety and is inimical to the proper working of our parliamentary democracy.'[15]

This Procedure Committee produced seventy-six recommendations on legislation, financial control, the organisation of parliamentary sessions and on the form and powers of Select Committees, some of which have been implemented over the succeeding fifteen years and which still provide the starting point for any discussion of parliamentary reform. It had a lively membership, including future senior ministers (Baker, Lamont, Ridley), Enoch Powell, and the keenest parliamentary reformers of the day (Beith, George Cunningham, Marquand, Radice, Whitehead, the author) and some formidable constitutional experts (Spearing, English), under the chairmanship of a patient and painstaking Labour lawyer, Sir Thomas Williams. Its far-reaching proposals were arrived at without much dissension, principally because it took care to demonstrate that it was advocating 'changes in practice of an evolutionary kind, following naturally from present practices'.[16] This is the secret of any successful proposal to reform Parliament because it lulls the traditionalists, who instinctively oppose anything presented as new, or a break with the past.

Many of the committee's proposals are discussed elsewhere in this book. Here we consider its recommendations for the reform of the Select Committees, which have had its most lasting effect on the House of Commons. It found that, despite the growth in Select Committees that had taken place since 1964 and the changes in their powers, facilities and methods of work, 'the development of the system has been piecemeal and has resulted in a decidedly patchy coverage of the activities of governmental departments and agencies and of the major areas of public policy and administration'.[17] While some departments such as the Overseas Development Ministry and the Ministry of Defence were subject to continuous and detailed scrutiny, other departments received scant attention. Some areas of some departments were regularly examined while others were not. Committee responsibilities overlapped, e.g. the Committee on Nationalised Industries, the Science and Technology Committee and the Race Relations Committee all conducted enquiries in the same fields as sub-committees of the Expenditure Committee. As a result of historical accident or sporadic pressures, there was an incomplete and unsystematic scrutiny of the activities of the executive. It was desirable that the different branches of the public service be 'subject to an even and regular incidence of Select Committee investigation into their activities'.[18]

The Procedure Committee accepted the argument for a structure of investigatory Select Committees based on the structure of government departments: a 'departmentally related' system covering all the responsibilities of departments, nationalised industries and quasi-autonomous non-governmental organisations. It recommended the establishment of twelve of these committees (with an average of ten members each), covering Agriculture; Defence; Education, Science and Arts; Energy; Environment; Foreign Affairs; Home Affairs; Industry and Employment; Social Services; Trade and Consumer Affairs; Transport; and the Treasury. The Expenditure Committee and the existing subject Select Committees (e.g. on Science and Technology) would be wound up. Government observations on committee reports should be produced within two months of the publication of a report and eight days in each session should be set aside for debates on the reports, which could be on specific motions proposed by the reporting committee.

A number of witnesses giving evidence to the committee had opposed the employment of a permanent staff by Select Committees, mostly on the grounds that experts would come to dominate the committee members. The Procedure Committee disagreed with this view: 'If the new Select Committees we propose are to call ministers and civil servants to account, to examine the purposes and results of public expenditure programmes and to analyse the objectives and strategies behind the policies of departments, they will require full-time, expert staffs'.[19] In addition, members should be able to call on personal research assistance, paid for centrally by the House: 'This would be particularly valuable for those members who served on Select Committees, since it could give them a source of advice independent of the committee staffs.'

The Procedure Committee tackled the controversial question of the powers of Select Committees to send for persons, papers and records. These committees had always been hampered by their inability to order the attendance of ministers or the production of papers by government departments, and by the absence of any effective means of bringing a case of refusal to the attention of the House and of seeking the support of the House to enforce their wishes. The report said, 'We believe that the powers of committees and the procedure for enforcing those powers need strengthening to bring them in line with the central requirement of Select Committees to secure access to the information held by the government and its agencies.'[20] The committee recommended that Select Committees should have the power to order ministers to attend to give evidence and to produce papers and records. In the event of a refusal to provide papers, the committee recommended a procedure whereby a motion requiring them to be produced could be put before the House with precedence over other public business.

In February 1979, seven months after the Procedure Committee reported, the government allowed a debate on its recommendations. There was overwhelming support for them, with the notable exception of the Leader of the House, Michael Foot, whose approval was essential if they were to be implemented, since he spoke for the government. He strongly opposed the proposed new committee system as likely to weaken the power of the Chamber of the House: 'The more powerful the committees have become in the United States, the more debased or ineffective have become the House of Representatives and, to some extent, the Senate,' he said. He foresaw a further draining away of attention from the Chamber and the strength of Parliament being increasingly transferred to such committees. He considered that the committees would become a shield for departments and would so be favoured by top civil servants. It would be a 'great error' for the House to proceed along these lines. It was a radical procedure, he said – and radical meant tearing something up by its roots. The House should move carefully before coming to a decision in the next session of Parliament. With this speech any further progress was blocked for the time being.

Soon after the May 1979 general election, the new Leader of the House, Norman St John Stevas, put forward a motion to set up the new committee structure, which was passed. In that year the Scottish and Welsh Select Committees were added to the list of twelve proposed by the 1978 Procedure Committee; later Trade and Industry were combined and in 1991 Health was split from Social Services, to make fifteen committees. Because of the difficulty in finding Scottish Conservative members to serve on the Scottish Affairs Committee, it has not met since the 1987 general election, a matter of frequent and acrimonious debate.

In his speech on the Procedure Committee's report, Mr St John Stevas said, 'Today is, I believe, a crucial day in the life of the House of Commons. After years of discussion and debate, we are embarking upon a series of changes that could constitute the most important parliamentary reforms of the century.'[21]

Departmental Select Committees since 1978

The Select Committees each have eleven members and on average the attendance by their members runs at over 70 per cent. Three of them – Home Affairs, Treasury and Civil Service, and Foreign Affairs – have set up sub-committees. They meet at least once a week, and often more frequently, for a session of two hours or more. Most of their meetings are open to the public and involve the examination of witnesses: ministers, officials, experts. They usually take as a topic a policy area of the department they 'shadow' and produce a published report. Some reports represent months of evidence-taking and can involve travel in Britain or abroad. Others are short, sharp reports based on one or two evidence sessions. In the twelve years to the time of writing, they have produced some 600 reports (and 230 special reports which are often the published response or observations of the department which has been examined).

They tend to proceed by consensus, on which their chairpersons usually place a strong emphasis. Some (Agriculture, Employment) regularly produce unanimous reports. Others have had a record of divisions – votes by members – on the content of their reports: in the Environment Committee between 1979 and 1983, there were no fewer than 159 divisions because at the time it concentrated on the controversial issues of housing and local government. In areas where party controversy is likely to break out in a big way (Defence, Treasury) committees generally try to avoid judgements on the merits of policy and stick to considering whether a policy resulted in what the department intended. Occasionally, dissenting members produce what amounts to a minority report.

The intention of the 1978 Procedure Committee was that the House of Commons should have a comprehensive Select Committee system covering each department of state. The result is that the organisation of committees reflects the organisation of government departments and not necessarily all the activities of government. This leads to one obvious gap in coverage: since there is at the time of writing no Ministry for Women, there has never been a committee forum for the examination of government policy towards women. It is also frequently pointed out that since the Environment Committee covers the work of the very large Department of the Environment, which deals with housing and local government, the heritage, construction, inner cities, new towns and land-use planning as well as environmental protection, the countryside and wildlife, it cannot give sufficient attention to green issues. In fact, in recent years the Environment Committee has produced important reports on these issues, but there is clearly a case for an additional sub-committee on environmental matters, given the growth of public interest in this area.

It is also often maintained that the Select Committee monitoring the work of the Department of Education and Science cannot give enough time to science and technology and a Select Committee to concentrate on these subjects should be revived. Sir Ian Lloyd, a champion of science and technology, has frequently pointed to the neglect of science policy by the House of Commons (the House of Lords has a Science and Technology Committee): 'Science and technology is relegated to the periphery of parliamentary consideration. There is no regular annual debate on science policy or the science budget, as there is on each of the armed services, foreign affairs or education.'[22] Sir Ian has been instrumental in setting up POST (the Parliamentary Office of Science and Technology), funded by members, firms and charities to provide an information service to Parliament on these subjects and it now seems likely that it will be financed by Parliament. But hitherto science and technology are subjects to which Parliament has done little justice.

Virtually all the Select Committees could produce reports on policies affecting women, green issues, and science and technology in the course of examining the work of their departments, but following current policy developments in each of these departments usually drives out the consideration of anything else. A structure which mirrors government departments, though probably the best way of organising the committees, also has the weakness of giving inadequate attention to government policies which cross departmental boundaries. It is surprising that the committees have never made arrangements for joint sessions for enquiries into such topics or for networking to mobilise the resources of several committees for an enquiry into a group of related government policies – especially as committees of the House of Lords have proved to be very successful in considering such policies (see Chapter 8).

The absence of an active Select Committee on Scottish Affairs, which receives most attention, is probably a temporary phenomenon, but there are other important areas of policy which have never been covered. First, there is the work of the security or intelligence services. In a report on the working of the Select Committee system up to 1982, the Liaison Committee (of committee chairpersons) made a disarmingly innocent observation: 'One government activity which already falls within the ambit of the departmental Select Committees is the work of the security services, and the question of their accountability to Parliament arises

Check history of the CHC.

from time to time.'[23] It went on to say that committees had refrained from enquiries in this field, but that such large expenditures should not go wholly unexamined when examination could be a spur to efficiency, nor had the security services had any parliamentary opportunity to put the record straight. One thing was clear, it said, the House had given the committees a wide and unambiguous duty in overseeing all functions of departments, though it had left them to decide for themselves whether or not to enquire into these matters.

These observations led to a sharp rebuke from the Leader of the House, John Biffen, in a letter to the chairman of the Liaison Committee: 'It is by no means clear to me that the security and intelligence agencies are to be regarded as being within the ambit of any of the departmental Select Committees ... As you know, there is a long-standing convention under which the government does not provide information or answer questions in Parliament on matters of security and intelligence, and the government would regard itself as bound by that convention in relation to departmental Select Committees no less than in relation to Parliament itself.'[24] There the matter rests. A voluminous study by the Procedure Committee on the working of the Select Committee system produced in October 1990 (see below) never even referred to it.

The Liaison Committee was surely correct in maintaining that Parliament had a right to enquire into the cost and conduct of the security services. Other Select Committees (e.g. Defence) examine highly confidential matters without any adverse effects. A committee of very senior members – former senior Cabinet Ministers, say – should be established to investigate and monitor the policy and administration of the security services, even if it rarely reported.

The second missing committee has been one which would cover the Law Officers' departments (the office of the Attorney General and the Lord Chancellor's department). In evidence to the 1990 Procedure Committee, the author and others pointed out that the Lord Chancellor employed 10,000 civil servants, was accountable for an annual spend of over £700 million and dealt with major issues of public policy; we concluded that its exclusion from Select Committee scrutiny was an anomaly which should be ended. The reason for the failure to set up a Law Officers Select Committee was that when the committee system was established, the Lord Chancellor of the time, Lord Hailsham, opposed the idea. The Leader of the House, Norman St John Stevas, decided to drop it, as a matter not of principle, but of tactics: 'I had no chance

INVESTIGATION

of getting the reform through the Cabinet against the opposition of the Lord Chancellor.'[25] An attempt to set up such a committee was later defeated by the government in a vote in the Commons.

The source of the government's unwillingness to allow a Select Committee to cover the Attorney General and Lord Chancellor's departments has been the fear that it might involve itself in particular legal cases and in the appointment of judges. The 1990 Procedure Committee proposed that these departments and the Crown Prosecution Service should be brought within the ambit of the Home Affairs Committee, whose terms of reference should exclude the consideration of the merits of legal cases. It did not favour a separate Select Committee on Legal Affairs because it thought that there would not be enough work to justify its existence.

There is an unanswerable case for placing the Law Officers' departments under the scrutiny of a Select Committee. This could usefully be a joint committee of Lords and Commons and should not be circumscribed as to its terms of reference. Better to trust its members to develop its enquiries as they think fit. As to whether it should examine the principles raised by particular court judgements, it is worth noting that while there is a system of judicial review of parliamentary decisions, there is no system of parliamentary review of judicial decisions. Judges often have a substantial effect on the implementation of legislation passed by Parliament and their work should be monitored. Such a committee should scrutinise the arrangements for judicial appointments, given their need for reform (see Chapter 2), and it could usefully examine some proposed appointees to high judicial office.

The third missing committee is on Northern Ireland affairs. This is a situation which should be remedied, given the exceptional powers of the Secretary of State for Northern Ireland under the present arrangements. Such a committee has never been set up because of the sensitivity of matters it might cover and because of the constitutional position of the province. When the 1990 Procedure Committee considered the matter, it felt that though the case for a Northern Ireland Committee was strong, the current initiative on future arrangements for the government of the province was of such extreme sensitivity that any proposal should await the outcome of negotiations. This conclusion seems to be the inevitable one for the time being.

The terms of reference of the Select Committees are to monitor the expenditure, policy and administration of departments and associated public bodies. They certainly examine policy (or rather, individual policies) in their consensual way and their coverage of policy issues of the day has ranged very widely. With a few exceptions, their examination of expenditure has been very limited. When the 1990 Procedure Committee enquired, about half of the committees claimed to have devoted some attention to the scrutiny of expenditure, while the rest did not make any mention of the subject. The Social Services Committee produces at least one report a session on spending on social services, and the Energy Committee has looked at particular estimates. More than any other committee, the Defence Committee has concerned itself with value for money, very frequently examining spending on weapons and on other programmes and issuing an annual report on the defence estimates. This is partly because the Ministry of Defence spends so much (£20 billion a year), partly because it is frequently culpable of huge overspending on equipment programmes and projects, and partly because such investigations enable the committee to avoid controversy on the merits of particular spending programmes. Particularly rewarding has been the committee's regular scrutiny of the cost and progress of the Trident submarine and its nuclear weaponry, which has frequently wrong-footed the Ministry of Defence and has clearly served the public interest. Unfortunately, its interest in spending has occasionally brought it into conflict with the Public Accounts Committee, which exists to scrutinise value for money and can hardly avoid reporting on the absence of it in many of the activities of the Ministry of Defence.

Mr Michael Ryle, a former House of Commons Clerk of Committees and an authority on the working of the House, has recently argued[26] that the Select Committees have failed to conduct a vigorous analysis of competing spending priorities and instead 'tend to argue for more for each service they look into'. His view is that there has been a failure, not only by Select Committees but by Parliament as a whole, to look intelligently at the control of public expenditure. He proposes that Select Committees should look at the balance of spending in departments and take a view on the implications of spending more in some areas and less in others. Mr Ryle illustrated a problem, but it is doubtful if his solution would work. If the committees really tried to decide on competing priorities, consensus would evaporate and they would never produce a coherent report. They have had over a decade in which to develop arrangements for the analysis of spending and they have chosen not to do so. In addition, as we saw from Chapter 5, financial and output information is now so voluminous, and of such a low quality, that a committee member or clerk would have to devote hours, even days, to teasing out comprehensible information from estimates, appropriation accounts, annual reports, trading accounts and volumes of statistics published by government. When, or if, departmental and agency reports become more informative the committees might tackle such subjects.

The deeper problem is inherent in the culture of the House of Commons: strong on single issues, weak on systematic analysis. In evidence to the 1990 Procedure Committee, the author wrote: 'I think that the structure of Select Committees has worked well. Their weakness lies in their style of operating. They seem to me to concentrate too much on events of the day, or policies which are in the public eye, and too little on a systematic examination of the performance of departments. They do not generally adopt what might be called a "systems approach". That is to say that they do not require departments to specify what their aims are and what are the objectives of, and justification for, policies and programmes nor require them to establish indicators of performance which would permit the systematic comparison of results with objectives. They should call the management of departments regularly to account for the consequences, effectiveness and impact of their decisions. Most Select Committees have lagged behind the development of management information in departments. The new information systems seem to me to provide the basis for a much more systematic and quantitative examination of the performance of departments. If Select Committees were more interested in these developments, and pursued them, civil service management would receive a useful stimulus to improve its reporting arrangements and its performance.'[27]

It is clearly impossible to persuade Select Committee members against their will to give more attention to spending, and the relationships of policy to spending, but they could be led in that direction if the available information improved in comprehensibility and if their committees had sufficient analytical staff.

The third task of the Select Committees is the examination of administration. Apart from the Treasury Committee, whose remit covers the civil service, only the Home Affairs and Foreign Affairs Committees have ever shown much interest in the management of the departments they monitor, and then rarely. This is a grievous omission given the influence on policy implementation of organisation structure, planning, personnel management and budgetary, programme and project control. Select Committees have dealt with many less important subjects. The problem is that management is an even less glamorous subject than financial control, so there would never be much media interest in reports on it, and most committee members do not feel competent in the field. In general it is not possible to examine and comprehend the style, competence and performance of management without investigative field work by qualified and experienced management consultants. Appraising management requires more than taking evidence from managers, staff representatives and academic experts, which is the way Select Committees proceed. This problem has become acute as departments have become more managerial in style, particularly as a result of the establishment of agencies. Here again, the difficulties arise from the inadequate levels of staff available to committees and their diffidence in demanding more resources.

Select Committees are extraordinarily sensitive about their own costs, which are tiny. 'Few aspects of the departmentally related Select Committee system cause more contention, within and outside the House, than its staffing and costs,' said the 1990 Procedure Committee.[28] The total cost of the Select Committees has ranged between £2.5 million and £3.5 million in the parliamentary years 1980–81 to 1988–89 (about £300,000 a year for each committee). In 1988–89 the total cost of £3.5 million was divided as to £950,000 for staff, £185,000 for special advisers, £346,000 for travel, witnesses' costs of £5,000 and printing costs of £2 million. By comparison, running the office of the Prime Minister cost some £7.7 million in that year.

The Treasury Committee, charged with monitoring the management of the economy, of the civil service and of government revenues and expenditures of £200 billion, costs about £250,000 a year to run. It is the most heavily staffed of all the Select Committees, with a principal clerk, an assistant clerk, a senior executive officer, two specialist assistants and a secretary. The Welsh Affairs Committee has to make do with a deputy principal clerk, a higher executive officer and a secretary. Six committees have specialist assistants on four-year appointments. The committees (apart from that for Home Affairs) also employ specialist advisers, who act as consultants and are paid £85–£115 per day if they are of professorial status. In general, they are very distinguished authorities in their fields and, but for the virtual donation of their time, most committees would be unable to function effectively.

For some perverse reason, this exiguous staffing is generally a matter of pride for Committee chairmen and most of their members. Though there have been many assertions, mostly by outside commentators, that the committees have to have substantially more staff to be fully effective, there is little support for the idea in the committees themselves.

Professor Phillip Norton, in evidence to the 1990 Procedure Committee, argued that 'the resources given to the committees had failed to match the tasks given to them'[29] and that they should have offices, dedicated research units, additional staff allowances for members and additional salaries for members and committee chairmen. Apart from a concern for extreme financial prudence and fear of popular and media criticism of the cost of more resources, the committees are also very wary of being dominated by their own staffs (as their American equivalents are commonly said to be). The present Clerk of the House has given his views on the matter: 'I would not want to run large staffs of so-called scientists, economists and what have you, because I do not think they would have the skill of the people we can obtain by short-term arrangements with specialist advisers we have at the moment.'[30] He saw the skill of committees as being to know what questions to ask and to receive the information they needed from witnesses and from memoranda sent to them. This is the model which Select Committees have always followed without question. It may explain the superficiality of most of their reports. It may be that the modest resourcing of Select Committees has influenced their approach – producing broad-brush reports on single policy issues – and that if they were more amply resourced, and particularly if they employed professionally qualified staff, they would get closer to fulfilling their terms of reference.

There are two further recurring matters of contention about the Select Committees: what happens to reports after they are published, and the behaviour of official witnesses. It has been a very sore point that after their publication most Select Committee reports just gather dust. Since 1979, only seven (out of some 600) have been the subject of a motion and a vote in the House and six have been the subject of a brief adjournment debate. A further 116 have been 'tagged' or notified on the Order Paper as being relevant to a debate. In evidence to the 1990 Procedure Committee, virtually all the Select Committees complained about the arrangements for debating their reports. The Transport Committee felt that the House had almost totally ignored its work and the Home Affairs Committee considered that on important subjects the government should allow time for a debate.[31] There have been a number of proposals for increasing the number of days (from three) for debates on Select Committee reports. However, unless a committee puts down a motion which is likely to lead to a vote, attendance at such debates will be thin and mainly consist of the committee members. Graham Allen proposed to the Procedure Committee that, as a minimum, each committee should be entitled to have one report debated each year, including the ultimate sanction of a vote on a motion: 'This in itself would bring Select Committees more into the mainstream of decision-making and end the current dislocation between Committee and Chamber which devalues committee work.'[32]

The Procedure Committee concluded that it could not recommend any increase in the number of days available for Select Committee debates, given the limited attendance they were likely to attract, but it recommended that the three Estimates Days should be used for debates on Select Committees' reports of general importance. If the proposal by the 1978 Procedure Committee that there should be eight days set aside for debates on estimates were approved there would be sufficient time for a mixture of full- and half-day debates on the committees' reports, so that annually each committee could mount at least a short debate. The new annual reports produced by government departments and agencies provide a basis for such an arrangement. If the proposals set out below for strengthening Select Committees were implemented, more members might be interested in participating in debates. Another change which would give more relevance to debates on Select Committee reports could be the fixing of a time limit – say three months – within which a government department would be obliged to reply to a report. At present, these replies can be so delayed as to make any debate outdated.

Select Committees have the power to send for persons (but only British citizens), papers and records. Members of Parliament may refuse to attend: see below. The conduct of civil service witnesses (a very important source of evidence) is governed by the 'Osmotherly Rules', the Memorandum of Guidance for Officials Appearing Before Select Committees, first issued within the civil service in 1972, published by the 1976 Procedure Committee and last updated in 1988. These rules have no parliamentary status whatsoever. They have never been considered by Parliament, nor have they been approved by Select Committees. In evidence to the 1990 Procedure Committee, the author wrote: 'The Osmotherly Rules governing the behaviour of civil servants in giving evidence to parliamentary committees are too defensive and restrictive. They consist of sixty-six paragraphs of warnings against saying too much. Luckily, senior civil servants have generally interpreted these rules in a liberal way. However, as presently written they give the wrong signals and should be revised and simplified into general principles.'[33]

Dr Peter Hennessy, a distinguished writer on civil service affairs, has been particularly scathing about the effect of the Osmotherly Rules: 'There are a few Osmotherlys which I think are an outrage ... The philosophy at the moment is this: that you will be able to say only a kind of residue; that once all the hot and delicate subjects have been removed, once anything to do with current policy has been removed you can say that. If they literally stuck to this rule book, they would be able to tell you only what was in Written Answers, oral questions, White Papers – and they could confirm the day of the week and the time of the day.'[34] He quotes Rule 30, which requires civil servants to refrain from commenting in any way 'on questions in the field of political controversy', and Rule 31, which rules out any answers on interdepartmental business (consultations between departments, e.g. between Agriculture and Environment on environmentally damaging farm practices) or any information on the level at which decisions are taken. The 'real outrage', he said, was Rule 41 ('it should enrage all decent parliamentarians'), which says that as Select Committees are not likely to accept a refusal to reveal a report from a departmental committee containing outside members, even less a refusal in the case of a wholly external committee, 'these implications need to be taken into account in deciding how much publicity should be given to the establishment of committees of this kind'. 'This is open government with a vengeance, is it not?' said Dr Hennessy.

The Procedure Committee could not bring itself to recommend any change in the Osmotherly Rules, worrying that a review at Parliament's behest would 'simply result in a new set of guidelines, which whilst superficially less restrictive would then be applied rigorously and to the letter. At the risk of accusations of defeatism, therefore, we believe that discretion is the sensible approach.'[35] The committee did, however, recommend that committees should be told what policy options were under consideration and their cost implications, matters at present forbidden by the Osmotherlys. Civil servants are usually more helpful to the committees than the Osmotherly Rules imply, though occasionally they use them to play every question with a dead bat. The rules should be abandoned not only because they do not enjoy any parliamentary authority, but because they also establish the wrong basis for the relationship between civil service witnesses and committees. Any rules for civil servants giving evidence to Select Committees should start from the opposite viewpoint: that they should be willing to discuss every aspect of the administration of departments and the implementation of policy, except in closely defined areas of great current sensitivity. Ministers are able to answer questions on these areas and on the reasons for, and the merits of, their policies.

The Procedure Committee's Review

As we have seen, in October 1990 the Procedure Committee reported on the working of the first ten years of the departmental Select Committees. It was a very dispiriting effort and certainly did not live up to the achievements of its predecessor of 1978. Far too deferentially, it avoided the question of the need for a committee to oversee the security and intelligence services and was timid on the reform of the rules governing the evidence given by civil servants to committees. It carried out no extensive examination of the failure of the committees to consider the spending and management of departments and did not consider what might be done to persuade them to do so. Its failure was one of imagination and vision: it did not contemplate what an investigatory committee system could do. It did not attempt to redefine the role of the Select Committees in the light of the increasing centralisation of government power; new management systems in departments; privatisation; the great leap in the amount of information produced in, and by, departments; European integration; developing research methodologies.

The final paragraph of the report summarises its tone: 'Would any government in the foreseeable future be prepared to abolish the system of departmentally related Select Committees? The fact that this last question virtually answers itself is in many ways the most eloquent testimony to the solid, unspectacular but undeniable achievements of the first decade of the new committees.'[36]

The report produced seventy conclusions and recommendations, but they are barely worth recording: that committees should be able to visit the EC without prior authorisation; that the allowances available to committees for entertaining visitors should be sympathetically reviewed; that the Treasury should be more helpful to the committees; that the committee which selects committee members should not be unduly influenced by the party Whips; that committee reports should be embargoed for two sitting days and not forty-eight hours; that improved co-operation between the Select Committees and the Public Accounts Committee should be discussed and that the government should make a serious effort to refer bills to Special Standing Committees (see Chapter 3).

As is often the case, the evidence to the Procedure Committee was more interesting than its conclusions. Lord St John of Fawsley (the former Mr St John Stevas, father of the committee system) thought they had been extraordinarily successful and that everybody had benefited. 'All gainers, no losers,' he said: backbenchers had found a vehicle to express their views in a sustained and effective manner; ministers had been afforded a platform to explain their views; the media had received a much greater flow of information; and, most important of all, the House of Commons had become a more effective check on the executive. The committees had succeeded because they did not try to do too much and what they tried to do and the basis on which they were founded grew out of the principles of the constitution.[37]

The then Leader of the House, Sir Geoffrey Howe, considered the committees an indispensable part of the work of the House of Commons. From the government's point of view, they provided a ready and public platform for it to explain and describe its policies; their scrutiny kept the work of government departments up to a high standard; the evidence they took could influence public debate and they could stimulate a reconsideration of policy.[38] He thought that the government could take some credit for 'getting the framework right, ten years back',[39] ignoring the fact that the framework was designed by the 1978 Procedure Committee. In a somewhat obscure passage, he said, '. . . It is important to recognise that the committee system exists not exclusively for the benefit of the government, not exclusively for the benefit of parliamentarians not in government; it exists for the amplification and increasing fruitfulness of that exchange for the benefit of those whom we represent in this place.'[40] On the whole, he did not think that committee enquiries placed too great a strain or cost on departments, except when a committee was examining a 'live issue', i.e. an issue of current concern when officials were already under pressure, or when officials were faced simultaneously by enquiries from Select Committees and the National Audit Office.

Most of the Select Committees reported to the Procedure Committee that their relationships with the government were satisfactory: 'polite', 'cordial', 'friendly', 'proper, courteous and arm's-length'.[41] A few of them were unhappy with inadequate or delayed replies to their reports from the departments they shadowed. The Transport Committee complained that it had been denied information by the Treasury which had already given it to the National Economic Development Council. The Foreign Affairs Committee also had a significant complaint about the difficulty of prising useful information out of the Foreign Office.

The most substantial complaint was by the Defence Committee, whose chairman, Michael Mates, referred to 'an element of the Ministry of Defence culture' which showed up as 'an unwillingness to answer frankly and in what seems to be a feeling that the less that is said to the committee, the safer the Ministry of Defence will be'. Occasionally, this had led to 'the giving of evidence that concealed a serious state of affairs' (e.g. cost overruns on the Trident submarine project).[42] The ministry had now realised that they could get away with less than before: 'To an extent we have got their attention.'[43] Tom King, the Minister of Defence, in commenting on these assertions, agreed that there was tension and a sense of friction and grievance on both sides and said that his department's ambition was a better and more constructive relationship between them. Unfortunately, within a couple of years, in December 1991, warfare broke out again between the committee and the ministry, when Mr King apparently refused to give military manpower plans to the committee, and the ensuing row assumed constitutional proportions. For the Procedure Committee, Mr Mates went into detail and at length on the overlap between the work of the National Audit Office (NAO) for the Public Accounts Committee (PAC) and that of his Defence Committee. In fact, he thought that more than 50 per cent of his committee's work overlapped with that of the NAO. He complained about a lack of co-operation from the PAC, in that it would not allow the Defence Committee access to NAO papers which were relevant to enquiries being conducted by the Defence Committee, though the head of the NAO (the Comptroller and Auditor General) was required by law to report to the House of Commons.

Mr Mates made a proposal to improve the relationship between his and other Select Committees and the PAC. It was that when the Comptroller decided on his work programme, agreement should be reached as to whether a particular NAO report might be taken up by the relevant departmental Select Committee rather than the PAC, which would take evidence on it, drawing on information and advice from NAO. He concluded by contrasting the 900 staff and £28 million annual budget supporting the PAC with the level of support for all the departmental Select Committees.[44] The Chairman of the Public Accounts Committee, Robert Sheldon, opposed the idea of Select Committees considering NAO reports because the NAO might then get involved in policy matters and its relationships with departments could be altered.[45] This matter has since blown up into a bigger dispute (see Chapter 6).

The government's response to the Procedure Committee's report was the usual mixture of condescension and negativism.[46] Early on, it administered a mild reprimand: 'The government trusts that committees will weigh their need for evidence against the expense and diversion from other work [in departments] that may be involved in producing it.'[47] It then proceeded to reject a long list of the Procedure Committee's requests and recommendations, some of them moderate in the extreme. It considered that it was 'inappropriate' for Select Committee reports to be debated on more Estimates Days and that Select Committees should not have unrestricted travel in the EC. It would not allow Select Committees to see working papers and internal files, nor to learn the details of consultations in departments. It justified this limitation on policy disclosure as being in the interests of government. The Home Affairs Committee would be allowed to cover the Lord Chancellor's department, but would not be allowed to consider individual law cases nor judicial appointments. It could also cover the Law Officers' departments (Attorney General, Treasury Solicitor, Crown Prosecution Service and Serious Fraud Office), but it would not be allowed to consider individual cases, appointments or *policy*. This exclusion of policy was said to be because the public view of the independence of the Law Officers in formulating and executing prosecution policy would be damaged if it were thought to be subject to political influence, which might happen if such policy were examined by Select Committees. As if the government did not politically influence prosecution policy!

The government made no commitment to the use of Select Committees in the process of legislation, issued an Awful Warning to the National Audit Office not on any account to involve itself in policy matters and finally gave the Select Committees a clean bill of health. It obviously did not consider them much of a threat. They should be.

If there is one overwhelming conclusion about the first decade's work by the departmental Select Committees, it is that they represent spectacularly good value for money. They have established an unequalled and irreplaceable archive of information on public policy, ranging from exhaustive studies of the justification and consequences of economic policy and defence spending, to brief reports on, for example, the future of the Theatre Museum and the effect of feed-stuff prices on the pig and poultry industry. The average cost of a report is a few thousand pounds.

An important reason for the exceptionally low cost of the Select Committees is that, in general, they have not adhered to their terms of reference. They have not examined the full array of policy, nor the

expenditure, nor the management, of the departments they are supposed
to scrutinise. They have examined individual policies, have occasionally
touched on some areas of expenditure and almost never looked at management. If they tackled policy analysis on a broad scale and systematically evaluated spending programmes, they would need a substantial
research staff, and if they investigated management they would need a
field force of professional consultants. They have never seen the need
for such specialist cadres because they have never sought to discharge
their full range of responsibilities.

There have been many academic studies of, and commentaries on,
the output of the Select Committees.[48] The reports which are singled
out as having had a direct effect on government decisions are always the
1980 report of the Home Affairs Committee on the 'sus' law (giving the
police powers to stop and search a person) which led to its repeal in
the 1981 Criminal Attempts Act, and the report by the Foreign Affairs
Committee on the patriation of the Canadian constitution (the North
America Act), also in 1980. There are a number of other reports which
have had some influence on legislation – on children in care, on drug
trafficking, on broadcasting, on electricity privatisation and on security
in military installations. A few committees have put down amendments
to government bills and one has brought in a bill of its own: the Football
Offences Bill, for which the Home Affairs Committee craftily used the
private member's procedure.

The Select Committees have had a number of other achievements.
The Energy Committee has systematically covered all the policy
areas of its (small) department; the Employment Committee regularly
combed through the corporate plans of the Manpower Services Commission; the Social Services Committee has made a point of examining its department's green papers and consultative documents in time to
influence policy. The Agriculture Committee has been influential on
animal welfare and, lately, on food safety, the Energy Committee on
energy conservation, the Trade and Industry Committee on company
investigations, the Transport Committee on policy on heavy lorries, the
Environment Committee on acid rain, toxic waste, the pollution
of beaches and rain-forest destruction (an excellent report, for
which it attracted a lot of criticism because it visited Brazil). There
have also inevitably been damp squibs and very many rebuffs from
government.

The most sensational events in the life of the Select Committees
have concerned the recalcitrance of witnesses, particularly government

witnesses, and leaks of draft reports. Some ministers (Michael Heseltine on the revival of Merseyside, Leon Brittan on Westland) have been heavily criticised for inadequate responses to committee questions. The former Health Minister, Edwina Currie, took a lot of persuading to appear before the Agriculture Committee to discuss salmonella in eggs, and Arthur Scargill, the NUM leader, had to be ordered to attend the Energy Committee.

The biggest scandal, and one which could have been very damaging to the government at the time, was over the Westland enquiry by the Defence Committee, when the government refused to allow five named civil servants to give evidence and sent the Cabinet Secretary in their place. This episode made it clear that, though Select Committees may have the right to send for persons to give evidence, the government does not have to comply. The refusal of the Ministry of Defence to allow named witnesses to attend was probably one of the reasons why the Defence Committee never unearthed the truth.

There have been several rows over allegations of leaks of draft reports to the media and to the government department concerned, to enable it to prepare its defences against criticism. The effectiveness of Select Committees would clearly be weakened if government departments were too well informed about the committees' proposed reports. There has also been the occasional rumpus over the apparent interference by party Whips in appointments to committees, allegedly to ensure that renegades and dissenters were not appointed. In July 1992 this issue became serious when a retirement rule was allegedly invented in the Conservative Party to evict a particularly effective Conservative chairman from the Health Committee.

The basic structure and terms of reference of the Select Committees are sound enough and they have provided a valuable service to parliamentary democracy. They have produced an enormous amount of information for Parliament and the public. They have enabled some MPs to build up formidable specialisms and have led to better informed debates in the House. They are the main forum in which government policy can be examined in depth and they have provided pressure groups and experts with the opportunities to challenge it. They have obliged ministers and civil servants to explain the origins and results of policy in public. Their dialogue with government has made an important contribution to public understanding and awareness of national policy. On the whole, they have avoided two traps into which it was predicted they would quickly fall: the government majority on each of them has not led to their being too deferential and producing uncritical reports, and they have not established too cosy a relationship with the departments they shadow. Most of their reports are honestly and often robustly critical of government, and though the relationship varies from tense and adversarial (Defence) to rather warm (Home Affairs), none of them has become a tame advocate for their departments.

In the author's experience, comparing today's Treasury Committee with its pre-1979 predecessor, it is noticeable how much slicker and more professional it has become. The old Expenditure General Sub-Committee was run on even more of a shoestring, was less well briefed, more spontaneous, more uninhibited and more dangerous, partly because of an unconventional chairman and partly because there were fewer conventions to follow. Now, the Treasury Committee has more support staff and a stable of seven distinguished economic advisers; it also has very thorough arrangements for briefing members and suggesting questions that they might ask of witnesses. It is, however, much more predictable and not much more effective.

The form and style of Select Committee enquiries has not changed much in a hundred years. They make no use of present-day technologies for forecasting or for modelling alternative policies and programmes; nor of cost/benefit analysis or social auditing techniques; nor of consumer surveys or polling; nor of environmental or social impact analysis – all of which would enable the better evaluation of government policies. Indeed, in some surprising ways, their reports are inferior to those of Select Committees in the nineteenth century. The ferocious report of the Select Committee on the Army Before Sebastopol (1854–55) on the 'intricacy and confusion' prevailing in public departments makes today's reports by the Defence Committee seem sycophantic. The report of the Select Committee on Distress from Want of Employment (1895) has a better research base, including detailed returns and narratives from every district in the country, than today's equivalent would have. The sixteen volumes of the Select Committee on the Poor Law Amendment Act of 1838 are much more comprehensive than we could expect today from a similar project. No report by today's Select Committee on Employment could match the vivacity and poignancy of the evidence heard by the Lords Committee on the Sweating System (1888) from Woolf Silverman, the presser; Myor Wilchinski, the ladies tailor or Charles Solomon, the secretary of the Jewish Mutual Boot Finishers and Lasters Trade and Benefit Society. If the Employment Committee of 1992 were engaged on such a study it would do little more than listen to a disquisition from the emollient Sir Humphrey in charge of some agency or division. (I was cheered to see that soon after I pointed this out to the chairman of the Social Services Committee he called a pensioner from the Maxwell pension fund to give evidence on the hardship caused by the mismanagement of the fund).

Reliance on the traditional arrangements for a Select Committee enquiry: sending for government papers, inviting opinions from interested parties and examining witnesses, is not only inexpensive but makes relatively few demands on members' time – maybe up to four or five hours a week. The disadvantage is that, not only do the committees focus on only a small part of their terms of reference, but their reports are often cursory, particularly when the subject is technical or complex. If committees used modern analytical and survey techniques for their studies of policy and also carried out financial and management studies, the time demanded from members could well increase. Many members would object, but most of those who were serious about investigating government would reckon the time spent worthwhile.

Another problem has become apparent at the time of writing, particularly in the work of the Treasury Committee. As departments and agencies produce more voluminous information, committees will be unable to cope with its amount and content. Committees do not have the means to employ the analysts who will soon be required, full-time, to examine the operations and systems of agencies, details of which are only now becoming available: with fifty-seven agencies in mid-1991 and many more to come, the resources of Select Committees will be stretched to breaking point.

Though the Select Committees have been successful, their success has been within unambitious limits and it is now time to redefine and widen their role, scope and operations. First, as discussed elsewhere, they should take on a regular and systematic examination of the objectives and the outcomes of the spending programmes of the departments and agencies they cover and they should regularly examine the efficiency and effectiveness of departmental and agency management. Secondly, they should undertake surveys of the clients of departments and agencies (e.g. the beneficiaries of social programmes, the recipients of overseas aid, industrialists and farmers) to establish the effects of government policies. Thirdly, they should undertake research into long-term issues of national importance. There are a number of such issues which they have never examined, from lack of inclination or shortage of resources: the social consequences of single parenthood; how the Treasury makes choices on spending; the redistribution of income from the poor to the well-paid in recent years; the formation and training of British managers; new health-care technologies, to pick a few examples. They should examine such evolving issues and develop a role as research institutes and consultants to the nation. Fourthly, they should join together from time to time on joint studies which cross departmental boundaries: on the relationship of poverty and health, for example. This would severely test departments because civil servants are forbidden to discuss inter-departmental business with Select Committees.

To develop in these directions would entail a substantial increase in their staffs, or in their budgets for commissioning outside advice, or both. They would need a new permanent, technically qualified body of staff even if they commissioned most of this work from outside organisa-tions. Neither the Clerk's department nor the Library's Research Divi-sion is staffed or organised to provide this depth of expertise. Some such staff should also be employed in a Department of the Opposition (see Chapter 3).

The question is whether each committee should have a technical staff of its own or whether there should be a common pool for all committees. On balance, the better case is for most of the additional staff to be in a common pool, first because of the varying workload of committees and secondly because most of the skills needed (statistical, accountancy, management, social survey, forecasting) would be needed by all commit-tees. This leads me to the conclusion that there should be a new Research Department in the House of Commons Service, which staff of the Clerk's Department and the Library could join, deployed to support Select Committees.

There is one other field in which it has often been suggested that the Select Committees could usefully develop: the examination of proposed government appointees to top jobs, e.g. chairpersons of nationalised industries, chief executives of quangos, ambassadors, judges. It can be argued that their terms of reference would permit this anyway, though they are certain to come up against a government refusal to allow such a witness to attend. Nevertheless, a Select Committee should issue an invitation to an appointee and we could see what reasons the government gave for refusal and what attitude the Commons took as a result. There is no good reason why Select Committees should not undertake such enquiries.

The problem with all these proposals is that at the moment there is little evidence that the present committees have any inclination to develop along new lines. Most of their members would probably be made nervous by the additional cost – or the media comment on the cost – of the additional resources required, and would be alarmed by the demands on their time. However, the changes could be introduced gradually, with frequent reference to precedent. What is needed is an intimation by the Liaison Committee and the House of Commons Commission that they would not refuse Select Committee requests for additional funds for research; a word from the Leader of the House that the government would not oppose a developing role for Select Committees; and a bid by an exceptionally bold committee chairperson for a lot more money (the Social Services Committee is at the stage where it might do so). The chances for such a congruence are slight, but one day it should emerge.

5
Financial Control

The arrangement for presenting and approving the government's annual estimates of the money it will need to appropriate for the financial year is called the Supply Procedure. To quote a Select Committee report on the procedure, 'From the earliest days of Parliament and the demands of the Plantagenet kings for money for their wars, the granting of supply has been the basis of power of the House of Commons over the executive. The power to withhold these grants of Supply enabled the Commons to ensure that their bills seeking remedies for their grievances were passed.'[1]

Constitutional practice dictates that it is for the Crown (i.e. the government) to demand money, the House of Commons to grant it and the House of Lords to assent to the grant. There is also a convention that the House of Commons may reject or reduce an estimate or a tax proposal, but it may not propose an increase in taxation or spending nor transfer spending from one head to another.

The main Supply estimates are presented in March for the financial year beginning in April, and winter, spring and summer supplementary estimates are laid before the House as extra funds are needed. The out-turn, or Appropriation, accounts are reported in the autumn following the end of the financial year to which they relate.

Since the early 1960s, government departments have produced 'projections' of their proposed expenditures for several years ahead for the Treasury's Public Expenditure Survey. Every January since 1969 a Public Expenditure White Paper derived from the survey has been published, setting out detailed expenditure programmes for each department for three years ahead and estimated and actual out-turns for the past six years. Since 1991 these plans have been produced in separate departmental reports, which include statistical and other information on the department's activities. In addition, a summary of departmental spending plans for the next three years, with the Treasury's latest economic forecasts, is presented to Parliament each November in an Autumn Statement.

Until the end of the nineteenth century Supply was examined at great length in the Commons. Each department's estimate was discussed in a Committee of Supply on the floor of the House. Individual members could move amendments to reduce or omit items of expenditure and governments were occasionally defeated on them. After reforms in the procedure introduced by Arthur Balfour in 1896, 'Supply Days' allocated for the discussion of estimates became days used by the opposition to discuss topics of their choice, thus recognising the changing practice of the House. In the early years of this century many members became concerned that government spending received so little attention from the House. Winston Churchill, in a debate on the Public Accounts in 1905, said that all were convinced that the present system of financial control was lax and ineffectual and that no proper scrutiny of the estimates or control of finance was exercised. So far as any systematic and scientific examination of the expenditure of the country was concerned, he said, they were a series of farces from beginning to end.[2]

In 1966, the Committee of Supply was abolished and the twenty-six Supply Days were formally detached from the consideration of spending estimates. In 1982, Supply Days were replaced by nineteen (now twenty) Opposition Days and three days were allocated for discussion of particular estimates chosen by the all-party Liaison Committee. The first Estimates Day debate in 1983 was the first time a specific estimate had been debated since that concerning the cost of the Lord Chancellor's bathroom in 1919. There are also three days nominally set aside for discussing the government's demands for supply which are used for private members to discuss subjects of their choice.

In March, the Chancellor's Budget sets out taxation for the coming year and this is accompanied by a Financial Statement and Budget Report which includes the Treasury's short-term economic forecast and medium-term financial strategy. The taxation changes in the Budget are legislated in an annual Finance Bill.

For nearly one hundred years, there has been very little detailed discussion of government spending and today billions of pounds are passed each year without debate. In contrast, taxation proposals contained in the Finance Bill are debated for a week on the floor of the House and considered in great detail for many weeks in Standing Committee. The longer-term spending programmes set out in the Public Expenditure White Paper also receive very little examination on the floor of the House or in committee. The most insignificant tax can be the subject of extensive debate, amendment and vote and yet a multi-million pound construction or defence project or public service programme could well not be examined at all, or only for an hour or two in a Select Committee.

In practice, parliamentary 'control' of the purse appears to mean authorising spending in general without any discussion and occasionally closely scrutinising a particular item of expenditure without any coherent analytical framework. This situation may be due to the traditional emphasis on debates in the Chamber, which is not a suitable forum for the detailed examination of spending proposals, though Select Committees have not been sufficiently interested in the subject to make much use of their opportunities in this field, either. It may also be due to the impenetrability of the estimates and public spending forecasts, which are not usually accompanied by any attempt to explain what an item of spending is intended to achieve. They do not fulfil the purpose of control, or management, information (see below). Both Parliament and the civil service have always appeared to find this concept quite hard to grasp.

Control Information

In management terms, 'control means the collection, analysis, comparison and distribution of information to permit the performance of the organisation and its constituent parts to be regularly compared with pre-determined standards so that action can be taken when the variance between achievement and standard exceeds acceptable limits.'[3]

A comprehensive system of financial and management scrutiny of government has to be supported by control information in three dimensions:

1. To establish the *regularity*, or the proper stewardship of funds, by the executive: to show that spending is properly attributed to estimate headings, is authorised by the legislature and properly accounted for at the end of the financial year. The purpose of this information is to demonstrate the propriety and legality of spending. It has to be organised in a way which suits the requirements of record keeping and audit, e.g. it identifies payments, purchases and grants. Supply estimates and appropriation accounts are designed to demonstrate regularity and

nothing else. From the 1830s, when they were introduced to prevent fraud and embezzlement, until the advent of the Public Expenditure White Paper in 1969 they were the only spending information regularly provided to Parliament and they are still the most voluminous – and least useful.

2. To enable the measurement and reporting of *efficiency*, i.e. the relationship of input to output, the cost per unit of service provided. Efficiency is measured by, for example, the cost per £x of taxes collected, or of social security benefits claimed, or of a licence issued or an inspection carried out. Most of the work of clerical, computing and technical organisations in the public service can be covered by such 'performance indicators'. They were first developed in the US federal government in the 1930s and were generally introduced there after the report of the Hoover Commission in 1949. Some experiments in their use were tried by the management services side of the Civil Service Department in the late 1960s, but widespread applications were not attempted until the mid-1980s and they are only now appearing in the annual reports of government agencies and departments.

To measure efficiency it is necessary to know the total cost of a departmental unit or activity and the volume of its output. This information has not been available until recently because the Supply accounts were not organised in a way which coincided with management units (divisions, sections, local offices) or with their particular activities, and because the recording of volumes of transactions was unreliable.

3. To enable the measurement and reporting of *effectiveness*. Effectiveness is the relationship of output to objective: i.e. the extent of the achievement of an intended result, or the impact of an expenditure on a specified public need or demand. To establish the effectiveness of an expenditure, a measurable objective is required and information has to be organised so as to track the progress made in achieving it. This involves categorising expenditures into 'programmes' attributable to specific policy objectives, such as the reduction of youth unemployment or homelessness; the provision of water of a specified quality; the reduction of the number of road traffic accidents or of deaths from specific diseases.

Measuring effectiveness can be an expensive and complicated enterprise, because it usually involves surveying the extent of a social, environmental, economic or other problem, setting an objective for dealing with it and then tracking the impact of the government's actions or expenditure on it. So, an attempt to discover the effectiveness of a regional or inner-city development programme should first describe and measure the economic or social conditions in the areas concerned, estimate what improvement is feasible, set objectives and then monitor the results of the spending or other intervention.

There are manifold problems involved in designing the survey specification for such an exercise, in gathering information and disentangling which actions caused what results. Many spending programmes take years to have any effect, for example achieving improvements in public health, or in the environment, or in educational standards, and keeping them under surveillance can be very expensive. Moreover, when the results are apparent they may call government policies into question and show that ministerial decisions were misconceived in the first place. It is not difficult to recall policies that have been ineffective: schemes of assistance for ailing industries, inner-city programmes, equal opportunities schemes, health education programmes, the 'short, sharp shock' treatment for young offenders, the poll tax.

It is not surprising, therefore, that governments are not keen on measuring programme effectiveness and very little of it has ever been done in Britain: spending programmes virtually never include a systems design for tracking their results. On the other hand, it *is* surprising that Parliament, and particularly Select Committees, have not shown much interest in it either, very rarely demanding reports from departments on the effectiveness of their policies and programmes and never commissioning such studies themselves. A system for analysing and tracking programme effectiveness, 'Program Planning and Budgetting' was developed in the US federal government in the early 1960s and briefly tried in Whitehall a few years later, but it did not attract any significant interest in Parliament.

A major problem with establishing control information systems for government is that the assembly of data on the performance of departments or agencies requires a different analytical framework for each of these three dimensions.* Regularity data has to be arranged 'subjec-

* New dimensions are now appearing. A few local authorities, to their credit, require reports on the performance of their departments in terms of equal opportunities and, more problematic, in terms of empowerment, i.e. enabling the participation of the people affected by a policy or programme.

tively', by reference to the nature of the goods or services purchased; efficiency data is organised by management unit and type of activity; effectiveness data by policy objective and programme. One might think that Parliament would not be much interested in regularity, as long as the auditor reported satisfaction; that it would be interested only in periodic reports on general trends in the efficiency of government departments and that it would be extremely keen to know whether spending programmes were effective. In fact, very few members appear ever to have been interested in any systematic analysis of the efficiency or effectiveness of government. The significant improvements in control information which have taken place over the last twenty years were prompted by a very small band of civil service reformers who have contrived to influence the Treasury and Procedure Select Committees. The Treasury, which has always defined 'control' not in management terms, but as limiting all spending, regardless of its merits, has been very slow to promote the development of management information, even for its own use. Its indifference to the development of management information systems is surprising in that they would have helped the Treasury itself to improve its control of expenditure, by enabling it to pick out inefficient and ineffective spending programmes and proposals and to evaluate the relative returns from spending programmes with long-term pay-offs, like training or child care.

The idea that government departments should construct information systems which enabled them to demonstrate their efficiency and effectiveness was first advocated by the management consultancy group which advised the Fulton Committee on the civil service in 1968. 'The system of vote accounting does not provide cost figures for particular aspects of departmental activities,' it said, and proposed that departments be divided into 'centres' or accountable units to which costs should be allocated and from which outputs could be measured: 'Regular provision of cost data in this form is essential to systematic management control.'[4] The Fulton Committee itself observed: 'Accountable management means holding individuals and units responsible for performance measured as objectively as possible'[5] and recommended that Management by Objectives (a performance appraisal system popular at the time) should be introduced into government. The Treasury maintained that to adapt the Supply Procedure to comply with these proposals would be too difficult a task.

The author and H. R. N. Jamieson, at that time management consultants, then tried a different tack, by taking the issue to Parliament. In evidence to the Procedure Committee in 1969 we pointed out that the Supply Procedure 'cannot be used to identify responsibility for costs, nor to show the costs of a period of working, they cannot be used for meaningful comparison, for the assessment of departmental priorities or for long-term planning.' We concluded: 'Departmental expenditure control procedures appear to be adequate to demonstrate the steward-ship of funds to Parliament, but they are not supported by an analytical substructure which permits the use of modern management systems of planning and control.'[6]

The Procedure Committee made encouraging noises and recom-mended that other Select Committees should take up the matter, but nothing happened. In the same year, the author and S. D. Walker of the Civil Service Department wrote a pamphlet for the Centre for Administrative Studies on Management by Objectives in the Civil Ser-vice which pointed to the feasibility of the adoption of that useful tech-nique if the service would reform its information systems.[7]

Interest in the subject faded away until in 1977 the General sub-committee of the Expenditure Committee (the equivalent of today's Treasury Committee) carried out an extensive survey of what had hap-pened to Fulton's proposals for civil service reform. This was the first time for 104 years that any Select Committee had enquired into the organisation and management of the civil service. It found management accounting haphazard and limited in scale: 'pretty embryonic,' admitted Lord Armstrong, the former head of the civil service, when he gave evidence to the committee.[8]

The committee described the Treasury's attitude as 'predictably con-servative'. The vote accounting system had not changed since 1866 and the Treasury saw no reason for changing it now, it said.[9] Lord Arm-strong put the matter in perspective: 'We give Parliament a combination of what Parliament wants and what ministers are willing to let it have, which is a funny thing.'[10]

The Expenditure Committee's report on the civil service recom-mended a reform of the accounts 'so as to provide a system of manage-ment information'. A year later, the Procedure Committee of 1977–78 (see Chapter 4) returned to the issue: 'It is clear to us that the present financial procedures of the House are inadequate for exercising control over public expenditure and ensuring that money is effectively spent.'[11] Its report quoted the Chairman of the Public Accounts Committee, Mr Edward du Cann: 'Broadly speaking, government expenditure is not within parliamentary control.'[12] It noted that the proposed reforms in financial systems had been around for a decade without receiving any response from government and recommended that a committee be established to look at the matter again.

The government accepted that recommendation and set up a special Procedure Committee to consider Supply, though it was established so late in the 1980–81 session that it could produce only a brief report.[13] It described effective control of finance by Parliament as 'a myth': 'The House's financial procedures are antiquated and defective and need a thorough enquiry'[14] and pointed out that only about half of government spending was covered by the Supply Procedure and was therefore never considered by the House; that loans raised by the government, which met a substantial part of spending, did not come before the House at all; that the form of the Supply estimates impeded any detailed examination of their purposes and justification and that Select Committees rarely examined estimates or long-term spending programmes. It proposed the creation of an Estimates Business Committee which would decide on which estimates would be considered on eight Estimate Days on the floor of the House. It pointed out that in other legislatures (Germany, Sweden, Japan, France, the USA) it was possible for a vote to be taken to increase an estimate, but decided without much discussion that such a revolutionary change was not yet acceptable to the House of Commons (i.e. to the government). The government's response to the committee's report was to allow three, not eight, days to discuss the estimates.

Many of these matters were considered by that committee's successor, the Procedure (Finance) Committee of 1982–83.[15] It recommended that new procedures should be developed to allow the House to examine government borrowing, the financing of nationalised industries, the rate support grant to local authorities and long-term capital projects, and to examine public spending as a whole. It also recommended splitting the annual Finance Bill into a Taxes Management Bill to tidy up existing taxation and a Finance Bill setting out proposals for changes in rates of taxation. Two very important issues, whether it would be possible to produce an integrated procedure for considering expenditure and taxation together each year and whether it would be possible to improve the presentation of information on spending, the committee referred to the House and its Select Committees 'for a view'. Parliament had still made little progress on specifying an information structure for the financial accountability of government, after fourteen years of sporadic outbreaks of concern about the matter.

The Civil Service Discovers Management

Significant developments in management information in government departments, which ultimately worked through to some improvements in financial reporting to Parliament, began in 1979. In the course of her initial programme of 'rolling back the state', Mrs Thatcher's Cabinet Ministers were invited to examine options for securing staff reductions of 2.5 per cent to 7.5 per cent in their departments. Faced with this challenge Mr Michael Heseltine, then Secretary of State for the Environment, decided to find out what went on in his enormous department and had produced a list of each management position in it and what the occupants were employed to do. This was then developed into a simple Management by Objectives routine for each of the Department of the Environment's fifty-seven directorates; the purposes and objectives of each unit were listed and work targets set for six months ahead. The scheme was called MINIS, or Management Information System for Ministers. 'This,' says Mr Heseltine in his memoirs, 'had not been done in the public sector before'.[16] In fact, it had been done a decade before in large areas of local government and in a number of experiments in central government, but had been allowed to wither away, because it had not had the support of powerful ministers. MINIS was further developed, by including a rudimentary costing system and, says Mr Heseltine, 'for the first time we could see what people were doing and what could be done with smaller numbers or cut out altogether.'[17] Four years later, the Department of the Environment employed 15,000 fewer people, an outcome which was partly attributed to the new information system.

At first, the Treasury was not impressed and the Cabinet was not enthused by MINIS, but given the record of the Department of the Environment in cutting its staff and the consequent plaudits showered upon its Secretary of State, most departments hastened to develop similar systems. So, for example, there was DEMIS in Energy, MAXIS in Transport, MAIS in Agriculture and APR in the Home Office.

There was a lot of exaggeration about the usefulness of MINIS and its offspring. For instance, MINIS accounted for only 1 per cent of the spending in the Department of the Environment: it covered only administrative costs, not the department's expenditure on services. The author observed at the time that MINIS told the Secretary of State the costs of the curtains and carpets in Marsham Street (the department's headquarters) but not the cost of Toxteth (an area of Liverpool singled out for spending after riots there).

However, MINIS had apparently been used to cut such a swathe through civil servants in the Department of the Environment that the government announced its universal application as the Financial Management Initiative (FMI) in 1982 in its reply[18] to a report from the Treasury Committee on the Civil Service. This had recommended that the annual Public Expenditure White Paper should set out the aims, objectives, resourcing and results of spending programmes and that the annual Supply estimates should give more detailed management, and budgetary, control information.

The government reply ignored most of these recommendations but announced that the FMI would promote in each department an organisation and system in which all managers had a clear view of their objectives; the means to assess or measure outputs or performance in relation to those objectives; and well-defined responsibility for making the best use of their resources. What it failed to mention was when all this improved information about management performance would be made available to Parliament to assist its processes of scrutiny and investigation. It did foresee that the Public Expenditure White Paper would contain more information on policy objectives and 'progress and performance indicators', but in fact information derived from MINIS-type systems and the FMI was never revealed to Parliament. A progress report on the FMI in 1984 never mentioned reporting to Parliament at all. All these changes in management information took place within the closed world of the civil service.

The FMI was not the civil service revolution it was cracked up to be, either. 'We are disappointed at evidence of its stunted growth,' said the Treasury Committee in 1988, after hearing from the First Division Association of senior civil servants that many civil service managers regarded the developments growing from the FMI as 'a meaningless and irritating waste of time'.[19] This failure was due to the inability of civil service managers significantly to affect the performance of their units because they had no control over recruitment, staffing, pay, promotion and the use of information technology. They were being given information about, and being judged on, performance they could not influence. A large expenditure on computing (£35 million in 1983–84) was used to produce information which could not be used for management and was not available for examination by Parliament. As the Fulton Report had foreseen, the next step had to be to delegate responsibility to civil service managers so that they had the authority to make decisions in the light of the new information available. Indeed, Fulton had proposed in 1968 that the delegation of authority, the breaking up of long civil service hierarchies into centres of accountability, had to be accompanied by information systems which allowed that authority to be exercised. These proposals were developed by Robert Sheldon and the author in a 1973 Fabian tract (No. 426 *Administrative Reform: The Next Step*), in which we introduced the idea that departments should be organised into small administrative branches and large executive, scientific and technical divisions constituted as departmental agencies.

The civil service arrived at the same conclusion in 1988. The reform it initiated was the breaking up of departments into centres of accountability, or agencies. The Treasury document which announced this development was called *Improving Management in Government: The Next Steps*[20] and the resulting organisations are often called Next Steps Agencies. These agencies, or PINGOS (Partly Independent Government Organisations), are units which carry out the executive functions of a department within a policy and resources framework drawn up by that department. Departments typically consist of small policy divisions, staffed by administrative mandarins and their support staffs, and large executive or technical divisions, run by managers and technical specialists, which deliver the department's services. The Next Steps document, a rather flimsy effort, proposed the separation of these two activities and the transformation of the executive and technical divisions into 'businesses' run by chief executives who would be given extensive powers over staffing, pay, investment, organisation and other aspects of management.

One of the reasons for the creation of agencies was said by the Next Steps report to be that departments paid too little attention to the results they achieved with the resources they were given – a criticism of the Treasury itself made for the preceding twenty years, often by parliamentary committees. Another reason was that there were 'relatively few external pressures on departments demanding improvements in performance'. That put Parliament in its place. One way and another (through constituency case work, debates, questions, committees) the greater part of the work of most MPs is about demanding improvements in the performance of departments. Worse was to come: 'Pressures from Parliament, the Public Accounts Committee and the media tend to concentrate on alleged impropriety and incompetence, and making political points, rather than on demanding evidence of steadily improving efficiency and effectiveness.'[21] This observation combined ignorance with impertinence to a breathtaking degree. The Procedure, the Public Accounts and, particularly, the Treasury Committees had regularly been demanding evidence of civil service efficiency and effectiveness for the previous two decades. The refusal to provide the evidence had always come from the Treasury, which had usually treated these demands with disdain and obfuscation.

The Next Steps programme began with a bang. Twelve agencies were announced on the day of the publication of the report and four more within three months. By May 1989 departments had identified eighty candidates for agency status employing 244,000 staff. In mid-1991 fifty-seven had actually been set up, employing some 200,000 staff. The government's aim was to have half of all civil servants employed in agencies by the end of 1991 and three-quarters within ten years. The earliest agencies were all small and in quasi-commercial areas of government; the Vehicle Inspectorate (1,600 staff); the National Weights and Measures Laboratory (50); Companies House (1,100); the QE2 Conference Centre (60). Recently very large agencies have been announced or established: Social Security local office operations (87,000 staff); the Training Agency (12,000) and the Employment Service (33,000).

These agencies are headed by Chief Executives with extensive delegated powers over staffing, organisation, pay and conditions, and investment. Their responsibilities are defined in 'framework documents' or 'contracts' produced by their parent departments and against which it is said that their managements will be held accountable. These documents are intended to include objectives and targets for agency performance: 'the setting of genuine indicators of agency performance is a mandatory requirement for establishing an agency,' reported the National Audit Office.[22] As agencies are set up, government departments will be reduced to small headquarters operations concerned with advising and supporting ministers, formulating policy and legislation and overseeing the activities of the agencies.

This process raises a number of important issues for civil service management (the end of a national civil service, the division between the mandarins in a department and the managers in an agency, the separation of policy from implementation) which are outside the scope of this book. It raises even larger issues of public and parliamentary accountability – Parliament has enough difficulty in scrutinising the operations of thirty main departments without taking on eighty or more agencies as well – which were discussed in Chapter 4. What concerns us here is what difference the existence of agencies makes to the information available to Parliament for the examination of the efficiency and effectiveness of government.

On the face of it, the difference is great. For an increasing range of government services, we are promised framework documents which set out the objectives of agencies and how their performance will be measured and it is intended that the agencies will report publicly on what they have achieved. The government proposes the review of framework documents every three years, but has never said if the performance of an agency will be reported annually or only when a new framework document is drawn up.

The nature of the performance measures imposed on agencies by departments is crucial. It is worth remembering that the agency concept sprang from the Financial Management Initiative and the FMI sprang from a determination to cut civil service numbers. This is very different from Fulton's (and later, Sheldon and Garrett's) advocacy of agencies as a means of improving the quality of civil service management and replacing administrative mandarins by professional managers. The performance required of agency heads has been to improve 'efficiency' and the simplest way to do that is to cut staff and other costs. Moreover, agency heads are the recipients of 'performance pay'; in other words, they are paid by results.

The activities of agencies in such technical, executive and trading areas as vehicle licensing, research and development, printing, driver testing and the care of historic buildings are relatively uncontroversial. Parliament has a quite different interest in agencies which handle such politically sensitive matters as training, job finding and social security benefits, where failures often end up in MPs' advice surgeries. Setting up agencies as businesses, the performance of which is judged primarily on accounting criteria, could be very contentious. The performance criteria for these public services should include not only the quality of service to applicants and claimants, but also the extent to which they reach *potential* claimants or beneficiaries from their services. For example, they should be required to improve the take-up rates of the services they provide. As we shall see below, the efforts in this direction have not so far been reassuring.

Information for Parliament

While government was modernising itself, the House of Commons continued to try to prise useful information out of it on the purposes and results of spending. In the eight years since the report of the Procedure (Finance) Committee in 1983 there have been no fewer than thirteen reports from Select Committees on the subject (ten from the Treasury Committee, three from the Public Accounts Committee) which have prompted six published replies from the government. The main aims of the committees have been to establish clear links between medium-term spending plans and the annual estimates, and to require government to produce analyses which show the purposes and effects of spending.

The Treasury Committee has proposed on several occasions that Estimates Days should be replaced by a series of debates in June when Select Committee reports on public expenditure spending programmes could be discussed. The Treasury appears to be unenthusiastic, probably because it has realised that a debate on a proposed spending programme would be much less closely circumscribed than a debate on an estimate and that the House could vote to increase the spending on a programme, which it cannot do for an estimate.

Since the Treasury claims that valuable improvements in public and parliamentary accountability have been made by the expansion of the Public Expenditure White Paper, changes in the estimates and the establishment of agency framework agreements and reports, it is worth taking a closer look at them.

The 1991 Public Expenditure White Paper came in twenty departmental volumes, amounting to 1500 pages (and costing over £200). Most of them were drab productions, in blue covers with a few hazy graphics. The Home Office, however, produced a volume which would not have looked out of place in the reception area of an advertising agency, with graphics printed over pictures of prisoners at work, computers and what appeared to be a fire in a chip pan, and with a signed foreword topped by a photograph of a smiling Home Secretary. The report by the Office of Arts and Libraries (on a spend of £500 million) was 20 per cent longer, at 34 pages, than the report by the Ministry of Defence (spending £22,000 million). The Defence report was largely narrative, with virtually no analysis. It informed the reader that its plan to improve efficiency by 2.5 per cent per year was going well and gave some descriptive examples such as its use of competitive tendering for army recruitment films and the cancellation of the overhaul of nine aeroengines.

The Inland Revenue, in one of the best of this kind of report, produced a management plan and set out its purposes and aims, its management strategies, its capital spending by project and such efficiency indicators as the cost per pound collected in revenue, the cost per taxpayer and a wide variety of measures of performance past and future.

Elsewhere, the information could only be described as haphazard and whimsical. All departments set out what they were spending, usually in great detail, but there were few meaningful indicators of what results they were aiming at. A few examples will give the flavour.

The Minister for the Civil Service recorded the ratings given to the Civil Service College by its students (on quality of training, accommodation and catering), but did not mention, or report, any progress in equal opportunities policies in the service. The Department of Employment recorded no objectives for youth or employment training or for placement in terms, for example, of those gaining qualifications or jobs. The report of the Department of the Environment – the largest and most expensive, at 178 pages and £17.20 – set out page after page of detail on spending but had no past analyses or future targets for the improvement of, for example, the quality of water or air. It reported the department's interest in preserving the landscape, but failed to report the extent of the damage to, or destruction of, Sites of Special Scientific Interest. It mentioned the extent of homelessness but offered no indication of how much it expected to reduce it. The Social Security report informed the reader on the ways in which take-up rates for benefits could be defined, but gave no analysis of what they were or how they might be improved. There were lots of apparently useful statistics in the Department of Health's volume on the costs of its services, the number of outpatient attendances, the average length of inpatient episodes, immunisation take-up rates, general practitioner list size and prescription costs. There were mortality rates for a number of diseases. There were targets for coronary grafts, hip replacements, cataract operations and bone marrow transplants. Unfortunately all these figures ended in 1989 or 1990 and there were no indications of how the government expected them to improve in future. On the key indicator of waiting-list sizes, we were told what special funds were being allocated to reduce them, but given no idea by how much the department expected them to be reduced.

The Treasury's slender report had an amusing selectivity. It grandly informed its readership that among its objectives (actually aims) were 'to maintain a general oversight of the financial system and help maintain its integrity' and 'to manage government debts and financial assets effectively and prudently'. One might therefore expect some figures relating to City failures and the effectiveness of investor protection, or to the Treasury's debt management and custody of assets, but a suggestion by the author to this effect in hearings held by the Treasury Committee was greeted with surprise by Treasury officials. On the other hand, the Treasury report did tell the reader about the productivity of pay clerks in the Chessington Computer Centre and offered an unintelligible graph on the caseload of clerical staff in its Pensions Administration Office. The mandarins of the Treasury appeared only too happy to apply measurement to the work of their clerical staff, but not to themselves.

The presentation of statistical indicators reached a somewhat eccentric peak in the report of the Welsh Office, otherwise one of the best of the departmental reports. There, a section on 'Indicators of a Healthy Lifestyle, 1985–88', recorded the percentages of the population normally using semi-skimmed milk and eating fruit daily, while a section on Indicators of Health reported that the department had under consideration the production of an indicator of emotional health and relationships among the Welsh.

Those of us who have argued for the past twenty-odd years that the Public Expenditure White Paper should set out, for as many spending programmes as possible, social and economic indicators describing the problem or conditions at which the spending is aimed and the objectives which future planned spending are intended to achieve, can only record dismay at all this. These first departmental reports showed either that departments were trying to swamp the reader with meaningless numbers or, more likely, that they had simply poured into the reports any old numbers they had to hand.

Only Customs and Excise appeared to have grasped the concept of measuring efficiency and effectiveness in its annual report (though the Scottish and Welsh Offices had a good try). It is true that Customs and Excise is a relatively easy department for which to construct these standards, because it handles large volumes of quantifiable transactions, but it was also better at explaining policy developments and strategic aims than the others. Its statement of purpose and aims at the beginning of the report makes the Treasury's equivalent list look fatuous – and the Treasury is supposed to set the pattern for all other departments!

A truly bizarre twist was given to this story by November 1991 when the Chief Secretary, David Mellor, admitted to the Treasury Select

Committee that the output and performance measures which the Treasury had spent so much effort promoting (and boasting about) were not used to make choices between, or to prioritise, spending programmes. He said that it was not possible to compare the benefits of various levels of spending on different programmes: 'Each department comes along with a shopping list,' he explained, helplessly.[23] What *was* the point of the exercise then? The argument for producing performance measures was primarily to enable government to replace shopping lists with rational priorities. If in practice they have so little importance, it is no wonder that the civil service has been so slipshod about them.

The Public Expenditure reports are followed by the Estimates, also claimed by the Treasury to have been much improved in recent years. The 1991–92 estimates came in twenty volumes totalling 1120 pages. Each volume covered a class of estimate which set out the money required for the coming year by a government department (thus Class 1, Ministry of Defence), divided into 163 individual estimates (five for Defence amounting to £23 billion, twenty-six for the Scottish Office, amounting to £8.6 million).

Each estimate is divided into sections (thirteen in Defence) and each section is divided into up to a dozen subheads. The sections in Defence vary from £5 million to £25 million; in Environment they range from £550,000 to £3.5 billion. Each subhead sets out what was spent in the penultimate year (the 'outturn'), what was thought to have been spent in the last year (the 'total provision') and what is to be provided for the coming year beginning in a month's time (see facing page).

This section provides a typical example of the wild variation in size and importance of items in the estimates format. The estimates are littered with these maddening inconsistencies in levels of detail: alongside items for scores of millions of pounds we can find £26,000 for two nursery schools in the Education estimates; £61,000 in payments to dentists compulsorily retired and £73,000 on courses for social workers for the deaf in the Health estimates; £4,000 to be recovered for incorrect ophthalmic voucher payments in the Welsh estimates; £1,000 for assessors for valuation services as part of the Sheep Compensation Scheme in the Agriculture estimates. The list of trivia is endless.

On the other hand, these volumes of estimates do now usefully set out the original estimate and the current forecast for the cost of capital projects and there the dedicated reader can come across some interesting nuggets, like the Old War Office Building Computer

DEPARTMENT OF THE ENVIRONMENT (CLASS VIII)
Miscellaneous housing administration and grants (Vote 2)

1989–90 Outturn £'000	1990–91 Total provision £'000	Subhead detail	1991–92 Provision £'000
		Central government expenditure:	
		Section A: Housing Corporation administration	
28,494	36,450	**A1 Housing Corporation: revenue support for special needs accommodation**	60,000
	36,000	(1) Grant in aid to cover the cost of Hostel Deficit Grant.	58,000
	450	(2) Grant in aid to cover the cost of Special Needs Management Allowances.	2,000
20,872	24,207	**A2 Housing Corporation: administrative and promotional expenditure**	28,988
	23,350	(1) Grant in aid for net administrative costs.	25,286
	857	(2) Grant in aid for grants, loans and payments by the Housing Corporation in support of promotional and advisory activities.	3,702
106	109	**A3 Housing Corporation: remuneration and pensions**	117
	105	(1) Remuneration of the Chairman and members of the Housing Corporation.	115
	4	(2) Payment of pensions to the retired Chairman and Deputy Chairman of the Housing Corporation.	2
49,472	60,766	**Gross total**	89,105
		Less:	
1	1	**AZ Appropriations in aid**	2
		Pension contributions from the Chairman of the Housing Corporation.	
49,471	60,765		89,103

Project (original estimate in 1988–89 £9.2 million; current estimate £42.2 million).

The estimates are followed after the end of the financial year by the appropriation accounts, which contain the same degree of detail. They show for each subhead the original grant of money, actual expenditure and whether spending was over or under the grant. Like the estimates, these are purely accounting documents showing only financial results and telling the reader nothing about what the money bought – the new homes, the trained workers, the improvements in the nation's health, a cleaner environment.

We should be entitled to expect substantial improvement in the information provided by government as a result of the creation of Next Steps Agencies. They were, after all, set up as managerial entities with extensive delegated authority over their own budgets and with the ostensible purpose of improving service to the public. Nearly all the first thirty of them were in quasi-commercial areas where costs and outputs were relatively easy to measure and their framework documents laid down some simple performance requirements. The Driving Standards Agency, for example, was to be measured on waiting times for 'L' tests, the time taken to make appointments, the promptness of replies to telephone calls, the level of complaints – though its framework document did not specify or explain any of them. This limited quantification of target performances by agencies was surprising, given that most of their managers were to receive an element of pay based on measured performance. The only agency with financial or statistical targets, HMSO (return on net assets, a specified percentage of orders delivered on time and of jobs produced without fault) produced them for the preceding year and not for the future.

The one agency in the first wave which operates in the field of social policy, the Resettlement Agency, which exists to provide board and lodging for persons without a settled way of life, had a framework document which nowhere mentioned the size of the problem with which it had to deal or what it proposed to do to reduce it. Its only objective appeared to be to abolish itself.

Now that more agencies are being established to implement social policy (employment, occupational health, social security benefits, training, planning) we shall need much more sophisticated information, showing their effectiveness in meeting important public needs. For example, the Benefits Agency should publicise its objective for increasing the take-up of benefits and the Training Agency should show what it proposes to do to reach out to the untrained: the results achieved by both should be reviewed by Select Committees.

The consequence of all these changes is that, though the annual information on government spending has increased to well over 3000 pages, most of the information in departmental and agency volumes and all of it in the estimates and appropriation accounts is of little value for parliamentary scrutiny. We now have exhaustive detail on the resources which are consumed by government, but still know very little about what is intended to be, or has been, achieved by the use of those resources. We are told what we are spending, but not what we are buying. We need a massive rationalisation and simplification of spending information and the development of directly comparable out-turn, or performance, information which would permit the examination of efficiency and effectiveness of spending.

One of the most useful proposals for a reformed structure of financial reporting to Parliament was made in 1984 in a report by Andrew Likierman and Peter Vass.[24] They suggested that only two sets of documents were required: a UK Budget covering expenditure and its financing, and reports on spending from each government department, to be published soon after the Budget.

The Budget would contain information on the relationship between income and expenditure, with taxation set alongside the main estimates for the coming year: 'The object of the UK Budget would be to enable an intelligent layman without a detailed knowledge of economics or public finance to follow major economic trends, including the government's public expenditure proposals'.[25]

Likierman and Vass proposed that the Budget should be accompanied by a special analysis volume of technical details such as assumptions, definitions and other details for specialist readers. They also proposed that soon after the Budget, departmental reports should be produced which would set out the coming year's main estimates, the main Appropriation Accounts for the last complete year and the public expenditure forecasts for two years past and two years beyond the coming year. These reports would include 'the objectives and policy context within which the expenditure proposals are being made, including volume trends and indicators of efficiency, effectiveness and performance'.[26]

They pointed out that the detail of the annual estimates would not need to be published in the departmental reports. They would not even need to be printed, but could be available as photocopied typescripts from the House of Commons Vote Office or the Treasury.

The advantages of these proposals were that Select Committee members were 'much more likely to put effort into understanding documents which also provide a policy framework than into the isolated and spartan figures of the supply estimates'.[27] They would also have a clearer basis for choosing and developing subjects for debates on Estimate Days. Spending would be seen in the context of policies and programmes and interest groups would be more easily able to focus on subjects which concerned them.

A number of reports, mostly by the Treasury Committee, have since recommended the development of spending and performance information for Parliament on much these lines. They have pointed out that the estimates and appropriation accounts are useless for scrutiny and that the annual debate on the Public Expenditure White Paper 'is not a distinguished occasion in the Parliamentary calendar',[28] being unfocused and overshadowed by the following Budget debate. They have observed that most performance indicators are not presented in a form which permits comparisons with objectives or with past performance, and are not related to programme or management structures. For the three days set aside for debates on estimates there is no information on how those estimates relate to government policy or to longer-term spending plans. Few Select Committees have ever tried to look at the spending of the departments they shadow, appearing to be unable to marshal the information in any systematic way.

Government replies to these complaints have sometimes appeared to try to be helpful, but either civil servants do not understand the requirement or ministers would rather not furnish Parliament with information which would enable members to ask penetrating questions. There is evidence to support either conclusion. The Treasury has never devoted much attention to management information except as a result of intense political pressure. It has always regarded management and its techniques with mandarin disdain as an activity for the lower ranks of civil servants. Nor has it recruited management accountants or other people familiar with quantitative analysis: there is not one accountant in the top forty posts in the Treasury. For ministers, as Likierman and Vass pointed out, 'the priority is that the figures are defensible, not understandable, and obscurity may even have its advantages.'[29]

Proposals for Reform

Though developments have taken place in this field since the Likierman and Vass report, their work still provides the basis for a reform of financial information for Parliament. The Autumn Statement should become an analysis of the state of the economy and a display of policy options, while the cycle of scrutiny should be based on two documents, published soon after.

1. An Integrated Budget, comprising the Financial Statement and Budget Report, with an economic survey, taxation proposals, national accounts and a summary of main estimates by department. This should be accompanied by a cheap and simplified version for general readership and a technical volume of background details, assumptions and definitions.

2. Departmental and Agency Reports, setting out:
 (i) the main estimates for the coming year and the appropriation accounts for the last completed year;
 (ii) public expenditure programme out-turns for the past two years and plans for the two years beyond the estimates year, together with outputs, performance measures and objectives for the past two years and the coming two years;
 (iii) the original estimates for, and spending to date on, long-term projects;
 (iv) statements of the value of assets held by departments.

Each departmental report should also include any special analyses of programmes requested by Select Committees. The Budget debate would occupy a week in January but would cover spending as well as revenue-raising. Select Committees should examine the departmental reports each year, taking evidence in February and March, and in the following couple of months there should be eight Expenditure Days, instead of the present three Estimate Days, on which reports on individual spending programmes would be debated as requested by the committees.*

* In his Budget speech of 10 March 1992, the Chancellor of the Exchequer announced that, from December 1993, there would be an 'integrated' Budget produced each December which would include the Autumn Statement and the Budget. On closer inspection, this proposal proved to be less integrated than might have been expected, because departmental reports will be delayed until late February and the estimates in March. There were no proposals for improving the quality of information, nor for giving Parliament greater powers of scrutiny.

The advantage of these Expenditure Days would be that Select Committees could make reports available for them, including ministerial, official and other evidence on a particular subject. In addition, a Select Committee could propose a motion which could set out its opinion of the expenditure instead of just taking note of it, the debate could range freely over a wider ground than that covered by one estimate, and the motion would not be limited by the rule that an estimate can only be reduced; in other words, it could propose an increase in spending. Once Select Committees started to focus this closely on spending and performance they would realise how uninformative the accounts and programmes are and would oblige departments and the Treasury to improve them.

What is needed is an information system which allows MPs and Committees to ask questions about each spending programme:

- what legislation governs it?
- what is its policy justification?
- what are its objectives?
- what was budgeted for and spent on it in the past?
- what will be spent on it in the future?
- how effective has it been, what impact has it had?
- how will its effectiveness be measured in the future?
- what has been, is expected to be, its efficiency?
- what other policies or programmes will it affect (e.g. in such areas as the environment, equal opportunities, European relations)?

Parliament has to learn to ask these questions, and the government has to learn to reply to them. Both questions and answers will depend not only on improvements in accounting systems, but also on substantial improvements in the coverage and reliability of official statistics.

Government Statistics

The monitoring of public policy depends on having a reliable statistical service providing information on social, economic, environmental and other conditions and trends.

In recent years there has been an increasing dissatisfaction among professional users with the reliability and coverage of government statistics. There have been allegations of a crisis of confidence in the statistical service provided by government, and demands for it to be reorganised in order to demonstrate a greater independence of ministers. The complaints arise from cuts in statistical staff, the abolition of some important statistical series, suspicious changes in coverage and some substantial errors.

Between 1979 and 1989 the number of civil servants dealing with statistics was halved. In 1981, a review carried out by the government's efficiency team recommended that the government should collect only those statistics which it needed for its own business, so as to relieve industry of the burden of reporting. As a result, Britain no longer collects detailed quarterly statistics about, for example, the output of particular industrial products and now has less information in this field than other European countries. The deregulation of financial transactions has removed another source of data. In 1988 a junior Trade Minister, Mr Francis Maude, was reported as doubting whether government needed to provide a statistical service to industry at all or whether inter-EC trade figures would be needed after 1992. In early 1989 Lord Young, the Industry Minister, proposed to cut by a third the statistics collected by industry which many users thought were essential for the evaluation of economic performance.

The Treasury Committee has severely criticised the quality of government economic statistics, particularly after what has been called 'the statistical fiasco of the decade', when the Treasury's underestimation of the strength of demand after a precipitous fall in the stock market led to the giveaway Budget of 1988 and the ensuing 'Lawson boom', followed by an unforeseen recession and more than a year of fictitious forecasts of recovery. In the summer issue of 1990 the *Treasury Bulletin* referred to such deep-seated problems with economic statistics that it had been difficult to devise a coherent and consistent picture of economic developments through 1986–89. In 1990 the Public Accounts Committee reported shortcomings in the calculation of the Retail Price Index, which is highly significant for wage settlements, pensions and benefits. There were grave suspicions raised by the coverage of statistics on social conditions, by the definitions of poverty, by the reduction in scope of such services as the General Household Survey and by discontinuities in statistical series which made comparisons difficult. Bristol University's statistical monitoring unit, in a report on the income levels of the poor, observed that some parts of the government statistical service had become 'excessively dependent on ministerial expectations, if not directions' and there was a readiness to allow ministers to dictate the kind of information collected for policy reviews.[30]

Then there was the celebrated case of the unemployment figures: to quote the *Economist* in July 1990, 'There is also a whiff of political trickery in the air. Some claim that the government is using statistics as a drunk uses a lamp-post – for support, rather than illumination. For example, the definition of unemployment has been changed no less than thirty times since 1979. By coincidence, twenty-nine of those adjustments helped to shorten the dole queue.'[31]

The Treasury Committee's report on the 1991 Budget returned to the subject of the gross unreliability of Treasury forecasts and requested that forecasts should be more frequent and that 'the results should not be modified by ministers'.[32] In 1991 the Social Science Forum produced a report which identified deficiencies in official statistics in four major areas: data discontinuities, changes in definition, gaps in statistics and problems with accessibility.[33]

Though there has never been any suggestion of doubt about the integrity of the civil servants employed on producing the statistics, there is genuine concern about the way in which their collection is managed, organised and resourced by government. New misgivings were aroused in January 1992 when it became apparent that the conversion of the Central Statistical Office to a Next Steps Agency could require it to generate a profit. Some researchers and users of statistics feared that some statistics (those which embarrassed the government) could be priced out of their reach and that the quality of official statistics could suffer if the CSO concentrated on profitable data.

The Royal Statistical Society and the Social Science Forum have called for a centralised government statistical service, a Statistics Act and an advisory National Statistics Commission to safeguard statistical standards. There is a very good case for legislative backing for the autonomy of a national statistical service, for a representative advisory body of users and specialists and for an additional sub-committee of the Treasury and Civil Service Committee to be convened on a regular, say quarterly, basis to monitor the provision of national statistics.

6

State Audit

Most national legislatures appoint an auditor and an audit department to verify that the money voted by the legislature has been properly spent for the purposes for which it has been authorised. Nowadays, many national auditors also report on the financial management and the efficiency (and sometimes, the effectiveness) of organisations in receipt of public money.

Britain was one of the first countries in the world to have a national audit body to verify government accounts and report to a committee of the legislature. However, the most notable thing about our arrangements, as we shall see, is that this great parliamentary institution, empowered by Mr Gladstone's reforms of public finance in the 1860s to scrutinise the executive, was gradually hijacked by the Treasury over the following century and became little more than a creature of the executive. Ironically, while the Treasury was blatantly encroaching on parliamentary rights, most parliamentarians believed that our system was a jewel of parliamentary accountability and many frequently commended it as a model to other legislatures. It was only after a campaign, starting outside Parliament and lasting some seventeen years, that Parliament reasserted most of its control over the national audit in spite of bitter opposition from the government. This achievement was the most important parliamentary reform of recent times, though its significance is not generally recognised. The civil service has always regarded its setback as temporary.

Prior to 1802, government accounts were presented to the Treasury by the Commissioners of Audit. In that year, a system was introduced whereby the Treasury presented annual accounts to Parliament, but these accounts simply showed issues from the Exchequer, and Parliament still had no means of checking whether money had actually been spent on the purposes for which it had been voted. In 1832, the first appropriation accounts, comparing actual expenditure with the sums which had been voted, were produced for the navy and this arrangement was extended to the army in 1847. In 1857, a Select Committee on Public Monies recommended that the system should be extended to the civil and revenue departments and all such accounts should be submitted annually to a committee of the House of Commons nominated by the Speaker. Meanwhile, in 1834, the old office of Auditor of the Exchequer was abolished and its functions transferred to the Comptroller of the Exchequer who, for the first time, was established as independent of the executive. His job was to ensure that all money that was issued was used for prescribed purposes.

In 1861, a standing order was passed which instituted the House of Commons' Public Accounts Committee (PAC). Five years later, the Exchequer and Audit Act was passed, producing a uniform system of accounting, and in 1869 the first complete accounts of the public service were laid before Parliament. The 1866 act also combined the functions of Comptroller of the Exchequer and the Commissioners of Audit in the post of Comptroller and Auditor General (CAG) at the head of the Exchequer and Audit Department (EAD). The act established the basic responsibilities of the CAG which still govern his activities today. On receipt of the Appropriation Accounts the CAG certifies them as satisfactory or 'subject to the observations in my report'. The accounts he certifies and the reports he makes are submitted by him to the PAC. This committee formally examines each Appropriation Account, but in fact concentrates on those topics on which the CAG has made observations. In pursuing these matters, the PAC may call before it the Accounting Officers of departments, customarily Permanent Secretaries, nowadays also the heads of agencies. The appointment as Accounting Officer implies a responsibility to appear personally before the PAC, because the holder of the post signs the accounts and accepts responsibility for them. The reports of the committee and the government's views on them are published. The committee can then examine officials on the government's reply and report again. Both reports and government replies are presented to the House of Commons and a selection of them are usually debated on one day per session.

It was not until 1966 that anybody pointed out that something was drastically wrong with our system of state audit. We owe a lot to Dr E. L. Normanton, a former member of the Exchequer and Audit Department.[1] He examined the powers and functions of state audit in Britain, the USA, France and Germany and showed that in Britain the CAG was under more direction from the executive than any other state auditor: 'At least in legal form the powers of executive direction could scarcely be more complete and they are incomparably more so than in any other Western country.'[2]

Normanton described how the General Accounting Office in the USA, the State Audit Office and in France the Cour des Comptes were all independent of government and their heads were officers of the legislature. He drew attention to the fact that other auditors examined all public expenditure, while our auditor's remit covered only about half of British government spending at that time. The nationalised industries were not subject to public audit, for example. He also observed that the Treasury prescribed the form of those accounts which were audited. In other countries, state auditors often examined the efficiency and effectiveness of the management of all the public bodies they audited, but ours did not. Our audit staff were recruited as A-level school leavers while other national auditors recruited staff with professional qualifications at graduate and postgraduate level. In Britain, the Treasury regulated the recruitment, grading and salaries of our audit staff. Our system, said Normanton, fixed 'the status and careers of the state audit staff at a level in the public service which is unquestionably and demonstrably the lowest of any major country in the Western world'[3] and he concluded that ours was the only state audit system in which the auditors were of a standing inferior to those whose decisions were being audited. The Comptroller himself, though appointed by the Crown, was nominated by the Treasury, usually from its own ranks.

It was at the time of the publication of Normanton's book that the author, having just been involved in the report of the Fulton Committee on the civil service, came to the conclusion that there had to be some force external to the civil service capable of making it take management seriously. Without continuous goading, the mandarin class was never going to introduce planning, costing and budgetary control, quantitative policy analysis and modern ideas of personnel management. Normanton showed what could be done by a seriously competent state audit body. Britain clearly did not have one. It was as old-fashioned and amateurish as the civil service we wanted to modernise. The only way to reform it was to stimulate parliamentary interest in the matter.

Normanton's work attracted no parliamentary comment at all at the time of its publication. The subject lay dormant until it was revived by the author and Robert Sheldon (later chairman of the PAC) in a Fabian tract in 1973.[4] The tract proposed a number of reforms in state audit in Britain, including the widening of the functions of the EAD to include

studies of efficiency, organisation and financial and management information systems in all bodies, public or private, which spent public
money, and the employment of professionally qualified staff. The EAD,
we said, should be totally independent of the Treasury and the civil
service and should undertake studies at the request of the Public
Accounts Committee and other parliamentary committees.

An important element in the argument for reform was what Parliament had originally intended the status of the Comptroller to be. The
1866 act had said, 'Every Appropriation Account shall be examined by
the Comptroller and Auditor General on behalf of the House of Commons.' Mr Gladstone, in moving the motion to set up the PAC, had
said that the object of the committee would be to revise (i.e. review) the
accounts of public expenditure after they had been examined by the
executive government.[5]

In a debate on the PAC in 1981, the author observed, 'After its second
reading, the 1866 act was referred to the Public Accounts Committee for
its committee stage. The Comptroller of the day suggested that the act
should say that the audit should be conducted according to rules laid
down by the House of Commons. The Treasury official in evidence
agreed that was the intent, but said there was no need to say so in the act.
In other words, even in 1866 the Treasury slipped the Public Accounts
Committee a fast one.'[6]

In 1903, the Select Committee on National Expenditure considered
the working of the audit system. The Comptroller of the day made the
interesting point that he conceived his functions to go beyond mere
audit and that, encouraged by the Public Accounts Committee, he
entered also into the merits of expenditure. This aside was not challenged at the time and it is worth noting that the legislation which
now governs the Comptroller's powers expressly excludes him from
examining the merits of expenditure, an injunction which has always
been insisted upon by the government. He then went on to say, 'I am a
parliamentary officer whose duty is not only to certify the correctness of
the accounts as rendered, but further I am directed by the act to report
to Parliament.'[7]

In a debate in 1912, Lloyd George (then Chancellor) observed, 'First
of all, the act appointed the CAG an officer of the House and independent of the Treasury.'[8] In 1916, the Comptroller produced a memorandum for the PAC on fifty years of the Exchequer and Audit
Department's governing act. He observed that he was an officer independent of executive government, examined the Appropriation Accounts

on behalf of the House of Commons and laid his reports before the House.[9]

In the debate on the 1921 Exchequer and Audit Bill, slightly amending the 1886 act, the Financial Secretary to the Treasury made a definitive statement on the position of the Comptroller who, he said, audited the accounts 'officially and formally on behalf of this House, so that the responsibility of this House over them through its officer, the Auditor General, is, as it were, signalised by statute'. The salary of the CAG was paid, he said, 'not out of Votes, but out of the Consolidated Fund, and that is done in order to mark the exceptional independence, freedom and dignity of the position of this great officer of the House of Commons'.[10] He later said, so as to give further emphasis to the point, 'As the House well knows, the CAG is a person independent of the executive and a servant of this House.'[11] In 1932, the Procedure Committee made the same point: 'The CAG,' it reported, 'is independent of the executive, responsible to Parliament . . .'.[12] In 1946, the Procedure Committee reported that the CAG 'is appointed by Letters Patent but is responsible to the House of Commons alone'.[13] The status of the CAG at that time was thoroughly understood.

The Reform of Audit

After being elected to the House in 1974, the author tried to interest it in reforming state audit in Britain, without any success. The first breakthrough came when the General Sub-Committee of the Expenditure Committee (of which the author was a member) was persuaded to have a look at our audit system. In the course of its study of the civil service in 1976–77, the sub-committee undertook the first critical review of our state audit arrangements for over a hundred years.[14]

In a memorandum to the committee,[15] the CAG said that for many years his audit had gone beyond questions of regularity and into 'value for money' in administration. His staff looked into the efficiency of departmental systems for monitoring and controlling expenditure: it did not, however, examine the operating efficiency of departmental management – in Britain this was a matter for the executive itself, with the central role being played by the Civil Service Department and the Treasury. Similarly, effectiveness (or results) audits of the kind carried out by the GAO in the United States were the responsibility of the department concerned, 'which is, or should be, best equipped in expertise and resources to make them and whose minister is best placed to inject the necessary policy guidance'.[16] An effectiveness audit, he said, would require a statement of governmental objectives and the means of measuring the degree of success in attaining them. It was likely to involve questions of policy, 'an area which the CAG and his department have over the years studiously avoided'.[17] In the course of being examined by the committee, the then CAG, Sir Douglas Henley, said, 'I am, of course, totally independent even of Parliament'[18] and later commented that the efficacy of his audit had not been constrained by the control over its staffing by the Civil Service Department and that he did not think it 'very terrible' that the Treasury had the final word in determining the form of the accounts.

The committee was not impressed by the revelation of the way the CAG saw his work and in its report expressed the opinion that 'by comparison with other countries our system of public audit is out of date'.[19] It recommended that the Exchequer and Audit Act should be amended to state as a principle that the Exchequer and Audit Department might audit any accounts into which public money went, even if public money was not the bulk of receipts into such accounts. It also recommended that the CAG should take over the staff of local authority auditors from the Department of the Environment; that the EAD should be empowered to conduct audits of the management efficiency and effectiveness of all the bodies that it audited financially and should recruit staff capable of carrying out these extended audits; that in future the CAG should be appointed after consultation with the PAC and that candidates from outside the civil service should be considered. Most important, the committee considered that the CAG and the staff of the EAD should become part of the parliamentary staff. These recommendations established the agenda for the reform of our state audit for the next six years that the campaign had to run.

The government's observations on these recommendations disagreed with the proposal that the coverage of the CAG's audit should be extended: it said that the cost of reinforcing the EAD was not justifiable and bringing local authorities into its field of activity had very important constitutional implications for the 'autonomy' of these authorities. The government was also not willing to allow the audit to extend into policy considerations, though it welcomed the intention of the CAG to develop further his operations into the fields of efficiency and value for money. It said that the recruitment policy and staffing of the EAD would be kept under review. In future, the chairman of the PAC would be consulted 'about the appointment of a CAG before the Prime Minister advised the Queen on it'. Most important, to the recommendation that the CAG and the staff of the EAD should become parliamentary staff, the government replied that it considered it of cardinal importance that the CAG should not be subject to directions 'from any quarter' in the exercise of duties 'laid on him by statute'.

The Expenditure Committee produced a report in reply to the government's observations. In doing so, it examined Sir Douglas Henley again and for his appearance the Treasury produced a note on his status and functions. It included a statement of great constitutional importance: 'The CAG's relationship with Parliament derives from the fact that most of his reports are presented to Parliament and he has by long practice established a close relationship with the Public Accounts Committee at which his formal status is that of a witness.'[20] There could be no clearer example of the bureaucracy taking power from Parliament. The great parliamentary officer of the nineteenth century had been reduced in status to a committee witness.

In oral evidence, Sir Douglas Henley said, 'I think it would not be right, as I have said, for Parliament or anyone else to, as it were, have the power to distract me from the way in which I and my department ought to carry out that responsibility' (for statutory audit).[21] He later quoted 'a note about my department' which said, 'The department is independent of all other public departments, including the Treasury, but at the same time it is an important instrument of the Treasury, since it is responsible for ascertaining that their directions relating to expenditure are duly obeyed; thus, the harmonious action and mutual support of the departments are essential to efficient financial administration.' 'I think,' said Sir Douglas, 'that sums it up.'[22]

In its report on the government observations, the Expenditure Committee said that it found the situation of the CAG disturbing as it was contrary to a 'proper constitutional principle that the auditor of the executive should be independent of it'.[23] It is interesting that, soon after, in April 1979, in an unprecedented move, a Treasury Under Secretary was transferred to the EAD as deputy to the CAG, linking the two departments even more closely.

In 1978 the National Executive of the Labour Party produced a statement on the reform of the House of Commons which proposed reforms in the system of state audit on the lines suggested by the Expenditure Committee and these were included in the party's 1979 election manifesto. In 1979 the PAC itself considered its work and the status and functions of the CAG, in the light of recommendations by the Expenditure and Procedure Committees. Its timid and confused report[24] dwelt mainly on the staffing problems the EAD would face if the scope and coverage of the audit were to be extended. It saw a risk that the 'independence of the audit could be jeopardised if the CAG were to be appointed by the House and if his department were subject to requests for assistance from the House . . .'.[25] It concluded that no changes should be allowed to jeopardise the independent audit work by the EAD, which it believed to be essential for a proper surveillance of government spending by Parliament. It never explained why it thought that an audit which was independent of the House could exercise more surveillance on behalf of the House than one which was under direct parliamentary control.

In January 1980 the Consultative Committee of Accounting Bodies representing the accountancy profession produced a paper on the EAD which it submitted to the Treasury. The accountants took it upon themselves to assert that the CAG should be independent of both the government and Parliament. They also, not surprisingly, considered that the EAD should occasionally operate in conjunction with professional accounting firms 'who have some of the capabilities required'.

The famous Procedure Committee of 1977–78 also examined the role of our state audit system. It repeated the Expenditure Committee's recommendation to amalgamate the EAD with local authority audit and to define the EAD staff as servants of the House. In response to this report and to a parliamentary row over the lack of authority of the CAG to examine the accounts of the publicly owned National Enterprise Board, the Labour government finally admitted the need for a review, by the Treasury, of the Exchequer and Audit Act and the new Conservative administration of 1979 accepted this proposal.

The Treasury produced a green paper on 'the Role of the Comptroller and Auditor General' in March 1980. It commented that 'his main duties under the Exchequer and Audit Acts are undertaken 'on behalf of the House of Commons'. This was quickly qualified: 'He is not, however, a servant of the House, although he has frequently been referred to in those terms.'[26] After that helpful start, the Treasury went on to say that nationalised industries should continue to be excluded from the scope of audit on the grounds of a possible threat to their commercial freedom of action and that the CAG should not examine the effectiveness of departments' management because such studies might put at risk the non-partisan nature of the PAC and compromise the independence of the CAG.

Thanks to this obstructiveness, a great tactical error by the Treasury, the reform campaign gained speed. In 1981 the PAC and in 1982 the Treasury Select Committee virtually repeated the recommendations of the Expenditure Committee five years earlier. In early 1982, 300 MPs signed an Early Day Motion calling for the implementation of the proposals for reform and in April 1982 an all-party alliance obliged the government to amend the Local Government Finance (No. 2) Bill to enable the CAG to produce general reports on the efficiency and effectiveness of local government.

Then came the strokes of luck which ultimately led to victory. Late in 1982, Norman St John Stevas came second in the private members' bill ballot. He had already established a reputation as a reformer by implementing the 1977–78 Procedure Committee's proposals for the creation of the departmental system of Select Committees. He introduced his Parliamentary Control of Expenditure (Reform) Bill – later renamed the National Audit Bill – in January 1983. It sought to re-establish the CAG as an officer of the House of Commons; to establish a National Audit Office and to ensure that Parliament had the right to follow public money 'wherever it went'. This last principle was significantly diluted by the exclusion of local government, other than what had been achieved in the Local Government Finance Act of 1982, and by a limitation of the powers of audit to bodies of which more than 50 per cent of the voting shares were publicly owned.

It was feared that the member who had come first in the ballot would re-introduce a bill to change the Abortion Act, which would lead to such a plethora of delaying tactics that the Stevas bill would have a very hard time making progress. However, this first bill dealt with diseases in fish and was soon out of the way; the Stevas bill reached its second reading.

The Chief Secretary to the Treasury, in replying to the second reading debate on the Stevas bill, while recognising that the EAD needed to be brought up to date and that the role and status of the CAG needed to be clarified, expressed the government's strong reservations about many of the provisions of the bill.[27] One of them concerned the proposed appointment of the CAG by the House of Commons. The Chief Secretary thought that since the CAG had access to highly sensitive papers, the government would have a substantial interest in the appointment. In addition, the Queen would be bound to look to the Prime Minister for advice on so important an appointment. Another concerned the scope of audit. The sponsors of the bill had, the Chief Secretary observed, 'correctly abandoned' the 'high constitutional principle' that the CAG should be able to follow public money wherever it went. However, the bill did bring the nationalised industries within the scope of audit and this he considered was a retrograde step. The examination of national-ised industries by a national audit body would affect their style of man-agement, would lead to a slower speed of decision-making, a reduced willingness to take risks and less commercial efficiency. The proposal would make it more difficult to attract top-class commercial manage-ment into the industries and could provide an obstacle to privatisation. Ministers would inevitably be drawn more and more into the day-to-day decisions of the industries. Bureaucracy in both Whitehall and the indus-tries would be increased. In the light of these matters, he felt he could not positively commend the bill to the House. In replying to the debate from the opposition front bench, Robert Sheldon said that it was clear that the Chief Secretary was utterly opposed to the very fundamentals of the bill. Nevertheless, the bill was passed at second reading by 111 votes to nil, because the government could not bring itself to appear so reactionary as to kill it at that stage.

The ministers concerned then let it be known that they were very alarmed at the prospect of the measure reaching the statute book. At a meeting between senior ministers and some of the sponsors of the bill (of which the author was one), ministers warned that the Commons' proposed involvement in the appointment of the CAG could well affront the Queen. They cautioned that the public would be offended by the addition of the EAD's several hundred members of staff to the House of Commons payroll. They repeated the warning about possible damage to the nationalised industries if they were audited by a parliamentary body.

The chairmen of the nationalised industries engaged in a ferocious campaign against the measure. In the second reading debate the author said, 'I have met some of the chairmen, with the promoter of the bill, and I was amazed at how little they understood about parliamentary control and the rights of Parliament. At the moment some of the chair-men of nationalised industries are telling Conservative members that privatisation will be hindered if they are examined by the Comptroller, and they are telling opposition members that it will inhibit public enter-prise ... It is rich for the [American] chairman of the British Steel Corporation to moan about the examination of his enterprise by the Comptroller and Auditor General under these new arrangements, let alone that his own position and remuneration need public examination, because he comes from a country whose Comptroller can follow every red cent of public money all the way down into a private steel company, and frequently does. The bill goes nothing like as far as the American equivalent. The American Comptroller turns over private companies that are in receipt of money from the state, yet the chairman of British Steel has the nerve to lecture us about being interfered with by a Parliamentary Comptroller and Auditor General.'[28]

The chairmen also managed to gain the support of some nationalised industries' trade union officers and a few Members of Parliament, who threatened to ensure the defeat of the bill if the nationalised industries remained within its scope. The media offensive on this element of the bill intensified. The twenty-one members of the Nationalised Industries Chairmen's Group were united in their opposition. The chairman of British Telecom threatened to resign if the bill became law.[29] 'Who'd want to run a nationalised industry in that situation?' asked Lord King of British Airways.[30] Opponents wrote letters to *The Times:* 'The centralised powers of vetting and intrusion which this bill provides are a move, however unwitting, towards the collective systems of Eastern European states which have proven a blight on initiative and enterprise,' wrote Lord Beswick.[31] The Council of the CBI unanimously denounced the proposal (though, remarkably, the Institute of Directors supported it).[32]

During the discussion of the bill in committee, a compromise clause was inserted to allow private auditors to carry out value-for-money enquiries into nationalised industries with the agreement of sponsoring ministers and of the industry concerned. These enquiries were simply to establish that arrangements existed to secure efficiency and effectiveness and were to be reported in the first instance to the minister who could, with the agreement of the chairman of the PAC, exclude from the report any matters which in his opinion could prejudicially affect the interests of the organisation in question. This proposed clause so weakened the principle of state audit that the Standing Committee defeated it by ten votes to seven on a cross-party alliance, and nationalised industries were therefore entirely excluded from the purview of the audit.

The other main issue of contention in the committee stage of the bill was that while the CAG was enabled to carry out examinations of economy, efficiency and effectiveness in a department or qualifying body, he was not entitled to question the merits of any of its policy objectives. It was pointed out in debate in the committee that any examination of the effectiveness of a policy or spending programme – i.e. the extent to which it met its objectives or achieved the desired results – would inevitably call for an examination of what those objectives were. An examination of the objectives of a policy would ultimately involve consideration of its merits: whether or not it could be implemented, for example. The issue was never clarified in committee. The last word on it was said by the Chief Secretary who summed up his view of the position as: 'If the CAG is saying, "I do not understand what the policy objectives are," that is a different matter from saying, "I think they are wrong." The latter he cannot do, but I do not see how one can stop him doing the former.'[33]

The bill squeaked into law on the last day of the Parliament in June 1983 and become effective in January 1984. Its achievements were to establish the CAG and the staff of the National Audit Office (the former EAD) as officers of the House of Commons and to equip them with an order of reference which included statutory powers to examine the efficiency and effectiveness of central government departments and some fifty other bodies. Those who had campaigned for the reform of audit had not secured all their objectives but had made the crucial breakthrough. It is worth remarking that though the CAG may not consider policy matters, there is nothing to stop the PAC from doing so, though it feels obliged to follow the same rule because of the risk of party controversy entering its deliberations.

The act also created a Public Accounts Commission consisting of the chairman of the PAC, the Leader of the House and seven other members, one of whom is elected chairman. The commission considers the estimate of spending for the NAO submitted by the CAG and presents it to the House. This has the effect of establishing the NAO as different from other departments of the House and reinforces the idea of its 'independence'. Matters would be clarified if the Public Accounts Commission were abolished and the estimates for the NAO were presented directly to the House of Commons Commission.

The next row over the constitutional status of our state audit arrangements came in December 1987 when the opportunity arose to appoint a new Comptroller and Auditor General. The author put down a motion signed by fifty-eight Labour MPs: 'That this House considers that, as the Comptroller and Auditor General is an Officer of the House under the National Audit Act (1983), appointments to the post should be made on a motion put down by the chairman of the Public Accounts Committee and that the appointment should not involve any consultation with the Prime Minister; and further considers that the requirement for the agreement of the Prime Minister to the appointment of an officer whose responsibility is to examine the financial management of the Government is constitutionally unacceptable.'[34]

On 16 December the Prime Minister, Margaret Thatcher, moved a humble address to Her Majesty praying that Mr John Bourn, a senior civil servant, be appointed to the office of CAG, saying that she had every confidence that he would be 'a worthy servant of the House'. The author and a couple of other members complained in the debate about the method of appointment. In winding up the debate, the Chief Secretary to the Treasury referred to the independence of the CAG 'not only from the executive, but from parliamentary direction'; then he said the Comptroller was subject to a degree of financial control from the House of Commons, 'but not operational control'; then he said, 'The government have the same interest in value for money as the House.' It was clear that the government still hankered after interfering with our state audit and as a result nine Labour MPs voted against the motion.[35]

Since then the new arrangements have been generally accepted, except for occasional complaints about the exclusion of the nationalised industries from the scope of audit, which have diminished as the industries have been privatised, and a continuing boundary dispute with the Defence Committee. However, as the debate on the Comptroller's appointment showed, the Treasury never considers itself defeated and there are some indications that it is still trying to recover its position. Michael Mates, in evidence to the 1990 Procedure Committee on Select Committees, pointed out that in an order under the Official Secrets Act 1989, the government had proposed that the CAG and the staff of the NAO would be defined as Crown (i.e. civil) servants.[36] In its response to the report of that committee, the government also refused to remove the Financial Secretary to the Treasury from the PAC, on which he has no justifiable place and which he never attends.[37] The Treasury still insists on examining the NAO's corporate plan and making observations about the costs of its staff. It also fixes the salaries of Permanent Secretaries, to which that of the CAG is tied, thus putting a ceiling on what can be paid to the staff of the NAO, which competes with private accounting practices for recruits.

In a debate in October 1991, the author referred to the conflict of interest raised by the Financial Secretary's membership of the PAC. The Financial Secretary, Francis Maude, said that his membership was of 'symbolic importance', reflecting the close relationship of the Treasury and the PAC. That is exactly what is wrong with it. It is symbolic of the Treasury's continuing wish to interfere in a parliamentary institution.

A potentially more serious issue arose in the summer of 1991 when the new Prime Minister, John Major, invited the CAG to Chequers to a meeting to discuss policy on the Citizen's Charter. This appeared to be a breach of the statutory position of the CAG in that an officer of the House of Commons was being engaged by the government on what could be construed as a political exercise, assisting in the drafting of a policy, the implementation of which he could later have to investigate. For example, the Charter was expected to lay down rules about the quality of service to the public in DSS offices on which the CAG might later report. The author wrote to the Prime Minister pointing out this potential conflict of interest. Mr Major found the matter 'quite ridiculous'. 'The Citizen's Charter is not a political exercise,' he replied and went on to say, irrelevantly, that the CAG could not do his job if members of the PAC tried to lock him up in his office 'poring over the books'.[38] Thus another constitutional impropriety was simply brushed aside.

The PAC produces forty to fifty reports a year across a huge range of issues in British public administration, having moved from its old staple – cost overruns in defence projects – to reports on privatisations, the management of the health service, support for low-income families, homelessness, the Common Agricultural Policy, coronary heart disease, the quality of service to the public in local DSS offices, charities, the new building for the British Library, the Social Fund, text processing in the civil service, invalidity benefit, the sale of Herstmonceux Castle, the Retail Price Index, national energy efficiency, inner-city policy, the measurement of farm incomes, falling school rolls, computer security, financial problems at universities and a new ship for St Helena, to take some titles from 1987 to date. Particularly since 1987, under the chairmanship of Robert Sheldon, the PAC has gone from strength to strength. It has grown in confidence and its members have developed an expertise and a network of contacts which have made them a very effective investigatory body.

The committee proceeds by considering reports by the CAG and taking evidence from the accounting officer of the department concerned and other witnesses, and then reporting their findings. An outsider would not notice that the PAC has to avoid the consideration of policy matters and from time to time senior civil servants have let it be known that they consider that the PAC has stretched its terms of reference too far in this direction. A strength of the PAC is that its enquiries are audit-based, i.e. it looks first at what happened to the money (on which it cannot be challenged) and is then inevitably led to how management discharged its responsibilities: readers of its reports can usually discern where policy decisions by departments have contributed to failures.

Many of the findings of reports by the PAC and the NAO have been dramatic and have attracted much media attention. At the time of writing, it has revealed that arrangements for people leaving the state earnings-related pension scheme to take out personal pensions have cost £9.3 billion, against £3.4 billion in savings – a government subsidy equal to 1.5p on the basic rate of income tax.[39] Other reports which have caused a stir include one on the undervaluation of the land assets of the Royal Ordnance factories when they were sold to British Aerospace,[40] and another pointing out that when British Aerospace bought Rover PLC they paid a mere £150 million for a business making a gross profit of £65 million, having surplus assets and other benefits of £250 million and having just had an injection of £547 million from the government.[41] A report on incorrect payments of social security benefits estimated annual overpayments of £9–£19 million and underpayments of £18–£30 million.[42] The PAC has reported three times on the unsatisfactory management of the Housing Benefit Scheme (annual cost £5 billion) and, by implication, the policy behind it.[43] It has produced some alarming reports on the monitoring and control of charities (annual turnover £17 billion) by the Charity Commission, which have led to an internal enquiry by the government and to legislation.[44]

Some of the most interesting reports have been on the National Health Service. From them we have learned that, at a time when 162,000 people had been waiting for more than a year for operations, only 50–60 per cent of operating theatre sessions were actually used;[45] that there has been inadequate measurement of the quality of clinical care;[46] that health departments have reacted slowly to the very high incidence of coronary heart disease in Britain;[47] that the NHS has failed to maximise its purchasing power of £4 billion a year (excluding drugs) to squeeze its suppliers' prices;[48] how the government has paid insufficient attention to outpatient services;[49] and why it takes seven to ten years to build a hospital.[50]

Time and again, the PAC has shown that the government has carried out inadequate research into the problems with which it has to deal: for example, in respect of inner-city regeneration on which it spends £3 billion a year;[51] of housing needs;[52] and of lone-parent families.[53] The

PAC has also been exceptionally critical of the quality of service to the public in DSS local offices, the NAO having established the time those offices took to deal with applications for supplementary benefit and the length of time personal callers had to wait for attention.[54]

Despite its remarkable record, the PAC has come in for some criticisms since it acquired its new lease of life in 1984. It has been said, for example, that its forty or fifty reports a year are too many and that some of them are superficial. It is true that NAO reports are not of a uniformly high quality and that the PAC itself usually devotes only one evidence session to a report, whether it concerns the mismanagement of billions of pounds or some fairly small mistakes by a department. On the other hand, this breadth of coverage has the useful effect of bringing most departments under its scrutiny at least once every couple of years or so and therefore keeps them all on their toes.

It has also been suggested that the gap of several months between the publication of an NAO report and the PAC's hearings on the same subject lessens the impact of an issue. However, this does at least allow the department time to put matters right before its officials are examined in public, and the public hearings are the better for the civil servants having had time to prepare for them.

There has been some criticism of the way in which NAO reports are agreed by departments before they are published and are therefore alleged to be less critical than they should be. In fact, members of the PAC generally have a very good idea of which matters were contentious between the NAO's auditors and the department concerned and usually manage to highlight them. There has been complaint that NAO and PAC reports are not prescriptive, in that they tend to point to a failure or weakness in a department's management without proposing a remedy. They often recommend that action be taken, or systems or staffing improved, without specifying *how* such action should be taken or setting deadlines for improvements. However, NAO staff are auditors, not management consultants, and it is not up to them to redesign management systems.

One mystery is why the departmental Select Committees do not take on a subject which has been reported on by the NAO and the PAC and then look at the relevant management and policy-making arrangements in the department in question. No such Select Committee has ever done so or invited the CAG to give evidence on one of his reports with a view to developing his enquiry into a wider study. One of them should try it.

In 1986, the author proposed some areas of advance for our state audit system.[55] One was to examine departments on the quality of their programme analysis, i.e. how they justified spending programmes and how they measured their results. Since then, the NAO has done some work on performance measurement,[56] but it does not seem to devote much attention to the government's planning of expenditure.

Another suggestion was that since the greater part of the direct costs of government were staff costs, 'there should be an attempt to audit the effective use of departments' human resources'.[57] There has always been evidence that the civil service underuses the ability of many of its employees, particularly women and members of junior grades, and this would be a legitimate field of enquiry by the PAC (though the NAO would probably need some additional specialist staff to undertake the work). Since then, the PAC has frequently referred to staff shortages in its reports; has made a report on clerical recruitment in the civil service[58] and on manpower planning in the service[59] and in the Ministry of Defence,[60] but these do not meet the point. The auditors should, for example, examine the qualifications and appraisal ratings of junior staff in a department and evaluate the jobs they do to try to weigh up the extent to which that department fails to use the talents of its staff. The PAC is always reporting on the waste of money by departments, but does not take the waste of talent sufficiently seriously.

On the whole, the National Audit Act has worked as well as the reformers had hoped, though it should be amended to bring every organisation in receipt of public money within the scope of audit. The Treasury is always waiting to envelop it again but, so long as the PAC is vigilant, its independence of the executive will continue and its impact will increase.

7

Cases and Causes

A very valuable feature of our parliamentary system is that MPs have access to ministers, government departments and other public bodies to whom they can make representations on behalf of their constituents. They can also usually get a hearing from private and corporate bodies. They have access to a variety of parliamentary procedures which they can use as platforms for drawing attention to cases, publicising causes or promoting campaigns. These facilities can be used for the highest motives of public interest or for low political advantage, but they are an invaluable means of serving constituents and of calling government to account.

Casework

The heaviest regular workload of an MP's office is the volume of mail concerning the problems and complaints of individual constituents. An MP can play an important role in redressing the grievances and securing the rights of constituents to benefits and access to public and other services. Most MPs hold constituency 'surgeries' at which aggrieved citizens seek their help.

It is impossible to generalise about MPs' constituency casework. In the author's urban constituency, the volume is reduced by a high level of casework activity by local councillors, who hold advice surgeries, and by the existence of easily accessible voluntary advice agencies. Even in this situation the volume of cases virtually doubled between 1983 and 1987, reaching about one thousand a year, mainly because of the reduction in the stock of council houses, changes in eligibility for social security benefits and the growth of unemployment. Half the cases are to do with housing problems and a quarter with social security, fairly common proportions. In an inner-city constituency, the volume of casework could well be double that level, again mostly concerning housing, but would include a number of immigration and citizenship cases which are usually particularly distressing and time-consuming. Some MPs greatly reduce the burden by refusing to deal with people with housing and other local authority problems and direct them to local councillors. The volume of business can be greatly increased by actively canvassing for problems, or by publicising the MP's surgery or the successful results of his or her interventions. Most casework is undemanding – except in time – and much of it can be handled by a competent secretary.

Securing the right to benefit or an improved chance of rehousing for a constituent is rewarding and the beneficiary is often touchingly grateful but it is not a very frequent experience. More often than not, the MP is the last resort for a constituent who has already exhausted other approaches to officialdom. Many constituents do not understand the differences between the roles and responsibilities of a councillor and a member of Parliament and many believe, or purport to believe, that the member has some power to command public bodies. An MP's constituency caseworker role is very worthwhile, given the difficulties many citizens have in securing redress or getting attention from public and corporate bodies, but it tends to be patchy in coverage and sometimes inefficient.

In addition to correspondence which involves taking some action on behalf of constituents, an MP will receive very many letters from constituents and others, seeking his or her views on a matter, offering the correspondent's opinion, requesting him or her to vote in a particular way or to sign a Commons motion.

Organised mail campaigns appear to be increasing in frequency and fluctuate according to the media coverage of issues of the day. Abortion law is the most dreaded subject, capable of generating many hundreds of irate letters in normally equable constituencies. Other matters which generate particularly heavy letter-writing campaigns concern the treatment of animals (some recent examples are pig-rearing conditions, the death of seals, the export of live horses, dog registration, the protection of wild animals, whale hunting), and green issues (nuclear power, the dumping of toxic waste, water quality).

The only comprehensive surveys of the total volume of mail (excluding circulars, promotional material and similar corporate correspondence) received by MPs were carried out in the late 1960s and in 1986. The earlier survey showed that most MPs received some 2,500 letters a year; the later that an average MP received 10,000 letters a year (which must have included a lot of corporate publicity and circulars). Tony Benn, who keeps an accurate tally of his activities, recorded 66,000 letters (and 8,300 constituency cases) in the five years from March 1984 to March 1989.

An active and alert MP can effectively draw the attention of the authorities to a case by a number of means. Most involve writing to district or county authorities, but a survey of ministerial correspondence in 1990 showed that about 70 per cent of MPs wrote up to twenty letters a week, and 3 per cent wrote over fifty letters a week, to ministers. Letters to ministers are normally answered in four to six weeks (except in the case of the Home Office, which usually takes much longer). Ministers will usually accede to the request for an interview on a case of any significance. Written or oral questions can be tabled in Parliament. Motions can be put on the order paper, published daily. Most valuable of all, a member can apply for a brief debate on a subject of his or her choosing, usually at the end of the day's business.

Parliamentary Questions

The first parliamentary question appears to have been asked in the Lords in 1721, about the disappearance of the chief cashier of the South Sea Company. In 1783 the Speaker ruled that any member had the right to put a question to a minister, who could answer or not answer, as he thought proper. This is still the rule. Tabling and replying to written and oral questions is now an important feature of the party battle in Parliament and much effort is devoted by ministers' staffs to avoiding or delaying answering inconvenient questions and by all parties to exploiting questions for political advantage. The partisan flippancy of ministerial answers to oral questions was noticeable in the run-up to the 1992 general election:

MR HATTERSLEY: Why has crime in this country risen by an average of 6 per cent per year since the war, but by 18 per cent – three times the usual average – in the past two years?

MR PATTEN: Being assaulted by the right hon. Member for Birmingham, Sparkbrook (Mr Hattersley) on such issues is rather like being attacked by a bread and butter pudding. It looks very substantial on the surface, but when one looks below the surface, one finds nothing of any substance. The right hon. Gentleman's question contains its own answer. If the right hon. Gentleman would only himself address the causes of crime, he would realise that they would certainly not be solved by the suggestion made at the Labour party press conference this morning – that we should empty our prisons to pay for more police. That is what was said by the Labour party which in 1979 left the police forces of this country 8,000 under strength.[1]

A member gives notice of ('tables') a question by handing it in to clerks in the Table Office. Oral questions usually have to be tabled a fortnight before the relevant Question Time to stand a chance of being called. Question Time lasts about an hour, from 2.35 p.m. on Mondays to Thursdays, with each government department being involved on a monthly rota. Questions to the Prime Minister are taken every Tuesday and Thursday from 3.15 to 3.30 p.m. Written questions, particularly, are a useful means of obtaining information which is often not otherwise available. They are answered by post and are reported in Hansard. A written question is usually answered in a week or so, though a speedier reply is possible if it is identified by the questioner as being in the priority category (about half are).

In 1847, the first year for which figures are available, 129 questions were tabled. In 1900 the figure rose to over 5,000 (forty a day), in 1950 to about 10,000 and in 1989–1990 to 66,000 (395 a day). In 1989–90 some 25,000 questions were put down for oral reply and about a quarter of them were actually asked as a result of being reached in the allotted time. The rest were replied to in writing.

Most oral questions to the Prime Minister are 'open', or not specific as to subject. Virtually all of them take the form of asking what his or her engagements are for the day. This enables the questioner to follow with a topical supplementary question on almost any issue.

Q1. MR SKINNER: To ask the Prime Minister if he will list his official engagements for Tuesday 18 February.

THE PRIME MINISTER (MR JOHN MAJOR): This morning I had meetings with ministerial colleagues and others. In addition to my duties in this House, I shall be having further meetings later today.

MR SKINNER: With only a few more bribing days left before the general election and in view of the fact that the House has been televised for more than two years, will the Prime Minister tell us whether he is prepared to take part in televised debates during the general election campaign with the Leader of the Opposition – yes or no?

THE PRIME MINISTER: As the hon. Gentleman knows, we hold televised debates in the House twice a week . . .

HON. MEMBERS: Frit!

MR SPEAKER: Order.[2]

There are many rules limiting the scope of parliamentary questions. A question should either seek information or press for action. Ministers may not be asked to confirm or deny reports, nor to interpret the law, nor about cases before the courts, nor about the activities of judges, nor about discussions between departments, nor about statements made by them outside Parliament, nor about the internal affairs of other countries (for example their records on human rights), nor may questions seek amendments to bills, nor ask for statistics for specific years in the past when a different party was in power, nor touch on any subject classed as secret. The 'Mayor of Sligo' rule prevents one member tabling a question relating to a minister's answer to a question asked by another member. A recent Procedure Committee proposed some amelioration of these rules and in January 1992, for the first time, questions about MI5, the security service, were allowed to be tabled, though the Home Office let it be known that it would not answer questions about MI5 operations or individual security cases. If a minister refuses to answer a question, he or she can be asked in the next session of Parliament if he or she will now answer questions on the subject. If a minister refuses to take action or provide information he or she can be asked the same question after three months.

The process of questioning ministers is the subject of much organisation and stage management. The widespread abuse of 'syndicating' questions, that is one member, often a Whip, tabling scores of identical oral questions on behalf of other members (so as to harass ministers on a single point), grew vigorously in the late 1980s. An attempt was made to tackle it in 1990 with the invention of a rule specifying that oral questions should be tabled only by a member in person or by another member acting on his or her behalf. The first few weeks of this rule produced a 40 per cent drop in the number of oral questions tabled, but at the time of writing syndication appears to be reviving.

Parliamentary Private Secretaries (MPs appointed as aides to ministers as an indication of future preferment, often unfulfilled) and shadow ministers often suggest or tout questions to their colleagues which can be used to score a political point. The practice of sycophantic government members asking 'planted' questions reached new heights of absurdity when the government was under pressure in 1991 and 1992 and very many of the questions asked by government back-bench members were simply devices to enable ministers to boast or advertise the more fetching parts of their policies. Planted, or agreed, questions by government backbenchers appear to be very common at Prime Minister's Question Time, judging from the way Prime Ministers read their answers. The Procedure Committee report of 1991 pointed in a disapproving way to the growing practice of asking a minister to list his department's achievements since a specified date. Such questions, it observed, generated 'inordinately long' answers, sometimes occupying several pages of Hansard and provoked opposition members to ask ministers to list their failures.[3]

In October 1990 Mr Michael Meacher found sixteen pages of briefing for Conservative MPs apparently produced by the Department of Social Security for use in that department's Question Time, including a series of 'bull points' for backbenchers to make in favour of the government. When it was drawn to his attention, the Speaker said he hoped this practice would cease.[4] In July 1991, the *Times* sketch-writer commented that nearly all back-bench Conservative MPs appeared to have been given the same question to ask the Prime Minister, which invited him '. . . to condemn Labour's links with the unions, or their minimum wage policy'. To such 'questions' Mr Major 'offered a word-perfect sound bite or had a handy quote'.[5] Many witnesses to this operation thought that such questions were out of order in that they did not relate to the Prime Minister's responsibilities.

In evidence to the 1991 Procedure Committee, the Principal Clerk of the Table Office referred to the increase in 'campaigns' using written questions: the tabling of large batches of questions with slight variations on the same point. Some of these appeared not to be concerned with gaining information, but 'to badger the minister or department concerned or to advocate some specific area of concern'.[6] Privately, the Principal Clerk supplied the committee with information relating to the activities of a small number of members involved in the tabling of a disproportionately high percentage of written questions. In the 1989–90 session, twenty members (3 per cent of the House) accounted for 9,999 questions (27 per cent of the total).

The committee reported: 'Examples of some of these questions appeared to indicate, *prima facie*, a degree of involvement by persons other than members which went beyond what we believe the House would regard as reasonable. Members must genuinely be an active party to the process. This implies some degree of interest both in the form of the question and the likely content of the answer, rather than simply passive acquiescence in the role of postman for outside persons or bodies, as appears to have been the case in some of the examples shown to us by the Principal Clerk. It was quite clear that one individual member was being used in this way, with his apparent connivance, in that according to the Principal Clerk, cards sent to him in connection with the high percentage of disorderly questions submitted in his name seldom, if ever, elicited any response.'

The committee concluded: 'We have no hesitation in saying that some of the examples given by the Principal Clerk constitute an abuse, pure and simple.'[7] It recommended the use of a rule which allowed the Table Office to refuse to accept questions recognisable as emanating from a particular individual who had already sought, via a number of different members, to have large numbers of disorderly, badly drafted or repetitive questions tabled.

A minister faced with an awkward or embarrassing admission will release it as an answer to a planted written question, often on a Friday, instead of in the form of a ministerial statement on the floor of the House, when he could be questioned personally. On the other hand, quite trivial news will often be made the subject of a ministerial statement in the House instead of an answer to a question if it is good for the government or if it delays (beyond prime media time) the start of a debate which looks as if it might be awkward for the government.

Ministers who wish to defuse the answer to a difficult question will reply that they will write to the member asking it. They will then delay the answer (and its publication in Hansard) until interest in the question has waned. They may reply that they will put the information requested in the Commons library, again avoiding publication. Sometimes, no indication is given as to when it will be placed in the library. Ministers may then provide only two copies, which may not be removed from the library. Sometimes statistical information is sent to the library in unprocessed form, so that expensive analysis is required to make sense of it. Ministers also use the 'holding' answer, saying that they will reply as soon as possible – and then take weeks to do so. They also sometimes reply that the information is not held in the form requested or that it would simply be too expensive to provide it.

A new device for avoiding the publication of answers to questions has been so effective that it has provoked extensive complaint. This is the practice of referring questions to the heads of executive agencies, organisations which, as we have seen in earlier chapters, are now operating in some highly sensitive policy areas, particularly social security benefits. Increasingly, a question to a minister is diverted to the head of the relevant agency who replies by letter, which is not published in Hansard. The letter should be copied to the library and its Public Information Office is supposed to supply it to enquirers, but it is clear that not all replies are finding their way to the office and it will supply copies only if they are 'reasonably short'.

In 1991 Paul Flynn, in a campaign against this practice, arranged for the publication of a number of answers from agencies. He pointed out that the library does not keep a record of the letters received. They are filed by members' names and not by date or by agency, so that anyone searching for letters from a particular agency has to search through the boxes of letters received in the current session of Parliament. The Procedure Committee has recommended that all answers from agencies are published in Hansard and in late 1991 the government yielded to pressure and announced that a separate weekly publication would include the answers to questions to agencies.

Ministers also not infrequently give inconsistent answers: at one time saying that an issue is not for them, but for an agency or other public authority (when it could be an embarrassment), and at another time freely answering questions on the same subject. Questions on, for example, recruitment or costs are answered by some ministers, but are referred to agency chiefs by others.

One kind of oral question, the Private Notice Question, is particularly useful for putting ministers on the spot. An application to raise a Private Notice Question has to be made to the Speaker before noon on the day on which an answer is wanted. The Speaker applies two criteria to the application: it has to be on an urgent matter, and relate to an issue of public importance. If the request is granted, the question is asked at the end of Question Time and therefore usefully catches the attention of the media. Recent Private Notice Questions have concerned disasters, strikes affecting public services and terrorist attacks. The most impressive one within living memory was asked in November 1967 by Robert Sheldon, later a Treasury Minister. His question concerned a loan being negotiated with foreign banks, and the Chancellor's answer to it and ensuing questions are said to have led to a run on the pound which caused a loss of $1500 million from the reserves in two days and which, according to Roy Jenkins, left the government 'debilitated and defence-less' for two years.[8]

Applications for thirty to forty Private Notice Questions are accepted each year. More should be. An application for a debate under Standing Order No. 20 is a similar device. A member asks the Speaker to allow an emergency debate on a 'specific and important matter that should have urgent consideration'. The Speaker has to decide whether the matter is sufficiently pressing to warrant giving it precedence over the regular business of the House. Applications are very seldom successful: about eighty are made every year and one or two are granted. Most are clearly not admissible, but a successful application under this standing order would be so awkward for the government (in prime media time, after questions) that there is a good case for the Speaker to view applications for them more leniently than in the past.

Motions and Petitions

It is frequently reported in the press that an MP has put down a Commons motion on a subject. Constituents then often request their MP's support, or vote for, this motion in the House of Commons. Invariably the proposition in question is an Early Day Motion: one for which no date has been fixed for debate and for which there is no prospect of debate or any further action. A century ago, members' motions were frequently debated, but as government business increased, members were obliged to put down motions for some future date ('an early day'). The procedure allows members to record their views on a subject and to seek support, by the adding of names, from other members.

The use of Early Day Motions is growing. In the 1950s they ran at about a hundred a year, in the 1960s four hundred a year and in 1989-90 over 1,400 were put down. Some fairly grand claims have been made for them: 'The last test of parliamentary opinion, unalloyed by party discipline, which is left to members'; 'Spontaneous unwhipped back-bench manifestos',[9] though, as usual, the truth is less impressive. The Whips like to be informed of proposed Early Day Motions and use their influence to try to stifle any which are critical of their party's policy or leadership. Most motions concern criticism of (or appreciation of) government policy; or a constituency matter, such as a hospital closure; or congratulations to an individual, a sports team or an institution for meritorious performance. The most effective ones are all-party motions with many signatures, calling for action on a subject by the government or for the redress of a popular grievance.

In an average session about six or seven motions attract over two hundred signatures. The record is 482 signatures in 1964 to a motion on service pensions. In recent years high scoring motions (over three hundred signatures) have included the protection of whales and baby seals, the treatment of widows of servicemen, the rights of grandparents, and resettlement grants for MPs. Opposition parties also frequently put down motions opposing statutory instruments (see Chapter 3), thus giving notice that they may seek a debate on an instrument.

The right to petition the monarch for the redress of grievance has been exercised since Saxon times and petitions to the Houses of Parliament date from the reign of Richard II. In 1571 a Committee for Motions of Griefs and Petitions was appointed. In 1661 an Act against Tumultuous Petitioning was passed because of the disorder commonly accompanying the presentation of petitions. In the nineteenth century petitions were very frequently used by members to secure a debate before the normal business of the House and their numbers grew from around a thousand a year at the beginning of the century to a record 33,898 in 1843. Even after a change in standing orders in that year which prevented debate on the merits of a petition, they were still very popular and thousands were presented every year at the end of the century. They dwindled almost to nothing from the 1920s to the 1980s, but have revived since then and now run at about eight hundred a year.

A petition must be presented in a specified form of words and must end with a 'prayer' which indicates what redress is sought. Its tone must be 'respectful, decorous and temperate'. A member may formally present a petition before the adjournment debate on Mondays to Thursdays or at the start of business on a Friday or may simply put the petition in a green bag hanging behind the Speaker's chair. A minister usually replies to the petition in writing. A standing order does allow an urgent petition to be debated, but it has not been used for thirty years. Typical petitions today would be against local hospital closures or for the protection of animals.

The Ombudsman

The office of Parliamentary Commissioner for Administration (or 'Ombudsman') was established in 1967 with the responsibility to investigate claims of 'injustice in consequence of maladministration' against government departments and some specified non-departmental bodies. The principle was derived from the Swedish Parliamentary Ombudsman (first appointed 1766) who has a much more extensive jurisdiction, covering alleged infringement of the Swedish Bill of Rights, and the more recently established Danish Ombudsman who has similar jurisdiction to ours, though the office holder can investigate complaints against the police and ministerial decisions. The British Ombudsman (an officer of the House of Commons) produces an annual report and his work is supervised by the Select Committee on the Parliamentary Commissioner for Administration, which on occasion has reprimanded government departments for failure to act on the Ombudsman's findings.

A case has to be referred to the Ombudsman by a Member of Parliament acting on behalf of a constituent. It is then examined by the Ombudsman's staff and is either rejected as being outside his scope or accepted for investigation. In 1990, some seven hundred complaints were referred by 370 MPs. Of the 724 dealt with during the year, 535 were rejected, 177 full investigations were completed and twelve were discontinued. In seventy-four completed investigations the Ombudsman found the complaint justified, in eighty-three he criticised at least some aspects of the way the case had been handled and in eighteen cases he found no justification for the complaint. He made no finding in two cases. The number of references increased by 13 per cent in 1991 alone. The average time for dealing with a case is about fifteen months. Most complaints were directed against the Department of Social Security (28 per cent) and the Inland Revenue (14 per cent). Successful complaints often result in reimbursements or compensation being paid by the department concerned.

Though the Ombudsman has no power to impose his findings, departments almost invariably accept and act upon his recommendations. This may be because the Select Committee could follow up a case if a department was reluctant to produce a remedy. The government does occasionally get into disputes with the Ombudsman, but usually backs down after a wrangle. For some years, the Lord Chancellor's department disputed the jurisdiction of the Ombudsman over the administrative actions of the staff of law courts, on the grounds that courts were independent of the department. The Select Committee eventually obtained a compromise on the matter. The actions of the staff of tribunals appointed by other ministers are not subject to investigations by the Ombudsman: an anomaly that should be corrected. The DSS has resisted the right of the Ombudsman to investigate the administration of the Social Fund, which gives loans to the needy, maintaining that the officers who administered it are independent, a matter still unresolved. The government also disputed the findings of the Ombudsman in the Barlow Clowes case that the Department of Trade and Industry had been guilty of significant maladministration, but in the end paid compensation without admitting fault. The Select Committee has maintained that the Ombudsman should have the right to investigate civil service employment procedures, but so far the government has refused it.

Both the Swedish and Danish Ombudsmen can initiate investigations without receiving a complaint, but our Commissioner cannot do so. The Select Committee recently considered the idea that our Commissioner should have a formal power to initiate investigations.[10] It concluded that the sparing use of such power would be compatible with the principles on which the institution rests and that it should examine the matter further. There must be a very good case for extending the powers of the Ombudsman in this way. Many MPs are apparently not aware of his powers: the Select Committee was concerned about the relatively small number of them who had ever used the Ombudsman's services. To raise consciousness among MPs about the role and work of the Ombudsman, the Select Committee recommended that there should be a debate in the Commons on the subject. The Leader of the House, Sir Geoffrey Howe, let it be known that this modest proposal was unacceptable to the government – and produced no fewer than five reasons for its view (no time, no demand, no need, system working quite well, MPs still unlikely to pay attention).[11]

There must be hundreds of cases of maladministration which are not picked up by the present arrangements, and the occasional inspection of the DSS, for example, initiated by the Ombudsman, could well bring some of them to light, with a salutary effect on the bureaucracy. A reserve power of inspection would be a useful development of public accountability. The role of the Ombudsman would also be substantially enlarged by the enactment of a Bill, or Charter, of Rights, since a powerful and independent inspectorate of administrative decisions is likely to be a necessary consequence of such legislation.

Investigations by the Local Government Ombudsmen (three for

England, one each for Scotland, Wales and Northern Ireland) can now be initiated by any citizen and are conducted on much the same lines as those investigated by the Parliamentary Commissioner. In 1991 they upheld two-thirds of the complaints brought to them, most of them about housing and planning. Some councils are notorious for ignoring the recommendations of the Local Government Ombudsman. The Select Committee has proposed that it should oversee the work of these officials, but the government has not accepted the proposal.

The Health Service Ombudsman can follow up a complaint by a private citizen and is empowered 'to investigate any failure to provide a service or any other action in consequence of maladministration leading to injustice or hardship'. However, his authority has some important exclusions: general practitioners, pharmacists, dentists and opticians (because they are independent contractors), and he cannot investigate actions which, in his opinion, were taken in the exercise of clinical judgement. The most common reason for the rejection of a case by the Health Ombudsman is that it involves clinical judgement, so that his criticisms tend to fall on nursing and administration. The Health Service Ombudsman is supervised by the Select Committee on the Parliamentary Commissioner, which has obliged the NHS to issue guidance to health authorities for the improvement of patient care, e.g. on the discharge of patients from hospital. There are also private sector Ombudsmen, covering banking, building societies, insurance, pensions, legal services and estate agents.

Adjournment Debates

Opportunities exist for members to initiate debates, most of them in the form of motions to adjourn the House. Such debates, usually lasting half an hour, take place at the end of business on Mondays to Thursdays. On Mondays to Wednesdays the opportunity to raise a matter on the adjournment is the subject of a ballot (there are about eighteen to twenty applications each week) and on Thursday the Speaker personally makes a selection from the applicants. A succession of similar debates are held on the last day before a recess. Adjournment debates are an exceptionally useful procedure for members to raise a constituency case or any other subject, usually of local concern, because a minister is obliged to attend. If the hours of the House are changed to allow an earlier finish to its main business, there is a very good case for substantially increasing their number. If, for example, the main business of the House were to end at 7 p.m., there is no reason why adjournment debates should not last for a couple of hours every day.

Private members also have the opportunity to draw attention to a subject in the all-night debates following the passage of a Consolidated Fund Bill which takes place three times a year. These bills authorise government spending and are theoretically debated 'in accordance with the historic principle of seeking the redress of grievances before granting Supply'.[12] Though the House now grants Supply before hearing grievances, these debates provide an opportunity to raise constituency or other topics. Two subjects are debated for up to three hours and the remainder (until 9 a.m.) for an hour and a half each.

A discussion of the MP's role as welfare caseworker inevitably spills over into the member as campaigner and promoter of causes. The Commons provides a valuable public platform for the promotion of causes and campaigns. Skilful parliamentary operators such as Alf Morris and Jack Ashley, championing the causes of the disabled, can make a significant impact on national policies.

Constituency casework, which has increased with the welfare state and the growth of legislation and has recently still further increased with cuts in public services, is now an important part of an MP's job. It is a very good indicator of the effect of government policies and decisions on individuals and organisations. To an extent, it demonstrates the weakness of the complaints procedure in local authorities and government departments. Many constituents have had their legitimate concerns ignored by the bureaucracy until an MP has intervened.

A new member receives no training in handling welfare casework and it takes some time to master the intricacies of the rights of benefit claimants, of local authority housing allocation arrangements and of the responsibilities of government departments. The provision of a manual of local and central government responsibilities and procedures would improve the induction process. A member's service to constituents could also be improved if today's casework load was recognised by the House authorities and the parliamentary research and secretarial allowance extended to the employment of an administrative assistant or fieldworker in the constituency who could follow up constituents' cases and evaluate how they had been dealt with by the authorities. If an MP is now expected to provide a citizens' advice service, then he or she should be properly equipped to carry it out.

8

The House of Lords

The House of Lords is claimed to be the oldest legislative assembly in the world. It is a uniquely undemocratic anachronism and its abolition or wholesale reform has been under active consideration for the past century. It has survived more or less untouched for the last eighty years because of a lack of agreement between its opponents on how to reform or replace it and an underlying fear that a replacement would challenge the power of the Commons. There are a number of very comprehensive recent accounts of the history and functions of the House of Lords:[1] this chapter briefly summarises its present role, analyses whether this role is a useful one, discusses the variety of proposals for reform on offer and considers what might practically be done about it in the near to medium future.

There are about 1,200 persons who are entitled to be members of the House of Lords. Two archbishops and twenty-four bishops – London, Durham and Winchester and another twenty-one in order of seniority – form the Lords Spiritual (formerly unkindly called the sacerdotage), who sit as long as they hold office (they now have to retire at seventy). There are about eight hundred hereditary peers (of whom twenty are women), the creation of which ceased in 1965 and was revived in 1983, and some 380 life peers (of whom sixty are women). There are thirty-three Law Lords: eleven of them Lords of Appeal in Ordinary created (for life) to form the final Court of Appeal for the United Kingdom (except for Scottish criminal cases), and twenty-two who are judges who are also peers. The Court, or Appellate Committee, usually has five members.

At the time of writing, of the 1,200 potential members of the Lords, about 133 have been granted leave of absence (because of, for example, infirmity or distance of residence), and about ninety have not received a writ of summons to the Lords, most of them because they do not wish to sit. Currently, twelve persons who have inherited peerages have disclaimed them for life.

In the 1987–88 Session of Parliament, 328 Lords attended 50 per cent or more of the daily sittings (or were there long enough to claim an attendance allowance): these were 140 hereditary and 188 life peers; politically they split 146 Conservative, 82 Labour, 40 Liberal/SDP and 60 Independent (called cross-benchers). The cross-benchers usually vote about two to one with the Conservatives. In addition, the Conservatives can call on 'a reserve army' of mainly hereditary peers – the so-called 'backwoodsmen' who attend irregularly but come up to London in large numbers when required by the Tory Whips.[2] About twenty peers are appointed, and paid, by the government of the day as ministers, usually junior, or Whips. Other posts in the Lords are also salaried: the Leader of the Opposition and the Opposition Chief Whip, two committee chairpersons and the Lords of Appeal in Ordinary.

The powers of the Lords are governed by the Parliament Acts of 1911 and 1949. From the mid-seventeenth century the Commons had regularly objected to the unrestricted legislative role of lords, and particularly their power to reject money bills passed in the Commons. The issue came to a head when the Lords rejected Lloyd George's 'People's Budget' of 1909 and therefore refused the government Supply. After two quick general elections, a bill was introduced in the Commons to restrict the veto of the Lords on legislation passed in the Commons to two years and to remove it altogether for money bills. The Lords gave the bill a second reading but amended it in a way that was unacceptable to the Commons. Prime Minister Asquith threatened to create sufficient new peers to carry the bill and it was then passed in the Lords on a close vote.

The Parliament Act was intended to be a temporary measure and proposals to reform the Lords were announced by the government in 1920, 1921, 1922, 1924 and 1927; and private members' bills on the subject were regularly introduced up to the mid-1930s. None of them proceeded. In 1917 a joint conference of both Houses, the Bryce Committee, recommended that the Second Chamber should consist of 246 members indirectly elected by MPs grouped regionally, together with eighty-one members chosen by a committee of both Houses. It proposed that disagreements between the two Houses would be resolved by a 'Free Conference Committee' of thirty members of each House. In 1922, the government rejected the recommendations of the Bryce Committee and put forward its own proposals for an Upper House of 350 members, consisting mainly of elected members, hereditary peers elected by their order and members nominated by the Crown. This idea lapsed, but was revived by the government in 1927 and dropped again in the face of opposition in the Commons. There has not been a broad-based enquiry into the reform of the Lords since the Bryce Committee.

In 1947 it appeared likely that a bill to nationalise the iron and steel industry would be blocked by the Lords beyond the life of the Parliament. The Labour government introduced a new Parliament Bill to restrict the delaying power of the Lords to one year. The Lords rejected it and it passed into law in 1949 under the 1911 Act. The result was that the Lords were left with the power to veto only private bills and statutory instruments and any legislation intended to extend the life of a Parliament beyond five years.

Also in 1949, an informal all-party conference agreed that there should not be a permanent majority assured for any political party in the Lords, that women should be admitted and that life peerages should be created. These proposals were not taken any further. By the mid-1950s, the Lords showed all the signs of the 'inward decay' or terminal atrophy that Bagehot had warned against in 1867. It usually met for only three days a week and for only three hours a day; over 50 per cent of its membership took the Conservative Whip and a mere 5 per cent supported Labour; and it made very little contribution to parliamentary life. It was then rejuvenated by the Life Peerages Act of 1958, the effect of which was modest in its first few years but became much more apparent after 1964 when the Wilson governments appointed over 180 life peers in six years.

The next milestone in Lords reform came in 1968 when the Labour government produced a white paper and a bill to end the hereditary basis of membership, to ensure that no one party held a permanent majority and to allow the government of the day usually to have a majority. The proposal was that there should be a two-tier structure of voting peers and non-voting peers. Voting peers would be created, some of them from the ranks of existing hereditary peers, and they would be expected to attend at least one-third of the sittings of the House, which would consist of about 230 members. It would be constituted in a way which would give the government a small majority over opposition parties but not a majority of the House as a whole. The House would be able to delay a public bill by six months and would not be able to reject, but could oblige the Commons to reconsider, a statutory instrument.

Voting peers would be paid and there would be a place in the reformed House for Law Lords and Bishops.

Between the publication of the white paper and the Parliament (No. 2) Bill which followed, the government dropped the proposal for salaried peers. The white paper was approved by both Houses. The second reading of the bill was passed in the Commons by 285 votes to 185. After twelve long days of clause-by-clause debate on the floor of the House discussion of the bill had only reached Clause 5, owing to fili-bustering by backbenchers on both sides, and it was abandoned.[3]

The question of Lords reform, and particularly its abolition, was strongly revived after 1974 when the Labour government produced controversial legislation in spite of having a tiny majority. This situation encouraged their Lordships to exercise their powers to amend bills passed up to them. This in turn obliged the Commons (in fact the extremely harassed Labour members) to spend time trying to reverse Lords amendments on, for example, devolution, labour relations legisla-tion and a bill to nationalise the aircraft and shipbuilding industries. The abolitionist tendency had also been strengthened by the dissolution of the Upper Houses in New Zealand, Denmark and Sweden in the preceding twenty years.

Labour's Programme for 1976 included the statement: 'We believe that the House of Lords is an outdated institution, completely inappro-priate to a modern democratic system of government. It should not, therefore, continue in its present form. Any Second Chamber which replaces it must be much more representative of the community as a whole, and we shall examine ways of bringing this about.' Also in 1976 the Labour Party conference voted to abolish the House of Lords and the National Executive requested the Machinery of Government Study Group of its Home Policy Committee, of which the author was a member, to produce a report on the matter. This group spent much of the following five years considering how to replace the Upper House. It concluded that the abolition of the Lords was fraught with difficulties, but should continue to be a commitment and that in the meantime a Labour government should appoint sufficient peers to ensure a govern-ment majority.

In 1977, the National Executive presented a statement to the party conference, 'The Machinery of Government and the House of Lords' which was debated and passed. This pointed out that during the 1964–70 Labour government, the number of divisions in the Lords was only forty, but that in 1974–75 the Labour government had been defeated in a hundred Lords divisions and in 1975–76 it had been defeated there 120 times (including twenty-eight times on the Dockwork Regulation Bill). It quoted a convention represented by the Marquess of Salisbury, with reference to the 1945–51 Labour government, that Conservative peers would not oppose legislation which had been set out in a Labour government's manifesto and concluded that this convention had now been abandoned. The Lords had deleted shipbuilding from the Aircraft and Shipbuilding Bill which had been a Labour manifesto commitment and had been passed in the Commons after two hundred hours of debate. It quoted the Prime Minister, James Callaghan, as saying: '. . . Time after time there has been a conspiracy between the Conservative front bench in the House and the inbuilt majority in the House of Lords . . .',[4] and observed that four out of five of the peers who had upset government legislation were hereditary.[5]

The statement went on to discuss possible reforms; creating up to a thousand new peers 'to swamp the Conservatives'; curbing the powers of hereditary peers; electing a Second Chamber directly or indirectly and having it composed of representative nominees (from trade unions, regions, local government, employers' organisations). All these ideas were rejected and the statement recommended that Labour's next general election manifesto should include:

> Should we become the government after the next general election, we intend to abolish the House of Lords. No doubt given such an electoral mandate, the Lords would agree to this, but should they not, we would be prepared to use the Parliament Acts or advise the Queen to use her prerogative powers to ensure this. Unless something else were done, this would remove the Lords' complete veto on an extension of the life of a House of Commons beyond five years. To safeguard the electors' rights, therefore, we propose that such extension should be subject to approval by a referendum or, in time of war, by a two-thirds majority of the House of Commons.[6]

In fact, in the 1979 Labour manifesto the abolition of the House of Lords was not mentioned, though there was a proposal to remove its remaining powers. Meanwhile, in 1978, a Conservative Party committee had produced a report proposing the creation of an Upper House which would eventually have two-thirds of its members elected, with one-third seeking re-election each year under a proportional system. This body would have powers to delay a Commons bill for two years and the right to call referenda on constitutional issues. This did not find favour with the Conservative leader, Mrs Thatcher, and no further proposals for reforming the House of Lords have emerged from her party.

In 1980 a committee of Labour peers proposed that hereditary peers should not continue as members of the House of Lords and that a body of voting peers should be appointed in proportion to the representation of the parties in the Commons after each general election. In 1983, the Labour general election manifesto included a commitment to end the legislative powers of the House of Lords forthwith and, later, to abolish it. The 1987 Labour manifesto did not mention the subject. In 1990, constitutional reform was back on the Labour agenda and the policy document *Looking to the Future* proposed to create a new, elected Second Chamber with the power to delay, for the lifetime of a Parliament, any change to legislation dealing with individual or constitutional rights. The new Second Chamber would also be able to prevent a government delaying an election beyond the five-year limit. It became apparent that the party was prepared to consider a reformed electoral system for the Upper House and that a number of its leading members had in mind constituencies based on Scotland, Wales and the English regions. Labour peers complained that they had not been adequately consulted on these proposals, which they did not support.

The Lords Today

The House of Lords sits for an average of seven hours a day for about 150 days a year. It spends about 60 per cent of its time on legislation, 16 per cent on general debates and 10 per cent on questions. Its proceedings have been televised since 1985, which has greatly increased public interest in its activities. It has also become somewhat more controversial in the last few years in that the Conservative government has suffered many more defeats in divisions there than in the Commons. In 1989–90 the government was defeated in twenty out of 186 divisions in the Lords and between 1979 and 1991 there have been 170 government defeats in some 2,100 divisions. Many of these defeats have been on minor matters, but others have included endeavours by the Lords to ameliorate the rules relating to child benefit, mobility allowances, housing benefit for students, community care, ophthalmic services, the Social Fund, housing for the homeless, access to footpaths, the sale of wild birds, and school transport. Most of them have been eventually overturned by the government majority in the Commons (in 1989–90, of the twenty government defeats only seven led to the government changing its mind), but the effect has been to strengthen the reputation of the Lords as the small voice of social conscience in Parliament at a time when the government appeared deficient in that department. This continued a tradition: early attempts to reform the abortion laws and to legalise homosexual relations had started in the Lords.

In general, the Lords have been suitably deferential to the Commons and have sought to avoid confrontation, though in the matter of the war crimes legislation (allowing alleged 1939–45 war criminals to be brought to trial) in April 1991 they carried their opposition all the way and the Parliament Act had to be invoked for the first time in forty years to override their decision. They have not used their power to veto secondary legislation, though they have carried motions deprecating some orders which have occasionally led to their withdrawal.

Bills go through much the same stages in the Lords as in the Commons, though the committee stage is usually taken on the floor of the House. Many amendments to bills are moved simply to improve their drafting and clarity and most of them are accepted by the government. Private members' bills originating in the Lords often propose useful amendments to the law; about twenty start out every year and two or three are finally enacted. General debates on motions are held on Wednesdays and debates are also held on one category of questions ('unstarred') and on Select Committee reports. Procedure is simpler and more flexible than in the Commons and there are very few rules of order or discipline because the Lords did not suffer, as the Commons did, the nineteenth-century turmoil over Irish Home Rule. Debates in the Lords are less adversarial, better tempered and often better informed than in the Commons: it is said to have more expertise in more fields than any other legislature in the world. Speeches are briefer and more reflective, though the advancing age of some participants encourages them to wander slightly. Recent debates on embryology, (7.2.89) in which distinguished scientists participated, and on war crimes, when lawyers and religious leaders spoke, were of an outstanding quality. The informal atmosphere has encouraged their Lordships also to debate unidentified flying objects and, on a memorable occasion, Lord Maelor (T. W. Jones of Rhosllannerchrugog) to sing the hymn '*Adenydd colomen pe cawn* . . .' in 'the language that Moses learnt after he ascended into Heaven'. (20.2.80 c.866) Given that the whole institution is run on a shoe-string, it is a relatively efficient means of scrutinising and revising legislation, of initiating less controversial legislation, of providing a forum for debate on issues of public concern and organising a Supreme Court of Appeal. In recent years the Lords has acquired a new strength: the development of some very effective Select Committees.

The Lords Select Committee on the European Communities was set up in 1974. It consists of twenty-four members (though about eighty peers are actively involved) and normally meets fortnightly. Most of its work is done in six sub-committees of twelve to seventeen members, on Finance, Trade and Industry and External Relations; Energy, Transport and Technology; Social and Consumer Affairs; Agriculture and Food; Law and Institutions; and Environment. Peers serve for a total of five years, the chairpersons of sub-committees for three years. In addition, ad hoc sub-committees are set up from time to time, for example on European union and on Fraud against the Community. Its staff consists of only five clerks, a legal adviser, two specialist assistants and nine secretarial and clerical staff.

The committee can investigate any community proposal and other matters which raise important issues of policy or principle. The chairperson of the Lords Committee (now Lady Serota) sifts out the most important proposals for further examination. Each sub-committee considers the documents referred to it and may clear them forthwith or conduct a small-scale examination, which may be followed by a published letter to the minister concerned, or may mount a full-scale enquiry including taking written and oral evidence, from, for example, the CBI, the TUC and the National Consumer Council. Members occasionally visit the European Commission in Brussels and other EC institutions. All its reports, over twenty a year, are sent to the Commission, the European Parliament and the UK's Permanent Representative in Brussels.

This committee has wider terms of reference than its equivalent in the Commons, and can examine the merits of proposals and EC proposals for future legislation. Its reports are usually debated, elicit oral responses from ministers and occasionally lead to government white papers. The Lords provides the most effective means we have of examining Britain's place in Europe and the development of European policies and programmes.

The Lords Committee on Science and Technology was set up in 1980, when the Commons disbanded its committee on the same subjects. It has three sub-committees and fifteen members and has the power to co-opt other members. It appoints specialist advisers and has very wide terms of reference which appear to enable it to take a more

dynamic attitude than Commons Select Committees. This committee
has produced some excellent reports on scientific advice to government
(1981); forestry (1982); engineering research and development (1982);
occupational health (1983); education and training for new technologies
(1984); hazardous waste disposal (1985); innovation in surface transport
(1987); space policy (1987); priorities in medical research (1988); and
innovation in manufacturing industry (1991). The reports on research
and development and on manufacturing industry attracted widespread
parliamentary and public interest and analysed some critical national
problems with dispassionate expertise. It is hard to conceive of any other
body in Britain producing such reports.

From time to time the Lords also appoint special Select Committees
to examine particular topics. These have included a Bill of Rights
(1978); Unemployment (1982); Overseas Trade (1984); and Murder
and Life Imprisonment (1989). Like those of the Science and Technology Committee, these reports were well received and widely discussed.
There are also a number of Lords Committees on House Affairs: the
Lords' Offices Committee, with sub-committees dealing with such matters as staff, computers, the library and works of art, and committees
for Privilege, Procedure, and Leave of Absence and Expenses. The
House of Lords has a small administration of some three hundred staff
organised into two departments. Its Serjeant at Arms is called Black
Rod (and is also Secretary to the Lord Great Chamberlain and Gentleman Usher to Her Majesty the Queen, as well as having other duties to
the Order of the Garter), a post which rotates between senior officers
of the three armed services (the next one will be an admiral, replacing
an air chief marshal). The estimates, or budget, for the annual expenditure of the Lords is agreed with the Treasury before being laid before
the Commons for approval. It is not clear why the Treasury's agreement
should be required.

What to do about the House of Lords?

Anybody concerned only with questions of efficiency would advise leaving the House of Lords more or less as it is. It provides a useful means
of examining and revising legislation; it saves the Commons a lot of time
in originating legislation and in handling private bills; it provides a forum
for expert public debate in a quiet and unassuming way; it provides a
very valuable, probably essential, means of examining legislation and

developments in the EC; it provides a very worthwhile public service in producing reports on science and technology and other matters of public policy. It does all this for a very small cost: some £34 million a year, including printing and building maintenance. Over a hundred years of attempts to abolish or reform it radically have ended in defeat. A serious attempt to abolish or reform it now would involve the Commons in months of debate on the floor of the House at the expense of many more worthwhile and popular activities and would open up a constitutional can of worms.

On the other hand, any self-respecting democrat has to argue that its existence is an affront and that it cannot be allowed to continue. The idea that some citizens should be able to influence legislation by accident of birth or by occupation is unacceptable. It reinforces social class divisions. It always has a majority for one political party. It can thwart the intentions of a democratically elected government.

As we have seen, reformers have veered between demanding its abolition and proposing its reform. Abolitionists have to face up to some tricky problems. There are two possible routes to abolition. One is to use the Parliament Act to ensure the passage of the necessary legislation. The use of the Parliament Act would lead to a delay of about a year after the passing of the second reading of the abolition bill. During the year's wait, the Lords would probably retaliate by holding up other legislation passed to them by the Commons. It has been argued that since the Parliament Act assumes the existence of two Chambers, it cannot be used to abolish one of them. It has also been said that since under the Parliament Act the Lords has the absolute right of veto over legislation to extend the life of a Parliament, it would be unconstitutional to, in effect, end that veto. Whether or not these are proper constructions to place on the Parliament Act, the likelihood is that they would be used to challenge abolition legislation in the Courts right up to the Court of Appeal – the House of Lords.

Even if, after all this, the Parliament Act proved to be a suitable vehicle for abolition, there might be a problem in securing the Royal Assent. The Queen's coronation oath undertook 'to govern the people of the United Kingdom ... according to the statutes in Parliament agreed on' and she and her advisers might conclude that abolition legislation would not properly constitute a statute in Parliament agreed on. However, it has been more plausibly argued that the Royal Assent would probably be forthcoming if the government's general election manifesto had made clear that abolition would require the consent only of the

Queen and the Commons. The upshot is that the Parliament Act could be an unreliable vehicle for abolition.

The other route to abolition is the creation of sufficient peers to ensure the passage of legislation (say a thousand of them, to be on the safe side). This would involve patronage on a scale that democrats might find distasteful. The Queen might balk at it without another general election (as Edward VII did in 1910), which might annoy the electorate so much that they could turn against the government which had caused it. As the Lords limits the introduction of new peers to two at a time two days a week, the installation of all the new peers could take longer than the lifetime of a Parliament to complete. If a way of short-circuiting this problem were to be found, it could be that the newly installed peers might take a liking to the Lords and refuse to support abolition. So the creation-of-peers route also has its difficulties.

Some of these problems might be overcome if the Abolition Bill were preceded by a referendum which authorised abolition. However, the British public has a soft spot for the Lords and, given the scares that could be run by opponents during the referendum campaign, might well not support abolition when it came to the vote, particularly if the government was unpopular at the time.

It is not surprising that most of the reformers with the House of Lords in their sights have nowadays dropped the idea of straight aboli- tion without replacement. A single-House legislature would impose an impossibly heavy burden on the Commons, including one or two extra stages for every piece of legislation and many new Select and Standing Committee sessions. The existing workload on the Commons is now so great that it could not possibly function in this way. The proposed creation of legislatures in Scotland and Wales would probably not reduce the workload on the Commons significantly for a very long time. The extensive growth in powers of a European Parliament might, but that is also a long way off. Abolition would require the construction of a new Court of Appeal, which itself could involve a tortuous piece of legislation and, most important, would also require a replacement of the Lords' present safeguard against the extension of the life of a Parliament by some such device as a two-thirds qualifying majority in the Commons.

The various ways of replacing the Lords with an elected Upper House could run into a number of the problems associated with abolition. However, such a measure might eventually get through via the Parlia- ment Act after a protracted and difficult progress through both Houses. The opportunity cost – the legislation foregone – would be very high.

Any government bent on the replacement of the Lords would probably best meet its objectives by proceeding in stages. It would be relatively easy to end the Lords' nominal veto on secondary legislation and to remove the right to a seat in the Lords of people succeeding to a hereditary title or becoming bishops. The second, more protracted, stage would be to remove the right of hereditary peers to vote in the Lords and to replace, say, 150 of them with appointed voting members so that the proportions of those eligible to vote reflected the composition of the Commons. Then we would have a wholly appointed Upper House which could last until a system of election to it could be designed, probably on a regional and proportional basis. Today's active roster of 350 seems to be about the right size. This stage might last for some time given that it has two advantages: the ending of the hereditary principle and the avoidance of the creation of a serious challenger to the Commons.

But, like all these schemes, this one has disadvantages. There would be an enormous increase in patronage. Some members would have to relinquish office on a change of government if the size of the Upper House were to be kept stable. However, it would be reasonable to appoint them all for one Parliament at a time. There would be a gradual loss of some useful cross-benchers, though the present Political Honours Scrutiny Committee could be given the duty of appointing a few distinguished people without party allegiance each year.

In the meantime the House of Lords should be encouraged – mainly by the allocation of more money for staff – to increase its activities in the area in which it performs best: Select Committee investigations of subjects not covered by committees in the Commons. A system of permanent Select Committees on, for example, women's rights, race relations, green issues, citizenship, could make a very useful contribution to public knowledge and awareness on these topics. Other committees could usefully be engaged on the examination of draft bills and post-legislative scrutiny: see Chapter 3.

In February 1992 a House of Lords Select Committee reported on the committee work of the House.[7] It pointed out that the European Communities Committee was considered by the EC Commission to be unique: no other Parliament attempted to undertake comparable analysis of material, let alone assemble and print such extensive evidence. Its role was essential and its influence significant. However, the government had warned of the danger that the committee's reports could become a 'critique of domestic policy'.

The Clerk of the Parliaments (the House of Lords Clerk) also had misgivings about its work and drew attention to the 'fundamental uncertainty' about the role of the European Communities Committee arising from its wide terms of reference.[8] It sometimes looked at the desirability of Community proposals from a Community perspective; sometimes scrutinised the impact of proposals on the United Kingdom and sometimes used these proposals as a peg to investigate domestic UK matters, he said – as if creating uncertainty in bureaucracies was not an important job of a parliamentary committee.

The committee seemed to accept these arguments and proposed a reduction in the number of sub-committees, and in the membership (from eighty to fifty), of the European Communities Committee, which seems a wilful act of abnegation given the increasing scope of EC institutions. However, it did propose some useful new links with the European Parliament.

Considering the work of the Science and Technology Committee, the committee on the committee work of the House noted that the government considered its reports to be authoritative but that it appeared to range 'to the very edges of its terms of reference, if not over them'. The Secretary of State for Education and Science, giving evidence in a personal capacity, said that he did not have a wide knowledge of its work, but that he regarded it in the main as 'a distinguished part of the science lobby'.[9] As if there was anything wrong with that.

The European Committees and the Science and Technology Committees thought that they needed some additional staff. On this matter the Clerk of the Parliaments urged a degree of caution: a strong case would have to be put for any significant increase and the implications for the career structure in his office would have to be borne in mind! The committee did bring itself to recommend a very small increase in staff.

The committee considered proposals for additional Lords' Select Committees: on foreign affairs; on the relationship between central and local government; on the scrutiny of bills with reference to the European Convention on Human Rights; and on justice. It could not recommend the establishment of any of them, but it suggested the greater use of ad hoc Select Committees and, very usefully, proposed a new committee for the scrutiny of delegated powers (legislation in the form of statutory instruments and orders which give ministers unlimited discretion – see Chapter 3).

Given the scope for new initiatives in the investigatory activities of the Lords, this was a disappointingly diffident report, showing the usual nervousness about incurring a little more expenditure, whatever the potential return.

In 1977 Lord Fulton, himself a great reformer of public administration, foresaw the right role for an Upper House in Britain: 'But is there not a strong case for us ... to do what we are specially well qualified to do, to give some of our minds to the more distant horizons of our times and to provide ourselves with appropriate instruments to help in laying the foundations on which those who have to take decisions can more safely build?'[10]

9
Services

Parliament is too under-resourced to do its job properly despite the efforts of a competent, dedicated (and sometimes exploited) staff. The government has too big a say on what services are provided for members and members themselves have been far too timid in demanding improvements in accommodation, equipment and increases in staff. In addition, the management arrangements of parliamentary services are outdated by present-day standards. These problems persist because too few MPs are bothered about them and because too often Leaders of the House – within whose remit these matters fall – are more concerned to defend the interests of the government than to advance those of Parliament and are much more motivated to limit spending on House services than to invest in them.

Accommodation

Parliament occupies the Palace of Westminster and seven haphazardly acquired outbuildings in the neighbourhood. The Palace, covering nearly 3.5 hectares, appears to have about a thousand rooms. Every flat roof on the Palace has had a hut put on it, several courtyards have been filled in with offices and staff have been squeezed into every available space. Overall, the space available to members and staff appears to be less than half of what is required according to health and safety legislation. The squalid conditions for catering staff, in particular, have been reported on several occasions. Until the implementation of the Ibbs Report on the management of parliamentary services in 1992, the premises were outside the scope of Health and Safety and Food Safety legislation.

About 3,500 people work in the parliamentary buildings, though some 10,000 people (in seventy-two different categories) hold passes which give right of access to the Palace and its precincts, including more than two thousand civil servants, about 1,500 members of MPs' staffs and two hundred people employed by the BBC.

At the time of writing, 280 members (mostly ministers and front-bench spokespersons) occupy single rooms; 230 share with one other member, 130 share a room with between three and twelve others. Some sixty members and nearly all their staff work in offices with no natural light. Five members have no office space at all. On average, members and their staff have eleven square metres of space per person (members of the Commons Clerk's department have double and under secretaries in the civil service have treble that amount). There are about 420 desks available for 1,600 members' staff.

Plans to provide a major new parliamentary office building on a site opposite the House of Commons were announced in 1960 and designs were produced, but later abandoned. New plans were produced in the mid-1960s, and in 1976 and 1979. These last two schemes were abandoned by the government on grounds of cost.

The present rebuilding programme aims to provide every MP with a single room by the year 1995, but this is now unlikely to be achieved. Phase 1 of a rebuilding programme, to provide additional space for a hundred MPs and sixty secretaries, a branch library, two small shops and apartments for six officers of the House, was begun in 1983 and, after acrimonious contractual disputes, completed in late 1991. Phase 2 of the rebuilding was due for completion in 1998, but it is likely to suffer delays because the underground station beneath it is also to be redeveloped.

The Palace of Westminster is closed to the general public except for access to the Strangers (public) galleries of both Houses, to attend public sittings of committees or to attend meetings with Members of Parliament. All other visitors have to be sponsored by members for a tour along a policed route, for a booked gallery seat or for functions. Facilities for visitors are virtually non-existent. Most of those who want to get into the Lords or Commons galleries at popular times have to queue outside the building in all weathers. There are no refreshment facilities for visitors unaccompanied by a member and handicapped people have great difficulty in getting into the House and its public areas. Admission to the Palace is distinctly unwelcoming. Visitors are universally referred to as strangers, and those who manage to get inside to view the Speaker's procession which opens each daily session are bellowed at by policemen to take their hats off. Most guided tours appear to concentrate on the interior decoration and the more anachronistic of parliamentary customs and rarely do much to explain our parliamentary democracy and the purposes of its procedures. Visitors to the public galleries are provided with a daily order paper, obscure in its presentation, which gives them little understanding of the process they are viewing. Graham Allen has sensibly proposed that it should be replaced by an Agenda of the House which is easily comprehensible and which should include a simple explanation of the day's business and a summary of the main issues under consideration.

The new parliamentary building should include a multi-media resource centre, with exhibition gallery, lecture theatre and cinema with live transmission from the Chamber and committees to help visitors, school parties and teachers understand what Parliament does. The present plans do not include these facilities. Their provision does not appear to have been considered.

The Organisation of the House of Commons

Up to 1978 financial control over House of Commons services was vested in Commissioners for Regulating Offices of the House of Commons as established by the House of Commons (Offices) Act of 1812. The Commissioners were 'the Speaker, the secretaries of state, the Chancellor of the Exchequer, the Master of the Rolls and the Attorney and Solicitor General for the time being (each of them being also Members of the House of Commons)': in effect, the government. In 1970, the Commissioners approved an arrangement known as 'the Statement of Principles' which delegated financial control to the Clerk of the House as Accounting Officer for the House of Commons vote, subject to his providing an annual statement to the Commissioners.

In late 1973, the Speaker appointed Sir Edmund Compton to report on the administration of the House. The Compton Report[1] was submitted to the House in July 1974. Sir Edmund concluded that the functions of the Commissioners, effectively the Speaker and the Chancellor, 'appear to be spent' and that the time had come to abolish the Commission. He proposed a unified House of Commons service (in place of the existing arrangement whereby the separate departments each employed their own staff), under a new Chief Officer of the House, assisted by two deputies – one for procedural services and the other for administrative services. He also observed, with great prescience: 'My assessment of members' requirements of service from the staff of the House, is that the time has come for a significant shift of activity from procedural services to administrative and management services – that is, to develop the organisation and staffing of the services that support and assist members in their life and work in the House.'[2] Less admirably, the effect of his recommendations was clearly to confirm control of the cost of the services of the House by the Chancellor of the Exchequer.

In 1975 a Commons committee under the chairmanship of Arthur Bottomley reported on Sir Edmund's review.[3] Without being specific, it noted a general opposition to the appointment of a Chief Officer on the grounds that it might 'inhibit the personal contact which senior officers of the House were accustomed to have with members and the Speaker'. Hostility to the proposed appointment of a chief executive was particularly strong from the Clerk of the House at the time, who wrote to the committee: 'Since, in the end, critical events in the Chamber are the most important and difficult with which the servants of the House have to deal, the Clerk himself has always been and remains the leading officer of the House. He holds this position not only by virtue of being the head of his department, but also because he is in close contact with the Chamber. If he were to lose contact with the Chamber the whole force of his advice would be emasculated. His place could not be filled by a "Chief Officer", sitting in an office and acting as the single channel for all advice, procedural and administrative. To sum up, the procedural services of the House must inevitably be the most important and the head of those services the senior officer of the House. This situation arises from the nature of the House of Commons itself and cannot be reversed by any administrative process. The whole idea of a "significant shift" from procedural to administrative and management services is in fact a delusion.'[4]

It is doubtful if many members would have recognised that description of the relative importance of the services they required. The idea that procedural services were more important to them than administrative support and facilities was one that belonged to a far simpler age. It was also strange that an officer of the House considered the existing arrangements irreversible.

The Clerk had an alternative scheme. It was that his department should take over the Official Report (Hansard) and, while the heads of departments continued to have right of access to the Speaker, the Clerk himself would, in the last resort, be in a position to give direction to any of them if he thought it necessary or desirable or if any of them asked him to do so. He produced an organisation chart showing himself in control of all departments.

The Bottomley Committee hastily dropped the idea of a Chief Officer, but recommended a reconstituted House of Commons Commission with direct responsibility for the employment of all staff in the departments of the House: 'We are convinced of the need, in the House of Commons, for an ultimate authority which can express the will of the House in respect of its own services, organisation and staff; which can provide a central thrust for the development of those services; and which can oversee and care for the interests of members of all parties and where necessary represent those interests to the executive.'[5]

The government accepted these proposals and went further than the Bottomley Report in deciding that the new Commission, instead of Treasury Ministers, should be responsible for the presentation of House of Commons financial estimates for staff costs. However, Treasury ministers would continue to present the estimates for members' pay, pensions and allowances (just a reminder about who really was in charge).

The House of Commons (Administration) Act was passed in 1978 and established the present organisation, which has six departments:

The Department of the Clerk of the House (130 staff)
This is organised into six offices and provides the clerks of Standing and Select Committees; prepares the order paper and receives questions and motions; gives procedural advice; ensures that bills conform to the rules of the House; compiles the minutes of the House and maintains contact with foreign Parliaments.

The Department of the Serjeant at Arms (229 staff)
This department has the duty of maintaining order in, and controlling access to, the Chamber and precincts of the House and of providing housekeeping services.

The Department of the Library (167 staff)
This department has four main divisions: the general library; the Public Information Office, including an Education Unit for schools; the Research Division, which handles some 9,000 enquiries a year from members and their staff; the Vote Office, which supplies official documents required by members.

The Department of the Official Report (135 staff)
This produces the verbatim record (Hansard) of the proceedings of the House and its Standing Committees.

The Refreshment Department (290 staff)

This runs a catering service which provides 150,000 meals a year for members and staff and 140,000 for private functions from twenty-odd cafeterias, restaurants and bars.

The Administration Department (190 staff)

This consists of the Fees Office, which keeps the accounts of House services and pays members and staff; the Computer Office; and the Establishments Office, which provides the personnel management for over one thousand staff.

There are also the Speaker's Office and the Parliamentary Works Office, which is responsible for building maintenance, new building and works services and was, until recently, part of the Property Services Agency of the DoE.

The six heads of departments form a Board of Management chaired by the Clerk of the House who is the Accounting Officer for the House of Commons Administration Vote, i.e. its budget, which includes departmental expenditures, superannuation, security, postage and telecommunications and computer charges. The Board of Management appoints an Administration Committee, chaired by the Head of the Administration Department and including the deputy heads of the other departments, to handle staff matters.

The Management Board and the six departmental heads are accountable to the House of Commons Commission of six MPs. Mr Speaker chairs the Commission and its other members are the Leader of the House; a member nominated by the Leader of the Opposition (usually the shadow Leader of the House); one senior backbencher from each of the two main parties and a representative of the minority parties (who answers questions in the House about the work of the Commission). Under the 1978 act the Commission has wide general powers over the staffing and expenditure of the departments of the House and lays before the House the annual estimate for its administration. The Commission employs the staff of the House and its approval is necessary for any proposals involving increases in staff costs. The Commission's power to appoint staff is delegated to the heads of departments except in the case of the offices of the Clerk of the House, the Clerk Assistant and the Serjeant at Arms, which are Crown appointments, and a few other senior posts which are delegated to the Speaker.

The interests of members in respect of the facilities, services and

administration of the House are represented by the Select Committee
on House of Commons (Services) which is appointed under a standing
order 'to advise Mr Speaker on the control of the accommodation and
services'. This Select Committee produces regular reports on, for
example, the accounts of the Refreshment Department, telephone services, the catalpa trees in New Palace Yard and accommodation for
members and staff. It has five sub-committees, covering accommodation
and administration, catering, computing, library and new building. The
Select Committee reports are inconclusively debated from time to time,
at the discretion of the government, and usually on motions to take note
which may or may not lead to action by the government.

The House of Commons Commission produces an annual report
which consists of remarks on the estimates for administration and
reports from each department, mostly relating to staff matters and new
developments in their services. There is also a section recording the
consideration by the Commission of applications by the Liaison Committee (comprising members who chair Select Committees) for funds
to enable Select Committees to travel abroad. The cost of overseas
travel appears to be an acutely sensitive issue. For example, in the 1988–
89 Commission report a request by the Liaison Committee for funds to
travel freely to the EC was refused by the Commission in the interest
of controlling expenditure. The Commission also refused any significant
increase in the special provision for members travelling in a representative capacity to international conferences and seminars.[6]

The Commission's report amounts to half-a-dozen pages. Attached
to it is a report from the Clerk of the House as Accounting Officer,
amounting to some two dozen pages. This sets out every change in the
numbers, pay and grading of the House of Commons staff in the year.
It records changes in night, late duty, morning duty, extra duty, Hansard
night duty and shift allowances for the staff. It records each increase in
staff numbers and each regrading of staff and the granting of new or
revised allowances. It records the salary and grade of every member of
each department including, from 1989, the performance pay of every
employee. So we are told, for example, that the Speaker's Deputy
Trainbearer was on a pay scale of £13,621 to £16,903 in 1990 with
performance points of £17,533 to £18,871; that the Second Principal
Doorkeeper was on £11,635 to £14,368 with performance points of
£14,892 to £16,006; sixteen watchmen, the nursing sister and the
steward of Mr Speaker's house were on performance points as well.
The only people not rewarded for performance appeared to be the

Speaker's Chaplain and forty-two cleaners. This performance pay scheme was copied from modern civil service practice and takes the form of salary increments based on annual report markings for 'overall performance'.

It would be difficult to design a more uninformative document than the House of Commons Commission's annual report. It tells the reader nothing of the Commission's policies for resourcing the services of the House or for planning its development; very little of the work of the departments of the House or the developments they propose and nothing about their standards of service or their costs. A reader can scan the report and not have the slightest idea of what the expenditures and the revenues of the organisation are. On the other hand, we are informed of the pay of the Annunciator Assistant Attendant and the Deputy Trainbearer and the allowances paid to the Head of Nights. The quaint titles and the scores of supervisors, assistants and assistants to assistants make the staff list look like the payroll of a Ruritanian palace.

The annual cost of Parliament appeared to be about £80 million in 1990–91 excluding members' salaries and allowances (another £53 million) and financial assistance to opposition parties (£800,000). The cost of the House of Lords was about £34 million. The costs of the House of Commons were allocated in seven different votes, some under the control of government departments: HMSO (which produces parliamentary papers), the Central Office of Information (publicity) and the Department of the Environment (building maintenance).

The top management structure is ambiguous. The Speaker appears to have the responsibilities of chief officer of the organisation in that he or she is chairman of the Commission and is a member put there by the Commons to safeguard its interests. Clearly, given his or her parliamentary and public duties, it is difficult for a speaker to manage a £130 million business. The Clerk of the House is now responsible, as Accounting Officer, for the financial control of House expenditure. An outside observer might think that the Clerk would have a relationship with the Speaker similar to that of a permanent secretary to a minister or a managing director to the chairman of a company. In fact, the Clerk has a more independent status. The office predates that of Speaker and its holder is appointed by the Crown, theoretically for life, on the advice of the Prime Minister, and at £82,000 a year, is paid twice as much as the Speaker. On taking office, the incumbent receives a Royal Warrant to fill 'the office of Under Clerk of the Parliaments to Us, our heirs and successors' and to attend upon the Commons. Combining the role of principal adviser to the Speaker and to the House and its members on practice and procedures, directing a department concerned with highly complicated legal and procedural matters and acting as Accounting Officer is a formidable task, particularly as the latter role has changed substantially in recent years. The Exchequer and Audit Act of 1866 simply required an Accounting Officer (usually the top official in a department) to submit, and vouch for, a department's annual accounts to the Treasury, but since 1987, the Treasury has laid on Accounting Officers heavy managerial responsibilities for planning and controlling the use of staff and other resources.

In May 1990, the House of Commons Commission came to the conclusion that an examination of its operations was required and announced that it had set up a review 'to examine whether the divided responsibilities for the management of the House of Commons and its facilities could be brought together within the control of the House so as to respond adequately to members' needs and to determine priorities between them'. The Commission invited Sir Robin Ibbs, the government's efficiency adviser, to direct the study, assisted by a small team.

The Ibbs Report

The report, published in November 1990,[7] noted that a survey of MPs conducted for it by MORI revealed strong dissatisfaction with office accommodation and with facilities for visitors: 58 per cent of members replying (and 69 per cent of women members) viewed the Palace as a fairly or very poor place to work and 69 per cent thought that it was a poor place for their staff to work. Some 40 per cent thought that services were not well managed and 37 per cent knew nothing about the work of the Commission, while 13 per cent had never even heard of it. Commenting on the most common cause of complaint, the accommodation available to members and their staff and to visitors, Ibbs observed that the members' requirements of the facilities and accommodation had risen significantly and the strains 'may soon become intolerable'.

The second most frequently mentioned group of complaints was about catering. There was disquiet about the way it was managed and some members disapproved of the growth of banqueting business – functions sponsored by MPs for constituency or other outside organisations. Ibbs commented on the seriously inadequate workplaces ('squalid and dangerous') for catering staff and observed that attempts to remedy these deficiencies over the years had failed to make any real impact.

The report was scathing about the management of the services of the House, saying there was a lack of clarity on how policies were decided and where responsibility rested for their execution. It noted that there were no comprehensive budgets, no usable financial information, no planning and no measurement of results. It commented on the divided responsibilities for the costs of the buildings (in which the House had 'minimal participation') and for other services. It found that the Board of Management did not exercise an effective corporate management role and was not well informed on financial management matters. 'Perhaps the most fundamental weakness we found in the House's administration was the absence of readily usable comprehensive cost information ... It is neither possible to identify the true cost of many activities, nor to match financial authority with operational responsibility ... Arrangements in the House are a complex anachronism. A complete overhaul of financial systems is an inescapable necessity.'[8]

The main Ibbs recommendations were that a Director of Finance should be appointed to head the Administration Department, with the responsibility of designing and installing a new cost-budgeting system. The director would also have a wider role in providing professional advice and support, through the Clerk, to the Speaker and the Commission. The Commission should assume responsibility for the total costs of the Commons by taking over the vote for works and accommodation from the DoE, the HMSO vote and the other small votes. The works vote would continue to be overseen by the Treasury, whose agreement would still be required for its authorisation. The estimates for MPs' pay and allowances would continue to be presented by the Treasury, and the Accounting Officer for them would continue to be the Clerk. A Director of Works should also be appointed, supported by a technical and administrative staff. The Works Director should report to the Serjeant at Arms, the House's 'housekeeper' who had the necessary standing to give the support and guidance needed by a director. There was a backlog of building work amounting to £220 million and the annual spend on it would have to rise by 50 per cent to £35 million a year.

Ibbs went on to propose a new management and advisory structure for House of Commons services. The Commission was a 'somewhat shadowy body', it said. It would need to play a more prominent role and should be responsible for an overall management and financial strategy. Issues with no financial element should continue to be decided by the Speaker. The Commission should delegate to a new Finance and

Services Select Committee the responsibility for detailed consideration of financial matters, including expenditure priorities. The existing Services Committee would be abolished and its five sub-committees replaced by four domestic Select Committees covering catering; accommodation and works; library, publications and information technology; and administration, which would make proposals on the development of services and act as consumer groups. The Finance and Service Committee would prepare annual estimates for submission to the Commission and would monitor the performance of departments.

Ibbs recommended that to be businesslike and effective all the new committees 'would need to move away from a process based on taking formal evidence towards a more deliberative style'.[9] He also made recommendations on the officer structure of the House. The Board of Management would remain, but instead of being primarily concerned with staff pay and conditions, it would become 'the point at which estimates, budgets, performance targets and actual results are brought together, assessed and then presented to the Finance and Services Committee'. The report went on: 'The Clerk of the House, as *primus inter pares*, is already in a position to exert the leadership that is needed and it is for this reason that we do not recommend that a separate Chief Executive should be added to the head of the organisation.'[10] It then moved on to familiar management prescriptions proposing that each department should agree with the Commission a statement specifying the services it would provide and the results it was expected to achieve, which should be published as part of an overall plan agreed by the Commission. Each department should also produce a report on its achievements against targets and its financial performance, published as an annex to the Commission's Annual Report.

The Ibbs Report was a useful summary of the inadequacies of the management structure and systems of the House. One of its weaknesses was that it was too deferential to the established order and conventions. First, it did not adequately explore the idea of a Chief Executive, but accepted the convention that the Clerk of the House had to be the Accounting Officer and was therefore 'first among equals' of the departmental heads.

In addition, Ibbs left in place the arrangement that major non-financial matters should continue to be referred up to the Speaker. This would presumably include such issues as industrial relations, security and site development. The Ibbs proposals would therefore leave overall control of the services of the House shared between two very senior officers with heavy personal responsibilities. Sir Edmund Compton, in his report of 1974, rightly identified the need for a chief executive to be responsible for the management of the organisation. That appointment is more necessary than ever, given the growth in demand for services, the bringing of all the costs of running Parliament under parliamentary control, the new building programme and the need for vastly improved information technology systems.

The report also failed to give adequate weight to the new post of Director of Works. It is curious that it proposed that an officer with the management responsibility for a building and refurbishment spend of £35 million a year and a backlog of work of £220 million should report to the Serjeant at Arms, who has a spend of under £3 million and whose responsibilities are primarily for security, housekeeping and ceremonial matters.

Surprisingly, the report made no mention of the Comptroller and Auditor-General. The peculiar history of the Comptroller was discussed in Chapter 6. Here we need only note that he is an officer of the House, though in 1983 the government carefully defined the status of his nine hundred staff to exclude them from employment by the House of Commons Commission. Whatever the propriety of that arrangement, the fact remains that if anybody was objectively to design a structure for an organisation with no apparent financial control they would want somebody like the Comptroller to be on its senior management body. There is clearly a good case that the Management Board of the House of Commons should most sensibly consist of the six departmental heads, a Director of Works and the Comptroller and Auditor General, chaired by a Chief Executive. The case is made elsewhere for another, research, department.

A further problem with the Ibbs Report was that it abolished the Services Select Committee, though it appeared to recreate it as a Finance and Services Select Committee. The proposed new committee is a management body, preparing estimates, advising the House of Commons Commission and carrying out tasks on its behalf. It is not an investigatory Select Committee, holding hearings, examining witnesses and producing reports with recommendations for change and improvement on behalf of the House. It would be there to serve, not prod, management. The House would lose its only machinery for advocacy in these matters. The distinction between the providers and the users of services should be quite clear, with a body representing the users being empowered to produce reports on the services they require.

The Ibbs Report also left far too much power with the Treasury. It frequently referred to the oversight of the Treasury and to arrangements for making applications for funding to the Treasury. There is a serious defect in arrangements which allow the executive to ration expenditure which makes the legislature effective. There is no evidence that the House would be profligate but for Treasury control – the Commission has a reputation for extreme financial prudence. The Commission should be trusted to produce a plan for the development of services and directly to present all the estimates for Parliament to the House for its approval.

Personnel Management

Unfortunately, the terms of reference of the Ibbs study excluded any examination of the personnel management of the House of Commons. There does not appear ever to have been such an examination. From time to time there have been complaints about the plight of the catering staff – understandably, given their working conditions – but in general the House has never shown much interest in the management of its staff.

Discussion with the staff and its representatives frequently reveals a resigned amusement (and some resentment) about its managerial style: 'Victorian', 'a museum piece', 'antiquated', 'the last pre-Fulton organisation in Whitehall' were some typical comments made to the author.

The definitive characteristics which prompt these remarks are the compartmentalisation of functions and the absence of corporate management; a waning, but still observable, 'them and us' élitism in some departments based on the method of entry and educational background; an excessive proliferation of grades (formerly eighty, now forty) based on minute job distinctions; the apparent absence of developmental personnel management and the feeling of a generally non-participative management style.

This is not to say that the House is a bad employer in material terms. On the whole pay is determined fairly; staff get a modest London weighting addition to their pay and some have lengthy summer leave. There is a certain amount of prestige attached to working for Parliament and a popular feeling of being at the centre of things. On the other hand, working conditions are generally bad and many junior employees

have to work in very unsatisfactory conditions. Some MPs are cantanker-
ous and demanding to deal with. Some front-line staff, such as attendants, are in possible physical danger from protesters or even terrorists.
The hours are long and unsocial for many employees. These burdens
are remarkably cheerfully borne.

Personnel management arrangements include some conventions
which appear antiquated. The Serjeant at Arms department's top management are usually former senior officers of the armed forces, while
its thirty-six attendants and doorkeepers must be ex-warrant officers of
at least twenty years' service (some would say that this requirement
could be held effectively to exclude the employment of ethnic minorities
and women). Other recruiting and personnel management practices
seem at least anomalous. The library recruits graduate library clerks
through the Recruitment and Assessment Services Agency, formerly the
Civil Service Commission. Many of them are specialists, lawyers or
statisticians for example, and they staff the Research Division. Professionally qualified librarians, who need not be graduates but often are,
are recruited by direct advertisement at a lower status. Research staff
are Officers of the House, a title that brings with it some privileges.
Clerical staff in the library are also directly recruited. In recent years,
the barriers between these occupational groups have been somewhat
reduced and three members of staff have moved from the librarian class
into the ranks of library clerk and eight (with library qualifications) have
moved from the clerical to the librarian class.

Arrangements in the Clerk's Department provoke comment from staff
in other departments because of some conventions peculiar to it. Clerks
enter the service of the House by the notorious Administrative Trainee
'high-flyers' scheme (the method by which a predominance of Oxbridge
arts graduates with the right background are brought into the mandarin
ranks of the civil service and given rapid advancement). This exclusivity
may be changing in that three members of the department have been
promoted from the lower ranks of its support staff in recent years. While
specialist researchers and librarians in the library are recruited to fill
specific vacancies, Clerk's Department clerks are brought in as a 'gen-
eralist' cadre each year. The different treatment of specialists and gen-
eralists is a marked peculiarity of the British higher civil service.

There are many more higher-graded posts in the Clerk's Department
than in the library: thirty-four posts at Grade 5 – £40,000 a year – in
the Clerk's Department to four in the library in early 1991. This is
partly because library staff have to be promoted into vacancies in their

department, whereas Clerks are usually promoted in post to Grade 5 when they are aged about thirty-five under a special arrangement called 'fluid complementing'. This arrangement was invented to allow talented members of the scientific civil service to be given additional reward while carrying on their research. The justification for these arrangements is far from clear when the differences between the qualifications of staff do not seem to be great. There should also be scope for staff with specialist and professional qualifications to provide support for Select Committees.

In the library, the Clerk's and the Serjeant-at-Arms Departments it has been difficult for a person who has joined in a lowly position to make it to the top, however talented they may be (a situation typical of the barrier-strewn civil service). There are vigorous complaints by junior grades in several departments about the lack of career development, of opportunities for cross-departmental experience and about the neglect of training. 'Training is abysmal or non-existent. I was told we have no time for training here,' a junior staff member said to the author.

The underlying problem is that the aim of the Bottomley Report, to create an integrated service for the House, has never been achieved because it could not bring itself to endorse the proposal for the appointment of a Chief Executive, free from departmental responsibilities, who could plan and manage the resources of the House and the development of its staff.

When the management of the services of the House was again reviewed in 1990, it was unfortunate that the Ibbs team was engaged to examine its organisation structure and accounting arrangements and not its management of people. Of course, departments differ substantially in their skill requirements but it is doubtful if the present arrangements have been subject to scrutiny in the light of present day needs. A modernised and effective House of Commons should ensure that it is up with the best in staff training and development. The House has a duty to be concerned about these matters. Clearly, a professional study of personnel development in the House of Commons service should now be carried out, with particular reference to training and other means of developing and utilising the abilities of its staff.

Information Technology for Members

By taking the MORI survey of members' opinions at face value, the Ibbs Report omitted to look into services which members need but did not have sufficient knowledge to articulate, or were not asked about. The poll showed that members cared most about accommodation and catering. Both of these problems are largely dictated by the size and age of the Palace of Westminster and until new buildings are available they will have to be lived with. However, to somebody trying to do a professional job as an MP, another issue which was largely missed by Ibbs looms much larger: the primitive state of the information technology at the service of members.

The only information technology equipment provided by the House to the offices of members of the Commons is a telephone and an annunciator which displays the business being taken in the Chamber and who is speaking. The annunciator system was installed in the late 1960s, is obsolete, can carry only one signal and is vastly expensive to maintain (£170,000 a year). Though press offices and ministers' offices in the parliamentary buildings can receive a continuous radio and television 'clean feed' of proceedings in the House, this has always been denied to members because of the fear that it would reduce attendance in the Chamber. From the beginning of 1992, a parliamentary cable TV channel has broadcast proceedings from the House of Commons so that members of the public who subscribe can receive live coverage, but MPs' offices cannot.

A majority of members now have individually acquired information technology equipment such as word processors and fax machines for their offices in the House and in their constituencies, paid for out of their office costs allowance. This equipment is often incompatible with that of other members or departments of the House, so that it cannot be used for electronic mail or paging, and new members and their staff have to acquire and teach themselves to use their own equipment. It is remarkable that governments which trumpet the crucial need for the nation to use information technology have not encouraged its development in Parliament, where, for example, wads of messages are carried round the premises by uniformed attendants searching for members. A modern multi-purpose cable network, such as other Parliaments now have, could be a national showcase for the electronic office.

The House of Commons Services Committee has had a Computer Sub-committee since 1979. In June 1984 it produced a report on

Information Technology: Members' Requirements[11] after commissioning a study of members' needs for information technology and examining computer services in the US Congress and the Canadian House of Commons. The report recommended the introduction of a local area network based on new broad-band cabling throughout the Palace of Westminster and its outbuildings, so as to provide all members, their staff and the departments of the House with centrally generated information services (e.g. the Parliamentary On-Line Information Service, POLIS, a library database of indexed references to current and recent parliamentary proceedings), television and radio reception, commercial information services and databases (e.g. Prestel and Ceefax) and to facilitate the use of word-processing and electronic mail by members.

The report was briefly debated on a motion for the adjournment of the House, together with another unrelated report from the Services Committee, in July 1985. Since the government did not put down a motion on the Committee's recommendations, nothing was done to implement them. The 1984 report assumed that the annunciator system was nearing the end of its life: this was confirmed in 1988 by consultants appointed in 1985, who concluded that it was not economic to preserve the present system for a further maintenance period. They observed that the system operated on the obsolete 405-line standard and could not receive many other signals, including television, which now operates on 625 lines. Because of their obsolescence, individual monitors cost £1,000 each! Christopher Chope, then a junior minister at the Department of the Environment, dismissed the consultants' conclusions as 'too pessimistic' and said that there were no grounds in the foreseeable future for providing a multi-purpose network.[12] The new parliamentary building, though cabled for annunciator signals and radio and TV channels, does not include provision for a modern information technology network.

In 1990 the Services Committee published another report on the subject: *Computer Services for Members*.[13] This noted the failure to make any progress on its 1984 report and said that there was a fairly widespread demand from members for access to the much wider range of television channels now available or shortly coming on stream and to other information services; it considered that there seemed no good grounds for preventing this access. A survey carried out by the same committee showed that a majority of backbenchers now needed personal computers, word processors, fax machines and associated equipment in their parliamentary and constituency offices. The use of such equipment had increased three-fold in five years and members had acquired a wide variety of equipment. The committee observed that this arrangement 'does not represent the best value for money in public expenditure terms'.[14]

The committee gathered information about the provision of information technology in foreign legislatures: 'Our overwhelming impression is that the provision of computer services for members is now regarded as a major priority by most European countries and by many countries of the Commonwealth.'[15] Most of them provided personal computer work stations and access to a wide range of central services at no cost to the member. The committee frowned on the number of staff required to support these computer services (e.g. 160 in Bonn, 250 in Ottawa) and rejected the creation of a 'bureaucracy' on this scale in Westminster, without saying why, but concluded that the United Kingdom Parliament was now out of step with the Parliaments of many other countries in leaving the acquisition of information technology equipment entirely to individual discretion and in not providing for members a range of mutually compatible computerised information services and technical support to members. The present practice of leaving members free to purchase and make their own arrangements for the maintenance of equipment meant that there were no economies available for the bulk purchase of hardware or consumables or through common maintenance contracts: 'No other large-scale user of computers would countenance off-the-shelf purchases at standard retail prices.' In addition, under existing arrangements, engineers from many maintenance companies had to gain admittance to the House, there were problems with the disposal of equipment when a member left and the present arrangements did not allow universal access to parliamentary databases nor to commercial services.

The committee concluded that the House should adopt as a long-term policy the aim of providing the best available information technology services for members and, ideally, install a new broad-band cable network throughout the parliamentary estate: 'There will inevitably be some additional cost to public funds. But some costs are already being met from public funds in the least efficient manner. We are convinced that better overall value for money would be secured by moving along the lines we have suggested, and that the efficiency with which members will be able to serve their constituents and the electorate at large will steadily increase by these means. Moreover, the House cannot continue to adopt a wholly amateur approach to the use of technologies which are already the standard tools of work in industry, business, education and government services of all kinds throughout the developed world.'[16]

The government has not yet responded to the Services Committee's report.

Pay and Conditions

MPs' pay, allowances and working conditions are extraordinarily sensitive subjects, mainly because of media interest. The tabloid press likes to add together the MP's salary, staff and equipment allowances and living away from home and travel allowances and call the total an extravagant reward. If in addition the readers' attention is drawn to the small attendance in the chamber for much of the working day, the conclusion is obvious. They neglect to point out that when a vote is called, within ten minutes some six hundred MPs record their presence in the division lobbies, drawn from their desks and committees and other meetings. In fact, the remuneration of an MP is about the same as a junior-to-middle manager in industry or public administration, well below that of a journalist on a national newspaper, and the hours of work of a conscientious MP are excessive. This chapter evaluates, particularly, the support costs (staff, equipment, accommodation) needed to do the job properly.

MPs' Pay

The payment of MPs appears to have started in the thirteenth century but it ceased from the late eighteenth century until 1911 when it was reintroduced at £400 a year by Lloyd George. He described it as 'not a remuneration, not a recompense, not a salary but an allowance: the only principle of payment in the public service is that you should make an allowance to a man to enable him to maintain himself comfortably and honourably, but not luxuriously, during the time he is rendering service to the State. That is the only principle, and it is the principle on which we have proceeded.'[1]

The payment stayed at £400 until 1931, when it was reduced to £360. Thereafter it was raised by governments irregularly and usually with great reluctance. In 1964, after seven years at £1,750, as the salary had been greatly reduced in value by inflation and as ministers' salaries had not been increased since 1831,* the government appointed a Committee on the Remuneration of Ministers and Members of Parliament under Sir Geoffrey Lawrence.[2] The Lawrence Committee tackled two issues about the payment of MPs which it recognised as controversial. First, it considered whether the salary should be in recognition of full-time or part-time service. A 'substantial number' of members replying to the committee's questionnaire had expressed a firm belief that the House would suffer considerably in the quality of its work if it consisted entirely of 'full-time professional politicians' and thus 'lost the benefit of the counsel' of those members who were actively engaged in occupations outside the House. The committee observed that it was frequently said that continuous contact with the outside world on the part of a substantial number of members 'contributed greatly to the reality of its debates'.[3] They decided that the salary of members should be such as to enable members who were without private means or the opportunity to earn income outside the House efficiently to discharge the duties of the service without undue financial worry and to live and maintain themselves and their families at a 'modest but honourable level'.

Secondly, the Lawrence Committee considered the suggestion that the MPs' salary should be linked to a level of salary in the civil service. They firmly rejected it, partly because they thought that any such link might involve the civil service in political controversy!

They found that an increasing number of members were 'forced to endure the discomfort ... of cheap and shabby lodgings in London; they cannot afford to use the Members' Dining Room; they have to submit to the humiliation of not being able to return hospitality even at the most modest level of entertainment; they are forced to impose considerable sacrifices upon their families and they find it necessary to cut down the number of days on which they can afford to attend sittings of the House. The result of all this is that if they do not receive help from some external source they are continually harassed by financial anxiety.'[4]

It was estimated at the time that for the average member all but £500 of the salary was taken up by the cost of living in London, postage and telephone calls. The committee recommended an increase in members' pay from £1,750 to £3,250 a year, which was implemented by the govern-

---

* The salary of the Chancellor of the Exchequer was £5,398 plus about £800 in fees in 1780. In 1964 it was £5,000.

ment after a debate which threw some interesting light on attitudes to members' outside occupations. Mr Albert Costain, for example, acknowledged that his financial position was 'a good deal different' from that of other members. 'I willingly acknowledge that I am grateful to my colleagues in my own companies for allowing me time to do this work.'[5] Sir R. Cary referred to the distinction that had been made between part-time and full-time members. 'What a wounding way to talk about members of this House!' he said. 'Anyone who has the privilege to embark on being a member of this House of Commons, and is elected here, is permanently preoccupied, always, with the privilege of being a member of this House ... Every waking thought, every other activity, in the law, in profession or in business, is dominated by the fact that one is a member of the House of Commons.'[6]

Another six inflationary years went by without any increase in MPs' pay and allowances and widespread hardship reappeared, so in 1970 the Leader of the House, William Whitelaw, announced that the matter would be referred to an independent body which would make recommendations to the House. The Top Salaries Review Body (TSRB) was given the task and produced its first report in December 1971. It has since produced fourteen reports on the subject, virtually all of which would have been unnecessary if it had initially accepted the principle of linking an MP's pay and allowances to a civil service grade. Few of its recommendations have been implemented at the time they were made, and governments have resorted to some remarkable devices to avoid or delay the improvement of parliamentary pay and allowances.

In 1975, after three and a half years without an increase, during which the cost of living had risen by 65 per cent, the government accepted the TSRB's proposal of £8,000 as a 'notional' salary for pension purposes, but actually allowed a salary increase to £5,750. In 1979 the proposed increase was phased over three years. In 1981 the device of a notional and a lower actual salary was revived. In 1983 the TSRB recommended an increase of 30 per cent and the government responded with one of 4 per cent. 'We still have to make our own political judgement about an issue sensitive in its economic and social consequences,' said the Leader of the House.[7] The House then voted itself a munificent 5.5 per cent, but at last succeeded in achieving a fixed link with a civil service grade: this was confirmed by a vote four years later and came into effect in 1988. On this, the fourth occasion that the House had voted for a link to a civil service pay level, the government accepted the decision (it led to a 22 per cent pay increase).

By the time it came into effect, MPs' pay was fixed at 89 per cent of that of a civil service Senior Principal (Grade 6). On an earlier occasion the vote (by a majority of one) had been to link to the level of an Assistant Secretary (Grade 5), some 15 per cent higher. Grade 6 in the civil service is at the top end of middle management and the entry point for a mature trainee for higher management; it is somewhat below the level of the average dentist, a Metropolitan Police Sergeant (including housing allowance) or, in the service of the House, a senior library clerk, a committee clerk or an assistant accountant. It is between two-thirds (France) and half (Italy) the level of pay of legislators in other European Parliaments.

The only occasion on which the job of an MP has been systematically evaluated by specialist management consultants was for the TSRB in 1983. The consultants concluded that on the criteria they used to establish the value of a job: know-how, problem solving and accountability, an MP's job ranked with that of a senior manager in industry.

The conclusion from this long and painful story can only be that the House has managed to cause its members the maximum injustice and the utmost embarrassment by its supine acceptance of the government's persistent refusals to implement an objective settlement on pay.

Occasionally, the TSRB has examined the extent of outside employment of MPs. In 1971, it found that 70 per cent of MPs other than office holders said that they pursued some other regular or occasional occupation. Some 19 per cent of MPs said they spent twenty hours or more a week engaged on outside work (30 per cent spent ten to nineteen hours a week). In 1983, the TSRB's questionnaire showed a similar percentage having a paid outside occupation, with about 40 per cent spending more than ten hours a week on it. Some 30 per cent received over £10,000 and 11 per cent over £20,000 a year from these occupations (an MP's salary at the time was £15,000).

In recent years concern has been expressed about the apparent growth of involvement by MPs in business activities and particularly in paid 'parliamentary consultancies', as revealed by the Register of Members' Interests, which was introduced in 1974. A study by the *Observer* in October 1990 reported that one MP in three acted as a parliamentary consultant. 'This can involve a wide range of activities ranging from advising on political tactics to putting down questions or speaking in debates.'[8] The survey reported that nearly forty MPs were directors or employees of PR companies: 'Though they list their financial links in the register, they do not have to disclose the names of the clients that their firms are representing.'

Members are required to declare relevant interests when speaking in debates in the House or in Committee (but not when asking questions or sponsoring motions) and to record in the register their directorships, employment, substantial shareholdings and overseas visits paid for by external organisations. They are supposed to register any interest within four weeks of acquiring it. They do not have to declare any income deriving from an interest, nor the business carried out by an organisation in which they have an interest, nor the business interests of their families.

A recent book by the journalist Mark Hollingsworth[9] maintains that MPs 'are increasingly hiring themselves out to the business community' and that they can easily double their salaries by taking on consultancies and directorships. He points out that of the 311 Conservative members who are not ministers, 256 have between them 522 directorships and 452 consultancies (seventeen of 230 Labour members have such occupations). He examines numerous relationships between parliamentary lobbyists (i.e. commercial organisations which seek to inform or influence legislators on behalf of their client and assist their clients to deal with legislative matters) and MPs and quotes the case of the MP who advertised for employment in the parliamentary *House Magazine*, saying that 'it was one way of drawing the nation's attention to the fact that I only had one consultancy and could take on more'.[10]

It is often argued that lobbying is pretty ineffectual in that MPs cannot deliver much more than contacts and limited advocacy for a lobbying organisation. However, lobbyists seem to think that it is very worthwhile and appear to make expansive claims to their clients about their influence. The public clearly deserves to know more about the activities of their representatives in this field.

Other legislatures take a firmer line on the outside earnings of their members. Members of the French National Assembly may not hold other paid positions. In the United States members of the House of Representatives (salary $125,000) are permitted to keep $23,837 in honoraria: anything more they have to give to charity. The amounts received and retained are recorded for each senator in the *Congressional Quarterly*. There are frequent attempts by senators to end the acceptance of these payments (one such motion was passed in August 1990). This passage from the Senate Congressional Record of 20 May 1991 (S6124) illustrates the difference from British practice:

Senator Boyd: 'The US Senate is the only institution in our Federal Government that still permits the acceptance of honoraria for personal use ... The Senate honoraria system is widely perceived as being one of the most serious ethics problems in Washington today. In recent years hundreds of newspapers across America have railed against this payola scam for Senators ... By voting to end honoraria acceptance here in the Senate, we can strike a new blow for our own self-respect.'

In the US and Canada legislators (and local councillors in Britain) may not vote on any matter in which they have a personal interest and in the US personal gifts have to be declared as well. We learn from a recent *Congressional Quarterly* that Senator Robert H. Michell received inaugural gala tickets from Reader's Digest and Senator Newt Gingrich was given a framed painting by Polk County Republican Executive Committee. Clearly, these restrictions and declarations may not prevent influence-peddling, but they do at least establish what is expected of legislators.

In December 1990 a Channel 4 poll of 173 MPs showed majority support for a public register of lobbying organisations; for tighter rules on MPs' business interests and for stricter controls on former Cabinet Ministers taking jobs with companies which were privatised while they were in office. Over a hundred of the respondents also considered that Select Committee chairmen should not have interests in organisations which operated in fields covered by their committees. One such alleged relationship led to the Select Committee on Members' Interests producing a report in March 1991 which proposed that chairmen should divest themselves of such interests and that MPs on committees should declare their links with businesses and withdraw from investigations where there was a possible conflict of interest. The same committee proposed in September 1991 that a register of political consultancy and lobbying firms should be set up (apparently, there are more than fifty of them with an annual turnover of £10 million) and that it should be supervised by a special Select Committee with the power to act on complaints about the activities of lobbyists and to suspend those who break the rules.

The outside employment of MPs has become so extensive that the only way to bring the matter into the open is at least to require all MPs to declare their outside earnings and the full extent of the activities of any company or organisation in which they have a declarable interest as an employee, director, adviser or shareholder. It would be better still to commission and implement a professional evaluation of the income appropriate to an MP's job – an update of the 1983 exercise – and then to prohibit all outside earnings, or all except limited lecture fees, on the American Congressional model. Motions on members' pay are still put to the House by the Treasury, though the motions on funding the services of the House are a matter for the House of Commons Commission (see Chapter 9). There is something wrong with an arrangement which gives the executive, rather than an independent body, responsibility for salaries paid to the legislature.

A pension fund was introduced for MPs in 1965 as a result of the Lawrence Report. Before that, the arrangements for retired members were based on the Members' Fund established in 1939, which operated like a charity. This fund made means-tested grants to ex-members, their widows and children (and, from 1948, their widowers). In 1965 the maximum grant to an ex-member was £500 a year, provided his or her income did not exceed £700; to a widow or widower £300 a year; to a child £30 a year. A committee of the House had recommended a contributory pension in 1955, but the government did not act on the proposal.

Oddly, when the pension fund was introduced in 1965 contributions and benefits were fixed in money terms; the pension was set at a modest £60 a year for each year of the first fifteen years of service (with a ten-year qualifying period) falling to £24 a year thereafter. This meant that inflation rapidly reduced the value of the pension and pensioners were soon again obliged to seek the charitable assistance of the Members' Fund.

The first report of the TSRB in 1971 recommended a scheme based on one-sixtieth of final salary for each year of service, which was improved to one-fiftieth in 1984, when apparently by an oversight the contribution payable by members was increased to an unusual 9 per cent of salary. Pensions under the scheme are indexed to the cost of living.

Yet another example of the attitude of the government appeared in 1990 when the Leader of the House proposed that the government contribution to the pension fund should be reduced to 4.4 per cent, less than half the level of the members' contribution, because the fund (worth £104 million) had accumulated a large surplus. It transpired that the governing legislation enabled the Government Actuary to reduce the employer's contribution but not the employee's so the government was able to adopt the device of many an employer of giving itself a contributions relief instead of improving the benefits for pensioners and their families.

In the brief debate on this proposal it was described as 'a rip-off'.[11] It was pointed out that it treated widows and widowers particularly badly. In addition, the government proposed ('slipped in,' said one member) in future, 'for the convenience of members and the House', that changes in legislation on members' pensions would be in the form of secondary legislation which could not be amended in debate. Sir Geoffrey Howe, as Leader of the House and the official defender of members' interests, hardly bothered to answer any of the complaints about the arrangements, but appeared embarrassed and muddled. The TSRB has since been required to re-examine the matter. There are still injustices to ex-members who retired before 1964 and their survivors, usually widows. The grants to them from the Members' Fund ran to £140,000 in a recent year, including £13,000 in hardship grants.

The Parliamentary Labour Party also has a benevolent fund to help ex-members and their spouses who are in difficulty. Labour MPs contribute £80 a year and the fund makes regular payments of £300 twice a year to those in need, as well as individual hardship payments.

Parliamentary pensions are another subject, like salaries, on which members are exceptionally reticent and fearful of media comment. This timidity has caused great hardship to some former members and their dependants. Another result is that elderly MPs may hang on to their seats longer than they would if they were better provided for: 'One way of keeping Parliament young is to provide adequate pensions,' said Harry Ewing in the 1990 debate.[12]

A discussion of the remuneration and worth of an MP's occupation illustrates both the government's intervention in every aspect of parliamentary life and the anachronistic, laissez-faire arrangements which encourage a significant number of MPs to undertake extensive outside employments. The conventional acceptance and continuation of these arrangements is amateurish and ultimately harmful. They hark back to the days when government was rudimentary and Parliament actually had very little to do. Now there are potentially damaging conflicts of interest and suspicions fanned by the media which diminish the standing and reputation of Parliament. Of equal consequence, the tradition leads to the continuance of eccentric hours of work (see below) and has helped to limit the resources – in accommodation, staff and equipment – provided for members. This directly affects the capacity of members to serve their constituents and to scrutinise government policy and spending.

Office Allowances

Until the Lawrence Report in 1964, MPs were allowed free telephone calls from the House only within the London area; free postage for correspondence with government departments and a railway season ticket from home to the House. They had personally to pay for postage on letters to their constituents, for telephone charges, for secretarial assistance and for accommodation in London. Many simply could not afford to handle constituency casework because of the cost of postage and employing secretaries.

After the Lawrence Report, free inland postage and telephone were provided, and a secretarial allowance was introduced in 1969. From 1984 onwards the 'Secretarial Research and Office Costs Allowance' was fixed at the level of the salary of a secretary in the civil service, after a management consultant's study for the TSRB had evaluated the workload and recommended a level some 65 per cent higher. In 1986 there was a memorable revolt when the government proposed a 6 per cent increase in the allowance and the House voted an increase of over 50 per cent (it involved ambushing the government in an unexpected vote). Since then, what is now known as the Office Costs Allowance is revised every year and is just about sufficient to pay for one full-time and one part-time secretary or assistant and a modestly equipped office.

In the 1980s the number of people claiming passes to the precincts of the House as MPs' staff rose rapidly and reached 1344 by March 1988 – an increase of 30 per cent in four years. This placed a heavy strain on the facilities – for example, there were only enough desks for a third of them. In 1987 the Services Committee was asked to consider control over access to the precincts of the House and in particular to consider whether the number of members' personal staff with access should be reduced. The origin of this resolution was the refusal, apparently on security grounds, of a pass for a research assistant employed by a member and concern about a growing number of such assistants sponsored by outside organisations. The Committee reported[13] that eighty-three members retained three members of staff and another eighty-three retained between four and sixteen each. It found that in early 1988 fifty MPs' staff had indicated a connection with parliamentary consultancy or research services or public relations organisations, and another fifty were employed by charities or other non-profit-making organisations or by professional bodies.

There had also been an increase in the number of American students accredited to members as assistants on temporary internships. There was a rule limiting these interns to 150 a year or fifty at any one time, but in March 1988 it was believed that there were another twenty-five to thirty of them attached to members as temporary secretaries and a further thirty who had attached themselves to members on their own initiative. The Deputy Serjeant at Arms, giving evidence to the committee, thought that American students paid their sponsoring organisations 'quite handsomely' to come to Westminster. They were a source of annoyance to many members and were said to bother the library staff with demands for basic information about Britain and its constitution.

The committee was particularly concerned about the influx of commercial lobbyists as research assistants with access to the library and to the arrangements for tabling questions: 'We, meanwhile, have received disturbing evidence of the direct approaches made by lobbying organisations to individual members, in some cases blatantly seeking the issue of a House of Commons photo-identity pass as a cover for commercial lobbying activities in return for "services" to the members concerned. We believe the evidence we have received represents the tip of a larger iceberg, and one whose progress should be halted.'[14]

One member referred to two permanent research assistants known to him who did a small amount of work for members but who were retained by corporations and lobbying groups to undertake work for them. Robin Maxwell-Hyslop submitted to the committee a letter he had received from an aspiring lobbyist:

Dear Mr Maxwell-Hyslop,

I have recently established a lobbying business and require a Pass for the House of Commons. Because of the lack of Parliamentary recognition afforded to the industry, such a Pass needs to be obtained via an MP. I wonder, therefore, if it would be possible for me to secure one through your good office, assuming that you have not filled your allocation.

With the position of lobbyists being rather a grey area, I would suggest that a pass be issued under the guise of a research appointment. In order to make this above board, but also to give something in return for sponsoring a Pass, I am prepared to undertake any work for you.[15]

The committee recommended a limit of three staff passes for MPs, restricting the use of library facilities by research assistants and freezing the total number of passes in use. It recommended that the House should have the power to withdraw the pass of any individual primarily engaged in commercial lobbying activities.

In December 1991 Brian Sedgemore claimed that examination of the Register of Members' Secretaries and Research Assistants, which is not published, showed that two hundred MPs employed research assistants who had full-time jobs outside Parliament and that many of them were public affairs consultants or lobbyists. He said that some MPs had an uneasy feeling 'that some people with passes are not working as research assistants to MPs at all, but simply have their passes to pursue their own ends' and had access to expensive documents and library research services.[16] The chair of the Members Interests Committee later referred to the need for 'greater transparency' in the relationship between MPs and outside groups.

All these potential abuses would be avoided if members were given a realistic office costs allowance. For a backbench MP with a normal constituency caseload, participating in the campaigning and policy-making activities of his or her party and taking an active part in the work of committees of the House, this should be enough to pay for a secretary, a research assistant and a constituency assistant – all full-time; a fully equipped office in the House and the rental costs of a fully equipped office in the constituency. This entitlement would amount to somewhat more than double the present Office Costs Allowance and would be about the same as that of a member of the German Bundestag or the French National Assembly. In July 1992, in the face of strong government opposition, the House voted for an increase of over 30 per cent in the allowance, which still did not meet the costs of a properly staffed and equipped constituency office.

The Transport and General Workers Union branch representing mainly Labour MPs' secretaries and researchers has long campaigned for proper pay and conditions for their members. They point out that the pay for full-time work in these jobs varies from £8,000 to £18,000 a year, that a number of their holders do not have contracts and are not covered by health and safety legislation. Payment for staff comes out of the same allowance as the costs of constituency offices and of office equipment, so that increased expenditure in one of these areas leaves less money for salaries. The TGWU proposes that every employee of an MP should have a contract lodged with the House authorities, who could then pay according to a civil service pay scale, and that office equipment should be provided and paid for centrally and excluded from the Office Allowance.*

Short Money

Opposition parties in Parliament receive an allowance from public funds. This allowance is called 'Short Money' after Ted Short (now Lord Glenamara), the Leader of the House in 1974. He explained in his autobiography how in 1964 he came to the conclusion that assistance to opposition parties was necessary:

> It was at the first meeting of the Queen's Speech Committee that I felt ministers were coming up against the facts of life in government. And the first of these was that there is a world of difference between putting an attractive vote-winning proposal in an election manifesto on an assurance from the research department at Transport House that it was feasible and workable and, once elected, hammering out a brief for the parliamentary draughtsmen to convert it into a bill.
>
> It became increasingly obvious that our manifesto had not been subjected to nearly sufficient expert appraisal as to its cost or, indeed, to its feasibility. I do not think that we were worse than any other government coming into office after a period in opposition. It was merely that the kind of appraisal that was needed was very costly and parties in opposition were unable to afford it. I was determined, if I ever had the opportunity to do so, to ensure that parties in opposition would have the resources to engage the best expertise available to examine and cost their proposals.[17]

The scheme was implemented from 1975, to 'redress the balance between government and opposition', in Mr Short's words. The amount of money available is determined by a formula based on the number of seats won by a party and the number of votes cast for it. For the lifetime

* There was an odd turn in the story of MPs' research assistance when the *Guardian* reported on 2 December 1991 that companies and lobbyists were willing to pay up to £30,000 a year to the employees of Labour's front-bench team in preparation for a new government.

of the 1987 Parliament this was fixed at £2,550 for each seat and £510 for every two thousand votes cast, giving the Labour opposition about £840,000. In the Labour Party, allocations from the fund were made by four trustees towards the costs of the Office of the Leader of the Opposition, the Whips' Office, opposition peers and research assistance for front-bench spokespersons. When the Conservatives were in opposition, the allocation of Short Money was in the hands of the leader of the party. The official opposition also has four civil servants allocated to serve in its Whips' Office.

Hours

The House of Commons meets for more days in the year and more hours in the day than any other Western legislature. The American Senate and the Canadian House of Commons sit for half as long and the Parliaments of France, Germany and Italy sit for one-third as long. The average annual session runs for 166 days and the average length of a sitting is about nine hours. In addition, many Standing Committees meet in the mornings and occasionally some go on beyond the rising of the House at night. In the last five years, when late sittings have been relatively rare, the House has had about 120 daily sittings after 10.30 p.m. and the average time of concluding business has been 12.30 a.m.

The only reliable estimates of the working hours of MPs were made by the Top Salaries Review Body in 1983 (and it is certain that they have increased since). They found the average hours worked per week by an MP were sixty-nine when the House was sitting and forty-two when it was in recess, giving an average of sixty-two for the year. The hours of the House inevitably have an effect on the domestic lives of members. They also act as a deterrent to the recruitment of women members. Married women and particularly those with young children are greatly disadvantaged by sittings (and votes) up to, and sometimes later than, ten o'clock at night. Every few years a campaign to change the hours of the House is revived among Labour MPs. There was one in the mid-1960s, another in the mid-1970s and the idea has now come around again, principally because of the campaign for more women MPs.

The only time that the demand for more social hours has made any progress was when Richard Crossman was Leader of the House. His proposals came from the recommendations of a Procedure Committee, on which Labour had a majority, in 1966.[18] This committee considered a number of ways in which the hours of the House could be reduced (automatic ending of proceedings at midnight, shorter speeches, bringing forward the parliamentary day so as to start in the morning, sitting for more days in the year) and in the end settled on moving some business to morning sittings on two days a week. The reasons the committee gave for rejecting the idea that the whole parliamentary day should be brought forward was that ministers had to run their departments in the mornings and that members would be inconvenienced; that added burdens would be placed on the Speaker because he was occupied with preparatory work in the mornings; and that members would be prevented from undertaking 'outside responsibilities' to which many of them attached importance 'for their value to the parliamentary debate'.[19]

It is disappointing that a committee with a reformist majority was taken in by these arguments. Only one or two ministers would have been required on duty in the chamber at a morning sitting and there was no clear reason why preparatory work should fall entirely on the Speaker.

Crossman instituted morning sittings on two days a week from 1 February 1967 for a sessional trial period. In an outstanding speech on the need both to reform and to modernise Parliament, he set out a number of proposals for change, including the trial of morning sittings.[20] He supported the Procedure Committee's recommendation that secondary business which was taken after ten o'clock on Wednesdays and Thursdays should be transferred to Monday and Wednesday mornings from 10 a.m. to 12.30 p.m. He observed that opposition to the proposal came from members who saw the experiment as 'the thin end of the wedge, which, if driven home, might exclude the part-time MP from the House altogether'. In answer to that view, he said that the composition of the House had now changed and more members were whole-time members. In former times 'the majority of Hon. Members belonged to business or the professions and expected to be able to earn their livings in the mornings and to come here late in the afternoon for a stint of public service and to spend an hour or two in the best club in the world.' The times of sittings remained as they were in Edwardian times, but legislation had increased greatly, engaging many more members on committees, and the social composition of the House had become more democratic, he said. The dominance of the country gentleman had disappeared, the dominance of finance and the learned professions was being challenged by the arrival of more and more backbenchers who had the kind of jobs which they could not carry on when they enter Parliament. 'Up till now, if we are frank, our timetable has been designed to suit the convenience of those part-timers who earn their livings outside in the mornings and the whole-timers, often without the economic advantages, have had to lump it . . . Is it not time we gave some consideration to the needs of those who keep the House of Commons going during the morning hours when the part-timers are earning their living?'[21] He saw much to commend in the view of many members that the proposal was a first step to conducting all parliamentary business in office hours, but that could be considered after the experiment had been tried.

The Conservative shadow Leader of the House, Selwyn Lloyd, got very excited. The proposal was absurd, he said. Members were already busy in the mornings – he had to deal with a hundred letters a week. They should be allowed a little recreation on Monday mornings. The Speaker would be inconvenienced. The doorkeepers would have to work longer hours. MPs who were journalists, businessmen and lawyers probably did twelve hours a day in the service of the House anyway and without their outside interests Parliament would be a poorer place. The most absurd proposal he had ever heard was that the House should start at ten o'clock on a Monday morning. 'Why ten o'clock? Why not make it half an hour worse and thus drive the barb in still further?'[22]

The experiment proceeded but was abandoned in the following session after much filibustering and the exploitation of procedural devices had shown that the Conservative opposition would not permit it to continue. Despite the morning sittings, the number of late-night sittings increased slightly. As Crossman pointed out, the government actually gained from the experiment.[23] In forty-six short morning sittings it secured twenty second readings, twelve committee stages, eighteen report stages and third readings, twenty-four orders and four considerations of Lords' amendments. 'While the opposition were busy harassing us late at night, the government was obtaining an easy passage for a remarkable amount of the kind of secondary departmental business,' he observed. Unfortunately, he went on, the full-time member had not gained any overall reduction in the hours and the staff of the House were strained to breaking point when a Wednesday morning session followed an all-night sitting. He did not want to give up, though, and simply revert to 'leaving the whole-time member as badly off as before and the House conducted for the convenience of the part-time member'. He had reconsidered a proposal supported by a number of members, that the House should meet for questions from 10.30 to 11.30 a.m. with the main debate running until 6 p.m., but had rejected it because of the need to run committees simultaneously. All that could be done was to institute an order which allowed a minister to suspend business at 10 p.m. and resume it at 10 a.m. the next day. This standing order is still in force, but has not been used since 1969.

So ended the only serious attempt to reform the hours of the House. Oddly, it has become the established view that the experiment failed because the government could not find any worthwhile business to put on in the mornings. In the hearings of the Procedure Committee nearly ten years later, the Leader of the House and the Government Chief Whip (both Labour) were convinced that this was the case.[24] The *Economist* got nearer to the truth, saying that 'the experiment was soon torpedoed by the self-interested group of lawyer MPs who thought (and still think) that the Commons should be organised to leave the mornings in court free.'[25] This issue was revived briefly in the 1970s, again by Labour backbenchers (and their spouses, who formed a delegation to meet the Labour Chief Whip of the time, and were brushed off).

In the Procedure Committee of 1977–78, which, as we have seen, produced far-reaching reforms in the investigatory powers of the House, the author moved the following amendment to its report:

We consider that the work of an assiduous Member of Parliament has increased so greatly that it should now be seen as a full-time job and that the arrangement of parliamentary sittings to enable members to pursue outside employment on the excuse that they need to 'keep in touch' with the everyday world of the Courts and the City is contradictory to our idea of a modern and effective parliamentary system. Inherent in the work of a member is the need to keep in touch with the outside world. Moreover, present sitting times virtually exclude women with domestic responsibilities from becoming members. We cannot believe it right to place obstacles in the way of a large group who would bring valuable experience to the House. The present hours of the House are also a deterrent to legislative efficiency, and are probably harmful to health and disruptive of family life. We therefore propose that the general rule should be that the House should meet in the mornings, afternoons and evenings up to 7.30 p.m. and not at night. We are convinced that the present pattern of sittings is quite unnecessary, that it is left over from a more leisurely age when Parliament was dominated by the tradition of the gentleman amateur – a tradition which, we are glad to see, is fast disappearing from other aspects of our national life – and that it is high time it was ended. A professional, full-time membership of the House has the right to fair remuneration and adequate accommodation and support services.[26]

The vote on this amendment was a tie, with Labour members voting for it and Conservative and Liberal against. The Labour chairman (a lawyer) used his casting vote to defeat it.

In the ensuing debate in the House on the report, the author aroused extreme Conservative ire by referring to the lost amendment. One prominent Conservative accused Labour members of foul play in even calling for a vote on it during what should have been a break for dinner after long hours of deliberation and, what was more, on his wedding anniversary.

The issue of parliamentary hours faded from view for more than another decade until its revival in 1991 by a study group of the Parliamentary Labour Party, set up to modernise the working of the party organisation. Women Labour MPs were particularly keen to see that the committee recommended a change to morning sittings. They pointed out that the party had already accepted a working day of 9.30 to 5.30 for the proposed Scottish Assembly. They emphasised that the present hours deterred women from seeking entry to Parliament because they could not adequately combine family responsibilities with evening sittings and commented that the hours also exiled many male members from their families.

The study group accepted these arguments and recommended that the House should change to an 11.30 a.m. start with Question Time, with the last vote of the day at 7.30 p.m., on Tuesday, Wednesday and Thursday. There would be no morning sitting on a Monday when many members are travelling from their constituencies and on Friday the House would continue to meet from 9.30 a.m. to 2.30 p.m. In a subsequent debate, the Parliamentary Labour Party voted to start at the earlier hour each day and to do away with Friday sittings altogether.

Apparently because of the interest of the new Prime Minister, John Major, in 1991 the government set up a Select Committee to enquire into the sittings of the House. The Shadow Leader of the House, Dr Jack Cunningham, giving evidence to it, proposed sittings beginning at 10.30 a.m. on Tuesday, Wednesday and Thursday with the main business ending at 7 p.m. and Friday sessions being abolished altogether.

The Liberal Democrats also called for morning sittings. Both parties proposed the greater use of timetable motions for bills. The Leader of the House, John McGregor, submitted a number of suggestions to the committee, including the abolition of Friday sitting, taking some private members' business in the mornings, timetabling bills in committee and reducing the time spent on such lengthy annual debates as the Queen's Speech debate, which opens each parliamentary year, and the Budget debate.

The report of the Select Committee on the Sittings of the House[27] was remarkably modest. It proposed that the main business of the House should be ended by 10 p.m. on Mondays to Thursdays; that on Wednesdays it should start at 10 a.m. to consider private business and private members' business; that it should not sit on ten Fridays in the year and on as many Thursdays as possible it should end at 7.30 p.m. This report represented a tiny move towards morning sittings, but made little contribution to meeting the problems of women members and was absolutely no threat to those members with outside occupations.

One particularly gruesome custom of the Commons is that if an MP is seriously ill, but is desperately required to vote (e.g. when the government's fate hangs on the result of a division), he or she is brought by ambulance into the precincts and is inspected for signs of life by a Whip (a member whose job is to mobilise the votes of his or her party) from the other party before a vote can be cast on their behalf. This was a quite common, and repelling, occurrence in the late 1970s. In fact, the Callaghan government fell in 1979 on a vote of confidence when a dying Labour MP was not allowed by his doctor to be brought to Westminster. The Parliamentary Labour Party has proposed that a severely ill member should be counted as voting if he or she could produce a sick note signed by two doctors. In evidence to the Committee on the Sittings of the House, John McGregor said he could see no viable alternative to the existing arrangements because an agreement might break down under pressure. The committee bravely recommended that the Speaker convene a meeting to consider proxy voting for seriously ill or incapacitated members.*

Those who oppose a change in the hours of the House have always used a variety of arguments which do not bear close examination. Some

---

* In the course of the debate on this report, one Conservative member told the House that he had to wait in New Palace Yard with a high temperature, when his doctor had insisted that he stay in bed, in order to form part of a majority of 126.[28]

say that wearing down the government (or opposition) by long hours of debate is an important weapon of parliamentary warfare, but it is difficult to see who gains from these tactics. Those with outside occupations say they fear that any change would reduce their contact with the outside world, though privately some of them admit that their standard of living would fall grievously without substantial outside earnings. The problem of income (if there is one) should be dealt with by a proper evaluation of the worth of the job and contacts with the outside world should be maintained without extra remuneration. There has also always been an opposition to an early closure of the House from some members (a diminishing number) who are worried about being at a loose end in the evening. The answer to that problem is to keep the library and other facilities open until 10 p.m. The hours of the House are ridiculous. They discourage women from entering parliamentary politics and they positively encourage part-timing, which, in addition to raising serious conflict-of-interest issues, reduces the strength of the campaign for better facilities.

Another uncertainty of parliamentary life is the future programme of work and the timing of recesses. The business of the House and the whipping is announced one week in advance, on a Thursday. This makes it impossible for members to plan activities with any certainty. There should be at least two weeks' notice of the forthcoming business. Only a couple of weeks' notice is usually given of the dates of recesses, which also makes constituency engagements difficult to fix. The summer recess, from the end of July to the middle of October (apparently originally arranged to coincide with the grouse-shooting season) makes for an extraordinarily exhausting and protracted summer session and in addition coincides with only two weeks of the school holidays in Scotland, a matter frequently complained of by Scottish members.

The government should publish a parliamentary calendar every year, setting out the dates of each recess. The House should go into summer recess at the beginning of July and return at the end of September. Party conferences could be brought forward to the first three weeks of September. These changes would make for a more rational allocation of time in the parliamentary year.

Personnel Management

Perhaps not surprisingly, there is no personnel management function for MPs and their staffs. The party organisations have no such responsibility and secretaries and research assistants are employed on an individual basis. There are therefore no formal arrangements for the induction of MPs or their employees (though briefing sessions are sometimes organised); no training arrangements; no appraisal system or guidance on self-development; no assistance in finding accommodation; no welfare counselling or assistance with redundancy. Proposals for a personnel service to meet some of these needs for members of the Parliamentary Labour Party were rejected by Labour MPs in June 1989. There have not been any proposals to provide them for MPs' staff.

II

Parliament and Europe

This chapter considers the relationship between Parliament and European institutions. The lack of formal contact between them is extraordinary, given the continuous shift of power and authority from the British government to the Brussels Commission and the limited supervision of the Commission by the European Parliament. The attitude of Parliament to the European Community is principally to ignore its existence until the Commission and the European Court legitimately exercise some power transferred to them by the British government (e.g. over fishing, or environmental protection or trade competition) and then to affect outrage. The chapter discusses the means by which the government's dealings with Europe could be more effectively supervised.

The Institutions

On 1 January 1973 the United Kingdom joined three European Communities: the European Coal and Steel Community, set up by the 1951 Treaty of Paris; the European Economic Community (now known as the European Community or EC), set up by the 1957 Treaty of Rome; and the European Atomic Energy Community, set up under the 1957 Treaty of Brussels. These treaties have since been amended, most notably by the Single European Act which came into effect on 1 July 1987. Treaties are not directly ratified by Parliament but are the subject of Crown Prerogative, hence the complaint by anti-marketeers that Parliament never had a hand in approving the Treaty of Rome. The effect of the Treaty of Rome was enacted in Parliament by the European Communities Acts of 1972 and 1986.

The main EC institutions are the Council of Ministers (thirteen ministers from member states); the European Commission (seventeen commissioners appointed by member states); the European Court of Justice (thirteen appointed judges) and the European Parliament (518 elected members). 'Summit' meetings of the heads of government of the member states are not referred to in the treaties and have no legislative power, but they are now known as the European Council, meet at least twice a year and increasingly deal with matters referred to them by the Council of Ministers. Proposed revisions of the governing treaties are considered by Inter-Governmental Conferences of which two were in session in 1990–91 to consider Economic and Monetary Union and Political Union.

The Council of Ministers is a legislative body which meets in private in some twenty different formations, e.g. in meetings of Ministers of Agriculture or of Transport. The senior body is the Council of Foreign Ministers (now called the General Affairs Council) which may resolve problems referred to it by 'subject' councils. Increasingly, decisions in the Council are taken by 'qualified' or weighted majority. A majority requires fifty-four votes out of a possible seventy-six. The votes are distributed among members roughly according to population. The UK, France, Italy and Germany have ten votes each; Belgium, The Netherlands, Portugal and Greece each have five.

As readers will know, the British government, having signed binding treaties, has always behaved as if any particular feature of membership were optional and to this day emphasises the escape routes open to us. For example, until recently it was maintained that Britain ultimately had a veto in the Council as a result of the 'Luxembourg compromise' of 1966 . Because of President de Gaulle's objection to the extension of majority voting, the six members at the time agreed that 'where very important interests were at stake' they would try to agree unanimously. This compromise has no status in European legislation, though British ministers invariably talked as though it had. Thus Mrs Thatcher at the end of 1985: '... The Luxembourg compromise will still be applied even when there is majority voting, provided that a very important national interest is involved.'[1]

Similarly, Mrs Lynda Chalker, a Foreign Office minister, told the Foreign Affairs Select Committee in 1986 that 'Majority voting will apply in areas where we want it to apply. Where we do not wish it to apply, it will not do so.'[2] The Foreign Affairs Committee was not impressed by this view: 'Despite what ministers say, we are extremely sceptical about the ability of British governments to invoke the Luxembourg compromise in future, particularly in those areas of decision-making which are now to be made subject to majority voting with the support and encouragement of HM Government.'[3]

EC legislation is implemented by the Commission, with which the British Parliament has no formal relationship. EC law applies in Britain with the force of domestic legislation and in case of conflict overrides British law. It usually takes the form of 'self-executing' regulations; directives, which are binding and enforceable but 'leave the national authorities the choice of form or methods'; and decisions, binding on those to whom they are addressed. The British government was hurt and surprised in late 1991 when the Commission warned it that its proposals to abolish restrictions on the hours miners can spend working underground (which had been in force for eighty-three years) were illegal under Community law and when the Environment Commissioner demanded that environmental assessments be carried out prior to the start of some destructive road projects.

The European Court of Justice exists to interpret Community legislation. It decides whether a member state has failed to fulfil a treaty obligation; reviews the legality of acts by the Council and the Commission and their fulfilment of treaty obligations, and gives rulings on points of EC law. In the 1960s and early 1970s, when the development of the EC barely made any progress, the *Financial Times* commented that 'It was the only Community institution which functioned properly'[4] in establishing the fundamental principles of Community law and its primacy over the national laws of member states. There is no appeal against its decisions. In recent years it has been so swamped by cases brought by the Commission against member states for failing to comply with Community directives that in 1989 it set up a Court of First Instance to relieve the load.

The Court of Justice has attracted much hostility in our Parliament when it has used its powers. For example, in 1988 it ruled that Britain must levy Value Added Tax on building works and water and sewerage charges. John Biffen, former Leader of the House, referred to the shock this decision caused: 'Taxes decided by judges with no possibility of amendment by Parliament were wholly alien to the Commons. For generations Westminster had been making the law, not being bound by it.'[5] In July 1990 there was a row about the Court of Justice ruling on the rights of Spanish fishing vessels in British waters which outraged a number of MPs who appeared to have discovered its powers for the first time. Roger Knapman, vice-chairman of the Conservative European Affairs Committee, asked, 'What exactly is the state of our sovereignty?'

and Lord Denning, former Master of the Rolls, was moved to describe the Court as impudent and 'a French court, dominated by continental thinking ... The Germans are coming in too.'[6]

The European Parliament is primarily a consultative or advisory body with powers (which it has frequently exercised) to alter, increase or even reject the EC budget, and the power to force the entire Commission to resign, which it has never used. It has the responsibility for 'sharing' budgetary power with the Council and has used it to try to alter Council policy or decisions. The recurring dispute on budgetary matters has concerned the right of the Parliament to increase allocations beyond the limit the Council had decided to be acceptable. In 1986 the Commission took the Parliament to the Court of Justice, which ruled that the two parties had to reach agreement and that neither could act unilaterally.

Parliamentary Scrutiny

The term 'democratic deficit' is widely used to describe the effects of the way in which national governments have ceded power to Community institutions which are not under any significant democratic control of either national legislatures or the European Parliament. Major EC legislation originates in the Council of Ministers and is implemented by the Commission. The Commission may also originate legislation, acting on its own authority under powers given to it by the Treaty of Rome or delegated to it by the Council. In the first quarter of 1989 over one thousand items of legislation were published by the EC, of which about one hundred were from the Council. Two-thirds of the legislation from the Commission related to agriculture.

British parliamentary scrutiny does not automatically cover legislation made directly by the Commission and it is not usually presented to parliament. The decision on whether any EC document falls within the scope of parliamentary scrutiny rests with the British government. The English text of such a document is usually deposited in the House of Commons about a month after its adoption by the Commission, followed within a fortnight or so by an Explanatory Memorandum produced by the responsible UK government department.

Most of the documents deposited in the British Parliament by the government are proposals made by the Commission to the Council for legislation, Commission communications to the Council and documents connected with the budgetary processes of the Community. All

PARLIAMENT AND EUROPE 219

deposited documents are considered by the Select Committee on European Legislation (the Scrutiny Committee – first appointed in May 1974) and are classified according to whether or not they are of sufficient legal or political importance to justify debate in the House of Commons. The Committee summarises documents which it considers important and gives reasons for its conclusions. It simply lists the other documents.

Ministers have undertaken not to agree in the Council of Ministers to any proposal which has been recommended for further consideration unless the Scrutiny Committee has indicated that agreement need not be withheld or the minister has decided that 'for special reasons' agreement should not be withheld. In the latter case the minister is obliged, as soon as possible, to explain his decision to the House. This is usually done in a written answer on which he cannot be questioned. The term 'special reasons' has never been defined, though the government has indicated that the criteria they had in mind were the 'need to avoid a legal vacuum' or the desirability of permitting a measure of benefit to the United Kingdom to come into effect as soon as possible.[7]

About eight hundred documents a year are presented to the House of Commons, of which about a hundred are recommended by the Scrutiny Committee for further consideration. Some (about 5 per cent) of the documents designated by the committee as raising important issues have been adopted by the Council of Ministers before they have been scrutinised by our Parliament. Debates on European Community documents may either be held in the House or be referred to a Standing Committee. Most of the debates in the House are begun after ten o'clock and may run for one and a half hours; Standing Committee debates may run for two and a half hours, though the sixteen debates which took place in committee in 1987–88 ran for an average of half an hour, and one took one minute. In Standing Committee, amendments can be moved but they very rarely are.

The working of the arrangements for the consideration of European legislation was examined by the Select Committee on Procedure in a report of November 1989. It reported that the Scrutiny Committee had presented it with two major complaints. The first was that it was prevented from considering policy trends and developments in the Community because some documents containing important proposals for the development of the Community and its institutions fell outside its terms of reference, since they were neither legislative nor published for submission to the Council of Ministers. Two examples of this category were the important Cecchini Report on the economics of the completion of

the Single Market in 1992 and the report of the Council of the European
Communities on progress towards European Union.

In a letter to the Chairman of the Scrutiny Committee replying to this
complaint, the Leader of the House refused to consider any alteration to
the terms of reference of the committee, without giving any reason for
his decision. The Procedure Committee observed, 'This seems to us to
be an unsatisfactory response, in that the government is blocking a
proposal to improve Parliament's scrutiny of the executive.'[8] It went on
to recommend that the terms of reference of the Scrutiny Committee
should be changed in the way that that committee had requested. In its
reply to this recommendation, the government said that it would not
wish to see the Scrutiny Committee making 'a major shift into the
examination of broad policy areas, particularly since this might tend to
detract from the committee's present effectiveness in its primary scrutiny
function' and that 'free-standing studies' of broad policy issues might
tend to duplicate the work of other committees.[9] In other words, the
government, which frequently complained about the speed of development of Community policy, would not allow the one parliamentary institution which could examine crucial documents relating to the future of
the Community to do so. As for duplicating the work of other committees, it is clear that the departmental Select Committees have little time
or inclination to look at Community developments in any systematic
way. The government also rejected the strengthening of those Select
Committees so that they could mount such enquiries.

The second complaint by the Scrutiny Committee concerned the
provision of documents. It particularly wanted access to those which
would give early warning of future legislative proposals, such as the
Community's annual programme of future legislation and its repertoire
of pending proposals. The government acceded to this request.

Other recommendations from the Procedure Committee concerned
improving the timing and frequency of debates and the need to allow
Parliament more opportunity to discuss EC proposals before they were
enacted. It reported: 'In the evidence submitted to us, there was general
agreement that the way in which the House currently debates European
legislation is profoundly unsatisfactory.'[10] The one and a half hour
debates after ten o'clock were particularly unsatisfactory, being 'cursory'
and not well attended. The Committee referred to the great unpopularity
of these late-night occasions, particularly among back-bench members
required to attend for divisions which seldom materialised. It considered
that the retrospective debates on the government's six-monthly White

Papers on Developments in the Community lacked focus. They were thinly attended, their timing was arbitrary, often taking place months after the end of the period to which they were supposed to relate and their atmosphere was of a 'dutiful attendance rather than clear purpose.'

In addition, the Procedure Committee complained strongly that Parliament was not consulted before meetings of the EC member states which decided on major developments in the Community. They instanced the Madrid meeting of heads of government in July 1990 which approved the launch of Stage 1 of the European Economic and Monetary Union. There was no prior debate on this meeting in spite of numerous requests from members and from the Treasury Select Committee: this, the Procedure Committee thought, was a breach of earlier undertakings: 'The failure by the government to arrange a debate on matters known to be on the Madrid summit agenda showed insufficient regard for the views of Parliament. We believe that the way in which the House was treated over the Madrid summit represented a serious breakdown in the scrutiny system.'[11] It recommended that the government should arrange, in the fortnight preceding each of the twice-yearly summit meetings, a full day's debate on that meeting, including its agenda, with a statement on the implications for the United Kingdom of each agenda item. The government accepted this suggestion.

Opposition spokespersons complained to the Procedure Committee that there had been occasions when no statement had been made to the House *after* important meetings of the Council of Ministers. In the previous year, for example, there had not been a single oral statement after the meetings of the Foreign Affairs Council. In fact, up to February 1990 there had not been a statement on the reports of the Foreign Affairs Council for two and a half years and even then a statement on its discussions of South African sanctions was made only after a request by the opposition.

The Procedure Committee considered whether there should be a special Standing Committee, or Committees, or even one Grand Committee (a very large committee) to deal with European legislation instead of having a fresh group of members nominated for every reference. John Wakeham, the Leader of the House, said he doubted the wisdom of 'umbrella' committees and said that such a body with permanent members would 'tend to encourage the specialist'.[12] On the face of it this was an eccentric observation: as EC law becomes more comprehensive and more interventionist, specialist scrutineers would seem to be exactly what the House of Commons needs. The word specialist in this context would be understood to be code for those awkward members, on both sides of the House, who continue strongly to oppose British membership of the EC and object at length (often with some justification) to all its legislation and activities.

The Procedure Committee concluded that five Standing Committees on European documents should be set up, with the power to cross-examine ministers but without the power to send for other witnesses and records (in case they infringed the rights of Select Committees) and without specialist support staff. They proposed such committees for Agriculture, Treasury, Transport and Environment, and a general committee. The government, without much explanation, announced that it would be difficult to find sufficient members to fill the places on five committees and offered to set up three of them. In January 1991 it further reduced their number to two, again because of an alleged shortage of willing members. However, it raised the membership of each committee from ten to fifteen, so that for the sake of saving four places it significantly reduced the coverage of the European Standing Committee system.

In establishing these committees the government craftily changed the basis of referral so that all European documents would automatically be referred to a committee unless a motion was tabled by a minister to hold a debate on the floor of the House. This was a not insignificant increase in the power of the executive. The Procedure Committee had also considered that the existing departmental Select Committees should have the opportunity to establish sub-committees to examine European legislation in their fields of interest. The government took a dim view of this, and said that it would have to consider such a proposal carefully, given the resource implications (i.e. it might require a small increase in committee staffs).

The arrogance of the government's comments on the competence of MPs to examine EC law and its refusal to agree to Select Committees having the resources to examine EC documents properly is part of a wider issue which crops up throughout this book. However, the Procedure Committee itself seems to have been short-sighted. It hardly referred to the likely increase in volume of EC laws and initiatives as the Community moved into new areas of social and security policy. It was content to observe that in the previous decade there had not been much increase in the volume of legislation and, as long as the Commission was checked in its alleged attempts to extend its influence and competence into fields not authorised by the treaties, the load of future legislation would be manageable. It did not attempt to evaluate the consequences of rising EC activity in fields which were already author- ised by treaty, like the environment, or potential extensions of treaties into immigration, employment or welfare law. It did not take evidence from the EC Commission on these matters. It barely considered whether British MEPs might usefully contribute to the examination of EC laws and proposals by Commons committees. It never resolved the question of whether EC documents are best considered by specialist Select Com- mittees as part of their examination of particular subjects, or whether the scrutiny of EC matters is a specialism in itself.

The House of Lords appears to have somewhat more effective arrangements for examining EC affairs (see Chapter 8). There, six sub-committees involving about eighty peers can examine any EC docu- ment or proposal for future legislation. They can take written or oral evidence from witnesses and visit EC institutions.

In December 1991, the Procedure Committee examined the work of the European Standing Committees in their first year.[13] They had produced twenty-eight reports on some technically complex subjects, varying from the quality of sheep carcases to protecting workers from radiation to lifting the embargo on trade with Kuwait. They had saved time on the floor of the House and had successfully exploited a pro- cedure which allowed each of their sessions to begin with questioning the responsible minister for an hour. However, the issue which had caused most concern was a procedural loophole which enabled the government to put to the House a motion different from that which a European Standing Committee had approved. This had happened when a minister had disapproved of a decision by a committee on the compul- sory use of seatbelts. The Procedure Committee considered this action had made a mockery of the scrutiny process.

The Procedure Committee considered the view of a number of members that the European Standing Committees should have research staff or specialist advisers, given the complexity of the subjects they had to examine. It concluded that this assistance was not justifiable, because these were legislative and not investigatory committees and because the advisers would generate more paper, and yet more reading, for their members. They were also influenced by the Chairman of Ways and Means (a Deputy Speaker), who thought that conceding specialist advisers for these committees would trigger off a demand for such advisers in other areas of the House's work, with a consequently signifi- cant increase in public cost. The Clerk of Committees drew attention to an additional difficulty in that a pool of advisers would have implications for staffing in his department for their appointment and management. If ever there was an example of the House denying itself the means to become more effective, this must be it.

British MPs are involved in a number of consultative assemblies in Europe. Eighteen representatives from Parliament are elected to the Consultative Assembly of the twenty-three-nation Council of Europe, which meets three times a year. The same delegation attends the twice-yearly meetings of the Western European Union, the parliamentary arm of NATO. The North Atlantic Assembly of delegates from sixteen countries meets twice a year. In November 1990 an 'assizes' of EC Parliamentarians was called in Rome and in the same month it was proposed that there should be a parliamentary assembly of representatives of thirty-four nations forming the Conference on Security and Co-operation in Europe. None of these assemblies has much influence on the British Parliament and it has no mechanism for considering their proceedings or reports.

The Single European Act

The SEA, which came into effect in July 1987, is a treaty between all members of the European Community. It made fundamental changes in the powers of the Community and in its relationship with Britain. It included a separate treaty for co-operation in foreign policy between members. It embodied the timetable for the completion of the internal market in 1992 and gave new authority to the Community in, for example, the fields of health and safety, regional assistance and environmental protection. It set out major changes to speed up EC legislative processes, extended majority voting in EC institutions and increased the role of the European Parliament in some areas via a 'co-operation procedure'. The British government demonstrated its view of the significance of, and Parliament's role in, these issues by arranging the consideration of the SEA with a report on recent developments in the Community in one six-hour debate. In it, the Foreign Secretary, Sir Geoffrey Howe, played down the importance of the SEA, while an opposition spokesperson observed: 'Institutional reform is the bread and circuses of European politics ... The SEA offers little or nothing.'[14]

The SEA obviously weakened the power of Parliament in relation to the Community. The extension of majority voting reduced the scope for Parliament to act through British ministers in Brussels and new arrangements for co-operation between the European Parliament and the EC Council created a new route for legislation not controllable by Westminster. At the time the Commons appeared to view these matters, as usual, with a blind eye.

The co-operation procedure adds a new stage to the Community's legislative processes. As before, the European Parliament is initially consulted on a proposal and then negotiations take place in the Council. Now, when the Council reaches agreement on a 'common position' by qualified majority, it is referred back to the Parliament, which has to give its opinion on the matter by majority vote within three months. If the Parliament proposes amendments to the common position, the Commission has one month in which to reconsider the matter and propose revisions to the Council. The Council then has three weeks either to adopt the latest Commission proposal by qualified majority or amend it by unanimity. If the European Parliament rejects the common position the Council may still adopt it by unanimity.

After the first eighteen months of the use of co-operation procedure, the Commission accepted some 60 per cent of the amendments proposed by the Parliament, of which the Council then accepted about a quarter. The best known example of a substantial change in legislation due to the Parliament's use of this procedure occurred when it succeeded in securing more stringent standards of vehicle exhaust emissions from the Commission and the Council.

The British government has played down the effect of this new procedure and the ministers have stressed that the 'last word' will remain with the Council of Ministers, but the fact is that the European Parliament has now acquired the right to require unanimity in the Council for proposals it has rejected, a significant strengthening of its powers.

European Union

In the preamble to the SEA the signatories declared that they were moved to 'transform relations as a whole among their states into a European Union'. This reaffirmed an objective regularly expressed in declarations by the community in the preceding twenty-five years.

British ministers have frequently said that European union does not mean what it says, but simply implies close co-operation. In 1985 Mrs Thatcher said, 'I am constantly saying that I wish they would talk less

about European and political union. The terms are not understood in
this country. In so far as they are understood here, they mean a good
deal less than some people over here think they mean.'[15] An objective
observer of the development of European political attitudes would say
that these terms usually mean much more than people over here think
they mean.

The draft treaty for a European Union, proposed by Signor Spinelli,
was approved by a large majority in the European Parliament in February
1984. It provided for a substantial transfer of powers from the nations
to EC institutions, with a greatly enhanced role for the European Parliament. Later in 1984, the Dooge Committee was set up to make suggestions for the improvement of European co-operation. Britain was
represented on it by a Minister of State at the Foreign Office. Its interim
report (December 1984) referred to demonstrating the political will of
the member states: 'In the last analysis that will must be expressed by
the formulation of a true political entity among European states, i.e. a
European Union.' This Committee's report, heavily played down in
Britain, led to the formulation of the SEA.

In a speech to the European Parliament in 1988, which shocked many
British MPs, Jacques Delors, President of the Commission, referred to
the need for a European government and said that most governments
had not yet woken up to the 'displacement of the centre of decision-
making. In ten years' time,' he said, '80 per cent of economic legislation
and perhaps even fiscal and social legislation will be of Community
origin.' Mrs Thatcher, speaking to the nation on the *Jimmy Young Show*
on BBC radio on 27 July 1988 strongly disagreed: 'I think he [M.
Delors] was wrong. I think he went over the top and I do not think he
should have said it.'

Undeterred, in March 1990 President Mitterrand and Chancellor
Kohl sent a joint letter to the then President of the European Council,
Charles Haughey, requesting that a Council meeting in April 'should
initiate preparations for an Inter-Governmental Conference on political
union' to reinforce the Community's democratic legitimacy to ensure
economic, monetary and political cohesion and to define and set in
motion a common foreign and security policy. At the end of that council
Mr Haughey said that the European Community was 'firmly, decisively
and categorically committed to a European Union'.

The Chair of the European Parliament's Institutional Affairs Committee has written: 'The European Parliament is clear on how to define
Political Union. Again this is not a new concept for the EC's elected

politicians. It refers to the same aspirations as those which lay behind Parliament's draft Treaty on European Union of February 1984. Parliament considers the essential elements of such a union to be:

Economic and Monetary Union

A common foreign policy

A completed single market with stronger policies to ensure economic and social cohesion and a balanced environment

Elements of common citizenship and a common framework for protecting basic rights

An institutional system which is sufficiently efficient to manage these responsibilities effectively and which is truly democratically accountable.'[16]

An example of the Community's development in this direction is the progress of the Social Charter or, to be precise, the European Community Charter of the Fundamental Social Rights of Workers. This document, which is now some thirty years old, was agreed by eleven of the twelve heads of government of the European Community's member states at their meeting in Strasbourg in December 1989 (Mrs Thatcher dissenting). It sets out a series of social rights in such areas as employment, pay, living and working conditions, collective bargaining, training, equal opportunities, worker participation and the protection of children, the elderly and the disabled. In November 1989 the Commission produced an action programme which listed the EC directives already in force under each of the Social Charter headings and proposed forty-three new initiatives, of which seventeen would be made in legally binding directives to be promulgated by 1992.

The Commission and most of the Community's member states support the Social Charter because they see that the introduction of the single market in 1992 has to be accompanied by measures of social improvement or it will be seen by the citizens of member states as simply an arrangement for the benefit of big business. Moreover, unless there are measures to harmonise such areas of social policy as conditions of employment, welfare benefits, training and trade union rights, competition will be distorted by 'social dumping' – the attraction of capital and enterprise to the parts of the Community where labour is cheap and industry is unregulated – and workers will tend to move to areas of higher social provision.

In general, Britain provides less social protection and fewer benefits than other member states – in such areas as low pay, equal opportunities, holidays, the hours of work of young people, the right to strike and participation in management. Some of the provisions of the Charter are very far-reaching:

> CLAUSE 24. Every worker of the European Community must, at the time of retirement, be able to enjoy resources affording him or her a decent standard of living . . .

> CLAUSE 26. All disabled persons, whatever the origin and nature of their disablement, must be entitled to additional concrete measures aimed at improving their social and professional integration. These measures must concern, in particular, according to the capacities of the beneficiaries, vocational training, ergonomics, accessibility, mobility, means of transport and housing.

Whatever one may think of the practicality of enforcing such general statements of intent, at least they provide a point of reference for those affected and a set of principles against which national provision can be tested. They would help to create in Britain the general idea of having 'rights' – a matter in which we are particularly deficient.

Mrs Thatcher described the Charter as disappointing: 'Britain does not accept that the Community should direct policy in these matters . . . nor do we see any need to seek uniformity among social policies which have been developed to suit the varied needs and traditions of the different Community countries.'[17]

She went further in the course of reporting to the House of Commons on the Dublin summit in June 1989, describing the Community's programme of social action as 'piffling little powers'.[18] At the time of writing (late 1991), Britain is opposing the implementation of the Action Programme in respect of parental leave, the rights of part-time workers, the right to four weeks annual holiday and the limitation of overtime, on the grounds of the detrimental effects of these proposals on business costs. In the Maastricht conference of December 1991, the British government 'opted out' of what had become the Social Chapter of the Maastricht Treaty, and progress in this field will go ahead in agreements between the other eleven members by which Britain will not be bound.

Subsidiary

The term 'subsidiarity' is increasingly used in discussions about the relationship of EC institutions with member states and is one of which much more will be heard in the future. In the Delors Report on Economic and Monetary Union it was elevated to the status of a principle and is now referred to in EC and British government circles as if it were a fundamental tenet of EC arrangements, though it has no legal status. It appears to mean that tasks should not be carried out at a higher level in an organisation (i.e. by the Community) if they can be carried out at a lower level (i.e. by a member state), though in current usage it is virtually devoid of meaning. The Foreign Affairs Select Committee has commented: 'We were offered various definitions, covering an assurance both to those who wished to avoid greater collective activity and to those who saw more centralisation as inevitable.'[19]

The term originated as an element of Catholic 'social teaching' derived from papal encyclicals of 1890 and 1931 and referred to the preferability of local, rather than state, action to deal with social problems. It is an anomalous idea for EC enthusiasts to endorse, given that the basic concept of the EC is that many tasks are better carried out by the Community in common rather than by the member states. In Britain, the increasing invocation of subsidiarity as a basic principle of the EC appears to be intended to play down the impression of excessive centralisation and uniformity often attributed to its activities. The legal adviser to the Foreign Affairs Committee observed that it was a 'manufactured term' and tried to ascribe possible meanings to it.[20] He considered that the definition which led the field was the 'attained better' test, e.g. as in the Treaty of Rome Article 130R(4): 'The community shall take action relating to the environment to the extent to which the objectives referred to in paragraph 1 can be attained better at the Community level than at the level of individual member states.'

He commented that the Commission is likely to take a more generous view of the benefits of Community action and of its own capability than member states may be disposed to do. However, the Commission in its programme for 1989 appeared to apply a 'common interest' test to subsidiarity. 'The autonomy of decision-making at whatever level . . . should be limited only to the extent dictated by the common interest. This principle has a long tradition in the Community . . . It is called subsidiarity.' The legal adviser pointed to another definition by Sir Leon Brittan, apparently based on democratic accountability: 'Decisions should be taken at the lowest level of government, rather than the highest, because decisions taken at the lowest level are taken by those closest to the people affected by them.' An odd remark from a former member of a government which had taken over more powers from local government than any of its predecessors. On this criterion very little would seem to be appropriate for Community action.

A third definition, the 'practicality test', was mooted by Francis Maude, a Foreign Office Minister, in a hearing of the Select Committee on European legislation: '. . . The principle of subsidiarity, that is, the principle that things should not be done at Community level unless they can be done at national level . . .'.

There have been suggestions that the matter would be clarified if the principle of subsidiarity were defined by treaty. The Foreign Affairs Committee's legal adviser observed: 'Any such suggestion would be received with alarm by lawyers brought up in the common law tradition. For written in as a pure statement of principle, it would serve no purpose. And if written in as something more, it could do great harm.' He pointed out that if it were defined, the European Court would have to rule on the purely political concept of whether member states were competent to carry out particular tasks. The Committee concluded: 'At a time when the Community is facing many uncertainties about its future orientation, anything to clarify a concept which is baffling even informed laymen would seem to be a public service.' It refrained from attempting to clarify it. From now on, arguments over subsidiarity between Britain and the institutions of the EC are bound to grow in such areas as monetary, taxation, regional and environment policy. Britain will demand the retentions of national autonomy in these areas, while our partners will support harmonisation and, eventually, common policies decided by majority voting.

Progress towards Unity

'A large body of opinion in the House of Commons has tended to regard the European Parliament with a degree of condescension,' said the Procedure Committee.[21] A small example of this attitude was shown in a debate in the Commons in 1989 on a proposal that MEPs should be eligible for passes which would entitle them to enter the public areas of the House of Commons (they are entitled to admittance on these terms to the Lords). The chair of the Accommodation Sub-committee, Stan

Orme, said, 'What special right have European members of Parliament to unfettered access to the building? It is completely wrong.'[22] The Procedure Committee observed that, prior to its own hearings, no MEP had ever been a witness or an adviser to a committee (even on European legislation) and considered whether MEPs might participate in the business of the House or act as advisers. It thought it best that informal contacts 'evolve organically' as the potential benefits are 'gradually perceived more clearly'.[23] The European Parliament allows members of national legislatures to attend and speak at their sessions, but not to vote. British MEPs who want to hear a Commons debate have to queue for the public gallery.

British MPs have no allowance or facilities for visiting the European Parliament or other EC institutions. Members wishing to telephone or write to Community institutions have to do so out of their Office Costs Allowance (MEPs can call the House of Commons on an internal government line). Neither the government nor Parliament makes any attempt to enable or encourage MPs to visit the Community and consequently the level of contact (and understanding) is very low indeed. In December 1991, the House of Commons Fees Office announced that MPs would be reimbursed for one two-day trip to EC institutions per year, the expense of which may be taxable.

The House of Commons Commission (see Chapter 9) authorises the expenditure of Select Committees, including travel expenses. In its 1988–89 report the Commission recorded that the Liaison Committee (of Select Committee Chairpersons) had indicated that the budget for overseas travel was becoming inadequate to allow Select Committees to keep abreast of developments within the Community. The Liaison Committee had therefore suggested that financial controls on travel within the Community should be relaxed or removed completely. If they were removed, committees would have the same freedom to 'adjourn from place to place', or meet, in the Community as they have in the United Kingdom. The Commissioners rejected these proposals, 'both on the grounds of principle and because they could lead to an uncontrolled growth of expenditure'.[24] It was not clear what the principle was: going to Europe to take evidence on developments there could only lead to a better understanding of how the EC works.

A closer union of EC countries as envisaged by the founders of the Community and now by the European Parliament is clearly well under way. At the Inter-Governmental Conferences of 1990 and 1991 most EC member states wanted the EC to take responsibility for such areas as immigration, drug control, health, energy, culture and social policy. They appeared to support the concept of democratic federalism, a union of states subject to a large and increasing body of EC law (most of it subject to majority vote) and common financial, foreign and defence policies under the supervision of the European Parliament.

Which brings us back to democratic deficit. What we have at the moment is undemocratic federalism. One MEP has observed that if the EC were a state and applied to join the Community it would be turned down on the grounds that it was not a democracy.[25] There have been many proposals for making the Commission and the Council more accountable to the Parliament which are outside the scope of this book. Briefly, they include requiring the Council to meet in public in its legislative role; extending the co-decision budgetary rules to all other legislation; extending Parliament's oversight to the coal and steel budget and to the fund for overseas development and to borrowing; allowing the Parliament to control and direct the Court of Auditors; increasing the Parliament's power of scrutiny over the Commission's implementing powers and individual spending programmes; allowing the Parliament to initiate legislation and to share power with the Council on policies adopted by majority vote; giving the Parliament the power to approve the appointments of, and to dismiss, individual Commissioners and to elect the Commission President. Progress on some of these aims was made at the Maastricht summit conference.

These proposals are a logical development, given the very limited democratic accountability of European institutions at the moment. Control, such as it is, of national Parliaments over their representative ministers does not give adequate democratic control over the Council's collective decisions, particularly when they are made by majority voting. The executive actions of the Commission in policy areas that have been ceded by national Parliaments can be effectively scrutinised only by the European Parliament and these actions are bound to be extended by the powers that the Commission already has. In addition, as competence and jurisdiction moves away from Westminster, the Parliament will have to shift from a restraining mechanism on the Council to a legislature which makes law on its own initiative. In Britain we cannot continue to ignore or denigrate the European Parliament while allowing powers to accrete to European institutions which cannot be held accountable by the Parliament.

There are a number of measures that can be taken to reduce the democratic deficit in our Parliament. It is important, at the outset, to establish that all Community documents and proposals, including those that originate from the Commission, should be available to Parliament and that the Scrutiny Committee, not the government, should decide what should be scrutinised. Since ideas for future initiatives are frequently floated and leaked by the Commission, there is no reason why the Committee should not have an official representative in Brussels, just as the government has, to pick up early warning of developments. The chair of the Scrutiny Committee could then discuss with the chairs of the subject Select Committees which of the topics, proposals or laws would be most suitable for extensive examination by Select Committee.

Every Select Committee should have the right to set up a European sub-committee, with powers and a budget which would enable it to visit Brussels or other EC institutions. Given the load on Select Committees, it is doubtful if these sub-committees would be able to produce more than two or three reports a year, but their very existence would make the government, particularly, and the Commission more aware of parliamentary scrutiny.

Having established the Select Committee system as the first point of referral, the Scrutiny Committee (not the minister) should decide what documents should be proposed for debate in the House or in Standing Committees. There is no reason why these should not have full Select Committee powers and be entitled to take evidence from British MEPs (who should have the right to attend anyway) and any other witness they wanted to cross-examine. This strengthening of the powers of scrutiny of Parliament and the relationship between the Parliaments is essential given the pace of development of the Community foreshadowed by the Single European Act. Of course, these proposals assume that Parliament has the will to take Europe seriously. Before the historic Maastricht summit the Foreign Affairs Select Committee could easily have mounted an enquiry into Britain's position on the issues which were to be discussed and the likely reactions of our partners, but it neglected to do so.

Throughout 1990 and 1991 the pace of European integration quickened and fears and expectations rose as the conferences on monetary union and political union rolled towards their conclusions. In June 1991 a draft treaty on political union, put before the EC Foreign Ministers, described the aim of the EC as a 'union with a federal goal': the first time the word federal had ever appeared in an EC declaration. The draft was accepted by all EC governments except Portugal, Denmark and the United Kingdom. The British Foreign Secretary, Douglas

Hurd, commented that in English 'federal' meant something 'tight and integrated'. It is curious that in Britain European federalism is taken to mean the centralisation of powers when we created federations in our former dominions and colonies to prevent the centralisation of diverse nations. At British insistence, the word 'federal' was removed from the Maastricht agreement.

It is very difficult to escape the logic that a common or single market has to lead to a common or single currency managed by a single monetary authority and to harmonised employment and social policies. Whether, under these conditions, sovereignty is lost, ceded or pooled seems little more than semantics. It seems excessive to characterise this process as the end of the governance of the monarch in Parliament and the eclipse of our national identity. It is also dishonest to invoke the Luxemburg compromise, the right of veto, the subsidiary 'principle', the right to 'opt out' and the inability to bind a future Parliament to give the impression that we can always back out of any EC decision we do not like while being 'at the heart of Europe'. The proclamation that the British Parliament must have the right to decide on whether or not to join a single currency is nauseating given the way government normally treats Parliament on this, or any other, issue. In fact, Britain is already in a Deutschmark bloc managed by the Bundesbank and could never resist joining a single currency if most of its EC partners did so.

The outcome of the Maastricht summit initially appeared to be a cleared route to a single currency and a central bank. Progress on integration in the social field was delayed by the British refusal to accept the Social Charter, but economic union will in the end drag social union through, as it has in the past. Our EC partners could argue that our intention that less regulated (i.e. inferior) working conditions in Britain will encourage investment from outside the EC would give us an unfair trading advantage, so our intransigence could well gain us nothing. A rather more robust realism is required. In spite of all the scares about European integration, there has been a continuous movement in public opinion in Britain in favour of the EC since 1979, to the point in mid-1990 that there was a 35 per cent majority for closer integration with the Community (LSE Eurobarometer Series). The British people seem less alarmed by these developments than their politicians. Parliament and government in Britain have not served the British people well in all these years of self-deception and foot-dragging. Our record, as the one member state of the Community which has persistently and wilfully failed to comprehend the nature of its enterprise, is shameful.

As George Orwell wrote fifty years ago: 'The insularity of the English, their refusal to take foreigners seriously, is a folly that has to be paid for very heavily from time to time.'[26]

The Danish rejection of the Maastricht Treaty in June 1992 provoked much apocalyptic comment in our Parliament on the future of the EC. The strongest likelihood is that now there will be some pause in the move to federalism, but progress will resume before long.

As for the democratic deficit, it will have to be closed by strengthening the European Parliament on those growing areas of policy ceded to the EC. It can also be closed by greater involvement of our Parliament in European affairs, particularly by having Select and Standing Committees empowered to investigate European developments as they choose. We have little right to complain about the European democratic deficit, given the impairment in our own affairs.

Postscript

While writing this book, I have had some cause for optimism in that a few useful changes have taken place in the way Parliament conducts its business (a little progress on altering the hours of the House; changes in the presentation of the Budget; an improvement in accommodation). On the other hand, the resistance to the strengthening of the powers of scrutiny and to improvements in the resourcing of Parliament, by many members and some officers of both Houses, has been depressing. I have regularly been surprised by the low expectations of my interviewees. Constitutional and parliamentary reform are issues which will have to be pursued by outside organisations for some time yet.

I began by saying that all my proposals were to be subjected to a severe test of practicality. Practical I am sure most of them are, but I would be failing in professional rigour not to put them in some kind of priority order.

I think that because of the long lead time, a reforming Parliament would have to make an early start on creating institutions to supervise the formation of the judiciary. Among other priorities would be a Freedom of Information Act; a start on reforming the Upper House; more effective arrangements for the declaration of members' interests and the more general use of the means we now have for the closer scrutiny of legislation.

The questions of creating and entrenching new parliamentary powers would properly be a subject for a special Procedure Committee (packed with independent-minded and disrespectful members – if they can be found), because this kind of reform has to have the agreement of a parliamentary body which parliamentarians recognise and accept.

The more fundamental question of electoral reform, now a necessary precursor to any significant constitutional change, should be examined by a Royal Commission, a lately neglected but valuable device for the

objective consideration of major matters of public policy, and any proposals for change should be the subject of a referendum.

While my belief in the institution is unshaken, my concern that it has
been too deferential has been confirmed and my conviction that it must
become more self-confident and assertive has been strengthened.

This book was finished at the time of the 1992 general election. I
think I can safely say that the new government will not pursue any of
the proposals herein. My readers will therefore have some years to
reflect on them. I am sure that the subject will continue to grow in
public concern.

References

Preface

1. J. A. G. Griffith, *Parliamentary Scrutiny of Government Bills*. George Allen and Unwin, 1974, p. 256.

Chapter 1

1. Roger Sands, 'Teaching Democracy'. *House Magazine*, 15 July 1991.
2. J. A. G. Griffith, 'The Constitution and the Commons'. RIPA Lecture, December 1981.
3. Quoted in Peter Hennessy, *Whitehall*, Secker and Warburg, 1989, p. 76.
4. House of Commons Debates, 26 July 1905, col. 411.
5. Robert M. Worcester, 'The Public's View of Parliament'. *House Magazine*, 3 May 1985.
6. Austin Mitchell, 'Consulting the Workers: MPs on their job'. *The Parliamentarian*, January 1985.
7. Martin Wroe, 'Pity the Poor Politician'. *Independent*, 30 January 1992.
8. 'May the Best Women Win', *The Times*, 30 November 1990.
9. Walter Bagehot, *The English Constitution. The Economist*, 1974, V, p. 275.
10. Hennessy, *op. cit.*, p. 326.
11. House of Commons Debates, 21 January 1992, col. 667.
12. Bagehot, *op. cit.*, V, p. 216.

Chapter 2

1. Anthony Lester QC, 'Bringing State Power to Heel'. *Guardian*, 2 May 1980.
2. Lord Hailsham, *Elective Dictatorship*. BBC Publications, 1976.
3. *A Bill of Rights*, National Council for Civil Liberties. Briefing No. 13, 1989.
4. *Legislation on Human Rights – with particular reference to the European Convention*. A Discussion Document, Home Office 1976, para. 2.11.
5. *Looking to the Future*, Labour Party, 1990, p. 42.
6. J. A. G. Griffith, *The Politics of the Judiciary*, Fontana, 1985, p. 225.
7. Alex Lyon, 'Looking Before a Human Rights Leap'. Letter to the Editor, *Guardian*, 6 February 1987.

8. E. D. Ewing and C. A. Gearty, *Freedom Under Thatcher*. Clarendon Press, Oxford, 1990, p. 13.
9. Maurice Sunkin, 'What is Happening to Applications for Judicial Review?' *The Modern Law Review*, July 1987, p. 465.
10. House of Commons Debates, 24 January 1992, cols. 667–670.

Chapter 3

1. J. A. G. Griffith, *Parliamentary Scrutiny of Government Bills*. George Allen and Unwin, 1974.
2. *op. cit.*, p. 203.
3. J. S. Mill, *Considerations on Representative Government*. Park Son and Bourn, 1861, p. 97.
4. *op. cit.*, p. 99.
5. House of Commons Debates, 26 October 1989, col. 1073.
6. Joint Committee on Private Bill Procedure, Report July 1988, HC 625.
7. *op. cit.*, para. 38.
8. Private Bills and New Procedures, Cm. 1110, June 1990.
9. Keith Puttick, *Challenging Delegated Legislation*. Waterlow Publishers, 1988, p. 20.
10. House of Commons Debates, 28 March 1988, col. 848.
11. De Smith and Brazier, *Constitutional and Administrative Law*, 6th edition. Penguin 1989, p. 334.
12. Andrew Bennett, 'Uses and Abuses of Delegated Power'. *Statute Law Review*, October–November 1990.
13. 'Government Backs Minister on Benefit Bar', *Guardian*, 22 February 1991.
14. 3rd Commonwealth Conference on Delegated Legislation. Report 1989, p. 38.
15. Quoted in Bennett, *op. cit.*, p. 24.
16. 'Working of the Select Committee System', Select Committee on Procedure, 1989–90, HC 19, Memo No. 11.
17. Bennett, *op. cit.*, p. 26.
18. Puttick, *op. cit.*, p. 23.
19. House of Commons Debates, 14 January 1991, col. 616.
20. e.g. House of Commons Debates, 27 February 1986, col. 627.
21. 'Public Bill Procedure', Select Committee on Procedure 1984–85. 2nd Report, HC 49, para. 26.
22. *ibid.*, para. 27.
23. 'Allocation of Time to Government Bills in Standing Committee', Select Committee on Procedure 1985–86. 2nd Report, HC 324, para. 2.
24. *ibid.*
25. Select Committee on Procedure 1977–78. 1st Report, HC 588, para. 2.19.
26. *ibid.*, para. 2.19.
27. 'Public Bill Procedure', Select Committee on Procedure 1984–85. 2nd Report, HC 49, para. 12.
28. *ibid.*, para. 12.
29. 'Public Bill Procedure', Select Committee on Procedure 1966–67. 6th Report, HC 539, para. 11.
30. *ibid.*, para. 11.
31. *ibid.*, para. 12.
32. 'Process of Legislation', Select Committee on Procedure 1970–71, HC 538.
33. 'The Preparation of Legislation', Report of the Renton Committee 1975. Cmnd. 5063, para. 9.2.

r r r r r3

34. *ibid.*
35. *ibid.*, para. 6.3.
36. Lord Renton, 'The Modern Arts of Parliament'. *House Magazine*, 11 February 1991, p. 14.
37. 'Process of Legislation', Select Committee on Procedure 1970–71, HC 538.

Chapter 4

1. Report from the Committee on National Expenditure, 7 July 1903.
2. House of Commons Debates, 26 July 1905, col. 411.
3. House of Commons Debates, 17 April 1912, col. 360.
4. Select Committee on Procedure, Report Session 1932–33, HC 129.
5. House of Commons Debates, 2 May 1933, cols. 69–70.
6. Select Committee on Procedure, Third Report Session 1946–47, HC 189.
7. Select Committee on Procedure, Session 1964–65 (1965), HC 303.
8. House of Commons Debates, 27 October 1965, col. 184.
9. House of Commons Debates, 14 November 1967, col. 260.
10. Select Committee on Procedure, Session 1968–69 (1969), HC 410.
11. Select Committee of the House of Commons (1970), Cmnd. 4507.
12. Select Committee on Procedure, Session 1970–71, HC 538.
13. Expenditure Committee, 6th Special Report 1971–72, HC 476.
14. Government Observations on the Expenditure Committee's 6th Special Report 1973, Cmnd. 5187.
15. Select Committee on Procedure, First Report Session 1977–78, HC 588, para. 1.5.
16. *ibid.*, para. 1.6.
17. *ibid.*, para. 5.14.
18. *ibid.*, para. 5.15.
19. *ibid.*, para. 6.39.
20. *ibid.*, para. 7.10.
21. House of Commons Debates, 15 June 1979, col. 35.
22. Sir Ian Lloyd. 'Science, Parliament and Democracy'. Science and Public Policy, February 1991.
23. Liaison Committee, First Report Session 1982–83, HC 92, para. 25.
24. House of Commons Debates, 12 May 1983, col. 444–5W.
25. Select Committee on Procedure, 2nd Report Session 1989–90, HC 19, Q742.
26. *ibid.*, Q73–75.
27. *ibid.*, Memorandum of Evidence 21.
28. *ibid.*, para. 77.
29. *ibid.*, evidence, pp. 139–150.
30. *ibid.*, Q765.
31. *ibid.*, para. 192.
32. *ibid.*, p. xlviii.
33. *ibid.*, Memorandum of Evidence 21.
34. *ibid.*, Q650–670.
35. *ibid.*, para. 157.
36. *ibid.*, para. 369.
37. *ibid.*, Q742.
38. *ibid.*, evidence, p. 28, paras. 4–9.
39. *ibid.*, Q85.
40. *ibid.*, Q86.

41. *ibid.*, para. 127.
42. *ibid.*, para. 134.
43. *ibid.*, Q328.
44. *ibid.*, p. 106.
45. *ibid.*, Q247.
46. Government Response to the Second Report of the Procedure Committee, May 1991, Cm. 1532.
47. *ibid.*, p. 3.
48. e.g. *Commons Select Committees – Catalysts for Progress?* ed. Dermot Englefield, Longman 1984; *The New Select Committees*, ed. Gavin Drewry, Clarendon Press, 1989.

Chapter 5

1. Select Committee on Procedure (Supply), 1st Report Session 1980–81, HC 118 Vol. 2, Memorandum by the Clerk Assistant, p. 2.
2. House of Commons Debates, 26 July 1905, col. 411.
3. John Garrett, *The Management of Government*. Penguin, 1972, p. 150.
4. Committee on the Civil Service, 1966–68, Vol. 2, paras. 368–373.
5. *ibid.*, Vol. 1, para. 150.
6. Select Committee on Procedure, 1st Report Session 1968–69, HC 535, paras. 169–170.
7. John Garrett and S. D. Walker, *Management by Objectives in the Civil Service*, CAS Paper 10, HMSO, 1969.
8. Expenditure Committee, 11th Report 1976–77, HC 535, para. 96.
9. *ibid.*, para. 99.
10. *ibid.*, Q1477a.
11. Select Committee on Procedure, 1st Report Session 1977–78, HC 588, para. 8.2.
12. *ibid.*, Q466.
13. Select Committee on Procedure (Supply), 1st Report Session 1980–81, HC 118.
14. *ibid.*, para. 37.
15. Select Committee on Procedure (Finance), 1st Report Session 1982–83, HC 24.
16. Michael Heseltine, *Where There's a Will*. Hutchinson, 1987, p. 20.
17. *ibid.*, p. 21.
18. 'Efficiency and Effectiveness in the Civil Service', Government Observations on the Third Report from the Treasury and Civil Service Committee 1981–82, Cmnd. 8616.
19. Treasury and Civil Service Committee, 8th Report 1987–88. Civil Service Management Reform: The Next Steps. HC 494, para. 7.
20. 'Improving the Management in Government: The Next Steps'. HMSO, 1988.
21. *ibid.*, para. 9.
22. 'The Next Steps Initiative', Report by the Comptroller and Auditor-General, HC 410, June 1989, para. 28.
23. Treasury Committee First Report 1991–92, para. 62.
24. Andrew Likierman and Peter Vass, *Structure and Form of Government Expenditure Reports: Proposals for reform*. Certified Accountants Publications, 1984.
25. *ibid.*, p. 17.
26. *ibid.*, p. 21.
27. *ibid.*, p. 22.

28. 'Structure and form of Financial Documents presented to Parliament'. Treasury and Civil Service Committee 1983–84, HC 110.
29. Likierman and Vass. *op. cit.*, p. 33.
30. 'Incomes of poor cut, says report'. *Financial Times*, 28 March 1991.
31. 'Numbers not worth crunching'. *Economist*, 26 July 1990.
32. Select Committee on Treasury and the Civil Service, 2nd Report Session 1990–91. 'The 1991 Budget', para. 19.
33. 'Improving Government Statistics', ed. Maria Evandrou, Social Sciences Forum, September 1991.

Chapter 6

1. E. L. Normanton, *The Accountability and Audit of Governments*. Manchester University Press, 1966.
2. *ibid.*, p. 273.
3. *ibid.*, p. 272.
4. J. Garrett and R. Sheldon, *Administrative Reform, the Next Step*. Fabian Tract 426, London 1973.
5. House of Commons Debates, 18 April 1861, col. 773.
6. House of Commons Debates, 30 November 1981, col. 64.
7. Select Committee on National Expenditure, July 1903, p. iv.
8. House of Commons Debates, 17 April 1912, col. 371.
9. Committee of Public Accounts, 1916. Memorandum by the Comptroller and Auditor-General, Cmd. 8337, para. 2.
10. House of Commons Debates, 5 August 1921, col. 1886.
11. *ibid.*, col. 1888.
12. Select Committee on Procedure, 1932–33, Cmd. 129, para. 9.
13. Select Committee on Procedure, 1946–47, HC 189, para. 39.
14. Select Committee on Expenditure 1977–78, 11th Report, HC 535.
15. *ibid.*, Vol. II, p. 582.
16. *ibid.*, p. 584.
17. *ibid.*, p. 585.
18. *ibid.*, p. 595.
19. *ibid.*, Vol. II, para. 153.
20. Select Committee on Expenditure, 1977–78, 12th Report, HC 576.
21. *ibid.*, p. 29.
22. *ibid.*, p. 30.
23. *ibid.*, p. xiii.
24. Select Committee on Procedure, 1978–79. HC 330.
25. *ibid.*, para. 15.
26. Role of the Comptroller and Auditor-General, 1980 Cmd. 7845, para. 56.
27. House of Commons Debates, 28 January 1983, cols. 1157–1222.
28. *ibid.*, col. 1173.
29. 'Audit Bill Condemned by State Chiefs'. *The Times*, 27 January 1983.
30. 'Open Book Rebellion by State Bosses Grows'. *Observer*, 23 January 1983.
31. Lord Beswick, 'State Enterprise on the Pillory'. *The Times*, 14 February 1983.
32. 'CBI Attacks Expenditure Control Bill'. *Financial Times*, 17 February 1983.
33. John Garrett, 'New Directions in State Audit', Public Administration, Vol. 64, No. 4, Winter 1986, p. 421.
34. Early Day Motion 427, 1987.

35. House of Commons Debates, 16 December 1987.
36. Select Committee on Procedure 1989–90. Evidence, Vol. II, p. 105.
37. Working of the Select Committee System, Government Response to the Select Committee on Procedure, Cm. 1532, p. 23.
38. Letter from the Prime Minister to the author, 25 July 1991.
39. PAC 8th Report 1990–91.
40. PAC 13th Report 1989–90.
41. PAC 6th Report 1989–90.
42. PAC 15th Report 1987–88.
43. e.g. PAC 3rd Report 1989–90.
44. PAC 6th Report 1987–88 and 7th Report 1990–91.
45. PAC 50th Report 1987–88.
46. NAO, March 1990, Report 328.
47. PAC 26th Report 1989–90.
48. NAO, April 1991, Report 357.
49. NAO, February 1991, Report 191.
50. PAC 18th Report 1989–90.
51. PAC 33rd Report 1989–90.
52. PAC 27th Report July 1990.
53. PAC 38th Report 1990–91.
54. PAC 44th Report 1987–88.
55. John Garrett, *op. cit.*
56. NAO, May 1991, Report 399.
57. John Garrett, *op. cit.*, p. 431.
58. PAC 4th Report 1990–91.
59. PAC 39th Report 1988–89.
60. PAC 41st Report 1988–89.

Chapter 7

1. House of Commons Debates, 23 January 1992, col. 474.
2. *ibid.*, 18 February 1992, col. 173.
3. Select Committee on Procedure, 3rd Report, 1990–91. Parliamentary Questions. HC 178, para. 108.
4. 'Spoon Feeding List for MPs'. *Guardian*, 17 October 1990.
5. 'Toadying: the Art of going Plonk'. *The Times*, 10 July 1991.
6. Procedure Committee, *op. cit.*, para. 102.
7. *ibid.*, para. 104.
8. Roy Jenkins, *A Life at the Centre*. Macmillan, 1991, p. 213.
9. Early Day Motions, Factsheet No. 30. Public Information Office, House of Commons.
10. Select Committee on the Parliamentary Commissioner for Administration, 1st Report, 1990–91. HC 129, para. 21.
11. *ibid.*, para. 31.
12. J. A. G. Griffith and Michael Ryle, *Parliament*. Sweet and Maxwell, 1989, p. 266.

Chapter 8

1. Lord Longford, *A History of the House of Lords*. Collins, 1988.
Donald Shell, *The House of Lords*. Phillip Allan/Barnes and Noble Books, 1988.
J. A. G. Griffith and Michael Ryle, *Parliament*. Sweet and Maxwell, 1989, pp. 455–513.

Andrew Adonis, *Parliament Today*. Manchester University Press, 1990.
2. Adonis, *op. cit.*, p. 159. This section is a very useful analysis of the voting behaviour of the Lords.
3. For a detailed account of this episode see Janet Morgan, *The House of Lords and the Labour Government 1964–70*. Oxford, 1975.
4. House of Commons Debates. 9 November 1976, col. 211.
5. *Guardian*, 27 October 1976.
6. 'The Machinery of Government and the House of Lords'. Statement by the National Executive of the Labour Party, 1978, p. 9.
7. House of Lords, Report of Select Committee on the committee work of the House, Session 1991–92. HL Paper 35.
8. *ibid.*, para. 71.
9. *ibid.*, para. 81.
10. House of Lords Debates, 5 July 1977, col. 211.

Chapter 9

1. Review of the Administrative Services of the House of Commons. Report to the Speaker by Sir Edmund Compton, July 1974, HC 254.
2. *ibid.*, para. 5.19.
3. Committee on House of Commons (Administration) 1975, HC 624.
4. *ibid.*, Memorandum from the Clerk of the House, paras. 11, 12.
5. *ibid.*, para. 4.5.
6. House of Commons Commission, 11th Annual Report 1988–89, p. 7.
7. House of Commons Services: Report to the House of Commons Commission, November 1990.
8. *ibid.*, para. 17.
9. *ibid.*, para. 33.
10. *ibid.*, para. 36.
11. Select Committee on House of Commons (Services) 1st Report, 'Information Technology: Members' Requirements'. HC 97, 1984.
12. Select Committee on House of Commons (Services) 4th Report, 'Computer Services for Members'. HC 614, 1990, Memorandum 1.
13. *ibid.*
14. *ibid.*, para. 12.
15. *ibid.*, para. 23.
16. *ibid.*, para. 68.

Chapter 10

1. House of Commons Debates, 10 August 1911, col. 1382.
2. Report of the Committee on the Remuneration of Ministers and Members of Parliament, November 1964. Cmnd. 2516.
3. *ibid.*, para. 31.
4. *ibid.*, para. 42.
5. House of Commons Debates, 18 December 1964, col. 802.
6. House of Commons Debates, 18 December 1964, col. 747.
7. House of Commons Debates, 19 July 1983, col. 273.

8. 'Something to Declare', *Observer* Magazine, 14 October 1990.
9. Mark Hollingsworth, *MPs For Hire*. Bloomsbury, 1991.
10. *ibid.*, p. 20.
11. House of Commons Debates, 17 January 1990, col. 339.
12. House of Commons Debates, 17 January 1990, col. 336.
13. Select Committee on House of Commons (Services) 2nd Report. 'Access to the Precincts of the House', July 1988, HC 580.
14. *ibid.*, para. 50.
15. *ibid.*, Q142.
16. MPs 'letting in lobbyists as aides', *Guardian*, 16 December 1991.
17. Edward Short, *Whip to Wilson*. Macdonald, 1989, p. 48.
18. Select Committee on Procedure, First Report 1966–67. 'The Times and Sittings of the House', August 1966, HC 153.
19. *ibid.*, para. 10.
20. House of Commons Debates, 14 December 1966, col. 489.
21. *ibid.*, col. 493.
22. *ibid.*, col. 506.
23. House of Commons Debates, 14 November 1967, col. 253
24. Select Committee on Procedure, 3rd Report, Session 1974–75, HC 491, Q64, 149.
25. 'The Late Parliamentary Show', *Economist*, 22 October 1977.
26. Select Committee on Procedure, 1st Report, Session 1977–78, HC 588, p. 58.
27. Select Committee on Sittings of the House, Session 1991–92, HC 20.
28. House of Commons Debates, 2 March 1992, col. 110.

Chapter 11

1. House of Commons Debates, 5 December, col. 432.
2. Foreign Affairs Select Committee, 1985–86, HC 442, p. 79.
3. HC 442, p. xii, para. 42.
4. Robert Rice, 'Europe Learns to Love its Court', *Financial Times*, 6 June 1990.
5. John Biffen, *Inside the House of Commons*, Grafton Books, 1989, p. 209.
6. 'Tory joins fight to curb power of European Court', *The Times*, 16 July 1990.
7. Official Report, 29 October 1984, cols. 798–800W.
8. Select Committee on Procedure, Report 1988–89, HC 622, para. 22.
9. The Scrutiny of European legislation: Government response, Cmd. 1081, May 1990, p. 1.
10. HC 622. para. 43.
11. HC 622. para. 46.
12. HC 622. Q73.
13. Select Committee on Procedure, First Report 1991–1992, HC 31.
14. House of Commons Debates, 23 April 1986, col. 328.
15. House of Commons Debates, 5 December 1985, col. 432.
16. David Martin MEP, 'European Union and Democratic Deficit'. John Wheatley Centre, West Lothian, June 1990.
17. House of Commons Debates, 12 December 1989, col. 858.
18. House of Commons Debates, 28 June 1990, col. 491.
19. 2nd Report of the Select Committee on Foreign Affairs, 1989–90. HC 82–i, para. 23.
20. HC 82–i, pp. 68–72.
21. HC 622, para. 105.

22. House of Commons Debates, 30 January 1990, col. 117.
23. HC 622, para. 113.
24. House of Commons Commission, 11th Annual Report, 1988–89, p. 7.
25. Martin, *op. cit.*, p. 22.
26. George Orwell, *The Lion and the Unicorn*, Penguin Books, edition 1982, p. 49.

Index